Life of Saint Cecilia

Virgin and Martyr – A Biography and Her History in the Christian Church

By Prosper Guéranger

Cantantibus organis, Caecilia Domino decantabat dicens: Fiat cor meum immaculatum ut non confundar. — *Offic, S. Caecelia,* V. A. M.

Published by Pantianos Classics

ISBN-13: 978-1-78987-467-9

First published in 1866

Contents

Saint Cecilia

Preface

In offering to the American public, a translation of the life of St. Cecilia, by the learned and laborious Dom Prosper Guéranger, the publisher feels assured he has made a valuable addition to our too narrow circle of Catholic literature.

The Church offers, in every age, in her Saints, Apostles, and Martyrs, brilliant examples of virtue, zeal, and heroic courage. While *all* are holy, there are still some, whose lives present features, at once so touching and sublime, that time can detract nothing from the interest which attaches to their names in every Catholic heart. Pre-eminent among these, is St. Cecilia, the gentle queen of Sacred Song, distinguished alike for her attachment to holy Virginity, her apostolic zeal, and the "unfaltering courage by which she won the martyr's crown.

The author has followed with fidelity, the ancient Acts of St. Cecilia, the authenticity of which the reader will find satisfactorily defended in his pages. For less important details, he has claimed the right generally accorded to historians, of receiving probable evidence, where certain proofs cannot be obtained. On such authority, he has, for example, assumed with the learned Bosio and others, that the virtues of our Saint formed the crowning glory of the illustrious family of Cecilia Metella. The recital does not terminate with the death of Cecilia. The discoveries of her tomb, in the ninth and sixteenth centuries, form not the least interesting portion of the work. The description of the church which was once her dwelling, and the witness of her sufferings and triumphs, brings those scenes so vividly before us, that Cecilia seems to belong, as all the Saints of God most truly do, as much to our own day, as to the period when she still combated on earth.

We will not speak of the pleasure and instruction the author has afforded by his faithful pictures of the celebrated Ways of Ancient Rome, and the sacred cities of the dead, concealed in the holy shades beneath. For this, and much other interesting information, we refer the reader to the following pages, content, if, by our own humble labors, we have contributed to the edification of our Catholic brethren, and to the glory of *Him* who is admirable in His Saints.

The Publisher

Chapter One - Alexander Severus. His Education. Tendency to Christianity. Defects of Character

The ninth year of the reign of Alexander Severus had just opened; [1] the consular fasces were in the hands of Lucius Virius Agricola and Sextus Catius Clementinus, and for eight years and a half, Saint Urban had been guiding at Rome the bark of Saint Peter. [2] Since the death of Septimius Severus, who had ordered the fifth persecution against the Christians, the Church had enjoyed a peace and tranquillity which had already lasted twenty years, and was destined to continue seven years longer, until the promulgation of the sanguinary edict of Maximinus, successor of Alexander Severus. During this interval, Christianity had made steady progress. Saint Callistus had occupied with honor, the Apostolic chair, and although his life was the forfeit of this perilous dignity, his martyrdom was not a signal for a general massacre of the faithful. The death of this pontiff was the result of the political jealousy of the Emperors, who dreaded the humble majesty of the Bishop of Rome more than they would have feared a competitor for the empire. [3]

St. Urban had, therefore, the prospect of sooner or later sealing with his blood, the elevated mission of presiding over the destinies of the Church, and, indeed, he was worthy of such a fate. The holy old man did not dread the trial for himself, but he felt great anxiety with regard to the flock of Jesus Christ; for, although the days of persecution were ever glorious for the Church, they were unhappily too frequently marked by the apostasy of many Christians. The fears of the Pontiff were based upon the well-known character of the head of the empire, who, although a clement and just prince, and kindly disposed towards the Christians, was weak and easily influenced. Alexander was at this time in his twenty-first year. His mother, Julia, not only loved and admired Christianity; but it appears that she even professed it. [4] While residing at Antioch, four years before the elevation of her son to the throne, she sent an escort of honor to Alexandria, requesting a visit from the learned Origen, with whom she conversed upon the Christian religion, the divinity of its origin, and the purity of its morals. She received this illustrious doctor with the greatest respect, and loaded him with honors. [5] Mammaea superintended herself the education of her son, and his contemporaries, as well as posterity, attribute to her influence his total disrelish for the dissolute habits of his cousin Heliogabalus, as well as the justice and humanity he displayed throughout the course of his life. [6] This princess directed Alexander in all his undertakings, accompanied him in his campaigns, and even shared his fate when he was massacred at the head of his troops, on the banks of the Rhine, in an expedition against the Germans.

If the policy of Alexander, who was only in his fourteenth year when the sovereign power devolved upon him, prevented his embracing the religion of his mother, he at least entertained for Christianity and its divine founder the greatest respect. The Lararium (oratory) of his palace included, not only the statues of the gods, and of the Emperors who had been signal benefactors to the human race, but also the statue of Jesus Christ, placed there by Alexander and honored by him with divine worship.

His admiration for the Son of Mary was so sincere that he even laid a proposition before the senate to admit to a rank among the gods, the founder of a religion, of which the moral code was so pure. The senate desired to consult the oracles upon this imperial fancy, and Lampridius, a contemporary author, reports their response to have been, that if this now apotheosis were celebrated, the temples would soon be abandoned, and all the world would become Christian. [7] The maxim: "Do unto others only that which you would wish them to do to you," was unceasingly on the lips of Alexander, and he freely acknowledged that he had borrowed it from the Christians. He caused it to be engraved on the walls of his palace, and on those of the new edifices. In obedience to his orders, a herald proclaimed it publicly at the punishment of criminals. [8] Alexander gave another proof of his respect for Christianity, by confiding many of the offices of his court to Christians whom he honored with his favor. Eusebius speaks of the excessive irritation of Maximums, on seeing these posts of honor filled by the followers of a religion, which he himself so unrelentingly persecuted. [9] An incident, related by Lampridius, and which throws great light on the situation of the Church in Rome, will serve to show the impartiality of Alexander in cases affecting the Christians. In the country beyond the Tiber, at the foot of Mount Janiculum, was situated the famous *Taberna meritoria,* from the soil of which, in the year of Rome, 718, a fountain of oil had burst forth and flowed during an entire day like a mysterious river. [10] Augustus, conqueror of Pompey and Lepidus, was inaugurating the era of universal peace, when this sign announced to the Romans the approaching birth of him, who, invested with the double unction of the Priesthood and of Royalty, would descend upon earth to be the pledge of the restoration of peace between heaven and earth. Under the pontificate of St. Callistus, this celebrated edifice, famed for so memorable a prodigy, passed into the hands of the Christians. This pontiff dedicated it as a church under the invocation of the Mother of God; since that time, Rome honors this sanctuary under the name of St. Mary beyond the Tiber. [11]

It is not known when the Christians obtained possession of a building which had formerly served only for profane uses; but Lampridius relates that the *popinarii* (tavern keepers) complained bitterly to Alexander, that a place hitherto free to the public, and profitable to them, had been taken from them and devoted to the service of a religion, not even recognized by the laws of the empire. The good dispositions of this prince toward the Christians were decidedly manifested in his decision of this case.

"I prefer," he replied, "that God should be honored in this place in any manner whatsoever, rather than restore it again to the venders of wine." [12] Such, with regard to the Church, were the dispositions of the prince who reigned over Rome and over the whole world. Nevertheless, St. Urban, as we have before stated, did not feel secure from the violent storms which had ravaged the Church even under the best Emperors. Trajan and Antoninus had persecuted the Christians, and, moreover, the defects of Alexander's character rendered a change possible, if not in his interior dispositions, at least in his conduct. Urban could not forget that his predecessor, Callistus, had suffered martyrdom in the early part of the reign of Alexander, and if the murder of this holy Pope could be justly attributed to political motives, it was not easy to forget, that, until that time, State reasons, as well as zeal for the worship of the gods, had dictated the edicts of proscription against the Christians. Alexander was opposed to violence, but his timidity rendered him very yielding. He was known to cringe to public opinion, and to fear literary men, lest they should transmit to posterity an unfavorable account of his character and reign. [13]

His weakness was particularly conspicuous in the exaggerated deference he paid Mammaea, to whose influence he was constantly submissive. This princess, distinguished for her noble qualities, but jealous and passionate, exercised complete dominion over her son, and, although her advice was generally most beneficial to Alexander, it sometimes led him to commit grave faults. [14]

It was at the instigation of his Mother, that Alexander repudiated, and exiled into Lybia, his first wife whom he esteemed and loved. Mammaea drove her from the palace and forced her to seek refuge in the protection of the army. [15] Alexander also caused Marcion, the father of his wife, to be put to death, a fate richly merited according to some historians, who assert that the unhappy man had been proved guilty of treason. However this may be, the weakness of Alexander's character was easily discovered by the courtiers. Interested and ambitious men took advantage of it to prosecute their designs with boldness, though opposed to his views, yet not without reason hoped for impunity, if not for favor.

[1] This prince had been proclaimed by the army, on the 11th of March, 222; the ninth year of his reign commenced on the 11th of March, 230.
[2] St. Urban had ascended the apostolic chair about the middle of October, 222.
[3] Such were, as we learn from St. Cyprian, the sentiments of the Emperor Decius, who ascended the throne a few years later: "Cum tyrannus infestus sacerdotibus Dei fanda et nefanda comminaretur, cum multo patientius et tolerabilius audiret levari adversus se aemulum principem quant constitui Roman Dei Sacerdotem." Epist. ad Antonianvm.
[4] Eusebius intimated this in his Ecclesiastical History, Book iv. chap. 21: Orosius, in the 18th chap, of his 2d Book. While St. Vincent of Lerins asserts it positively. (Commonit. cap. xxiii.)
[5] Euseb. lib. vi. cap. xxi.
[6] Herodian, a pagan historian of Alexander, unhesitatingly acknowledges this. Lib. v. p. 571; Lib. vi. 574, 575, Frankfort edit. 1590.

[7] Lamprid. Augusta, histor. Paris, 1620, p. 129.

[8] *Ibid.* p. 132.

[9] Euseb. Histor. Eccles. lib. vi. cap. 28.

[10] This incontestable fact is reported in the Chronicles of Eusebius, and in those of St. Prosper, Idacius, Orosius. Previous to these Christian writers, Dio Cassius mentions it in his History of Rome. Lib. xliii. p. 383. Edit, of 1606.

[11] See Moretti, de S. Callisto Papaet Martyre ejusque Basilica S. Mariae, trans-Tyberim noncupata. Rome, 1752.

[12] Lamprid. Alex. vita. pag. 131.

[13] Lamprid. Alex. vita. pag. 115.

[14] Herodian. Hist. August, lib. vi. pag. 575.

[15] Herodian. *Ibid.*

Chapter Two - Dispositions of the Magistrates of the Empire with Regard to Christianity. Ulpian. Unceasing Trials Imminent for the Christians of Rome

If the influence of Julia Mammsea at times induced Alexander to act in opposition to the dictates of his heart, there was at least no reason to fear that, with respect to Christianity, this princess would lead him into the path of persecution. But unfortunately the bitterest and most formidable enemies of the Church had found an asylum in the palace of the Emperor, and were favored with his confidence. Elevated to the throne at an age when the character is still unformed, he needed a council to direct him in the art of governing. The members of this council, sixteen in number, were chosen by Mammaea herself, and were principally skilful juris-consults, who were highly esteemed in Rome. Papinian, Domitius Ulpian, Julius Paulus, Celsus, Pomponius, Modestinus, Yenuleius, Hermogenes, and Callistratus, successively formed part of this council, and many of them retained their seats several years. These legists, adorers of the coercive principle decorated with the pompous name of Law, *that* law of which they were the oracles, witnessed with profound antipathy, the progress of Christianity, which revealed to men the principles of an eternal jurisprudence, calculated essentially to modify the mutual relations of mankind. A spiritual, and at the same time, cosmopolitan society, which rejected the control of political power, and propagated itself in spite of all the edicts of repression, seemed to them a monster which the empire could not stifle too soon. Jurisprudence and philosophy united their efforts in repelling the common enemy which was advancing so rapidly against them, and would inevitably, sooner or later, crush them in their own domain, by assigning faith as the guide of intellect, and erecting in the conscience of each man a tribunal from which he would judge the law. Edicts of persecution had been the sole reply to the pretensions of this new society.

The ferocious autocracy of Nero, the benevolent genius of Trajan and Antoninus, the philosophical instincts of Marcus Aurelius, had all conspired in the general massacre of the Christians. From the very beginning, the empire felt that it had either to bend under the yoke, or conquer by carnage. The personal disposition of Alexander, as well as his education, seemed almost a guarantee that the Church, during his reign, would not be harassed by any addition to the long series of proscriptive edicts against the Christians; but the tolerance of the emperor for the religion of his Mother, was not so great as to banish from the Arsenal of Roman laws, those weapons of tyranny, the use of which a clement prince would have prohibited. Pagan superstition and Roman policy watched together over the maintenance of those sanguinary edicts, and Alexander dared not brave public opinion, nor expose his popularity, by revoking them. Lampridius, in a few words, perfectly expresses the politic measures of the emperor with regard to the Church: "Alexander," he says, "*tolerated* the existence of Christians." [1]

Daring this truce, the legists of the imperial palace compiled several times the Roman laws, carefully bringing together in their compilations the ordinances which condemned the faithful to death. The assessors of Papinian, in his office of Prefect of the Praetonum, were Domitius Ulpian and Julius Paulas, two men whose names are as imposing in the history of jurisprudence, as they are odious in the annals of Christianity. Daring the reign of Alexander, the former published his famous books, *De officio Proconsulis,* in which he collects the different edicts of the Emperors against every kind of crime. We find there the numerous constitutions which outlawed the disciples of Jesus Christ. Lactantius brands with eloquent indignation, this sanguinary concession to the passions of the Prsetorium, [2] which rendered the reign of Alexander a cruel and cowardly transition from the persecution of Septimius Severus, to that set on foot by Maximinus, and which broke out immediately after the assassination of Alexander. Herodian and Lampridius eulogize in the most extravagant manner, the virtues and qualities of Ulpian. Pagans like himself, they considered it no crime to sharpen the sword destined to massacre the Christians. Moreover, the degree of morality necessary to satisfy the writers of this epoch, is well known. According to Dio Cassius, Ulpian would never have enjoyed the honors of the Praetorium, had he not murdered his predecessors, Flavian and Chrestus. [3] The blood of the Christians could hardly be more precious to Ulpian than that of the first magistrates of Rome. Such was the man who exercised unbounded influence over Alexander, and enjoyed to an unlimited degree the imperial favor. Mammaea at first watched with great anxiety, the influence of Ulpian. She knew his violent opposition to Christianity; but Ulpian was too politic to solicit new edicts against a religion favored by the Mother of the Emperor, and respected by Alexander himself. She therefore soon calmed her fears, and even contributed towards advancing the fortunes of Ulpian. [4]

The tranquillity which had been restored to the Church, was destined to be of short duration; the brief respite from persecution seemed merely granted to increase the number of victims, who never for a moment lost sight of the arena of their brethren recent combats. The reigns of the emperors were frequently short, and even during that of Alexander, a favorable opportunity was alone required to give free vent to the hatred of the proconsuls, ever eager to persecute the Christians. Even a limited knowledge of the laws of the empire at that time, is sufficient to show how little dependence could be placed by the citizens of Rome upon their liberty, their fortunes, or even their lives. Exile, confiscation, or judicial murder, were calamities which often fell upon patricians, senators, and even consuls, whilst tyranny was exercised against the plebeians — to which class the majority of the Christians belonged — with the greatest ease and impunity; the law branding them as despicable and vile. The perils which the Church had reason to dread from the Roman legislation, were considerably aggravated by the hostile dispositions of a large portion of the inhabitants of Rome. Tertullian, in his Apology, published thirty years before the epoch of which we treat, remarks that in public calamities, or in seditions, the multitude never failed to cry out: — "The Christians to the lions!" The mild, but weak reign of Alexander was more than once agitated by tempests, which converted the capital of the world into a theatre of carnage, where free vent was given to the violence of passion. Even Ulpian, with all his skill and power, frequently failed in crushing these disturbances. His office gave him supreme authority over the praetorian guard. This body having displeased the Romans, in some trifling matter, war was declared against them. The civil contest lasted three days, and resulted in many deaths on both sides. Encouraged by their superiority of number, the people fought with such success that they were gaining a decided victory, when the praetorians commenced to fire the city; fear at once overcame the exasperation of the people, and paved the way to reconciliation. [5] A short time after, in the fifth year of Alexander's reign, Ulpian was assassinated by the praetorian guard, thus expiating by his own violent death, the murder of Flavian and Chrestus. His efforts to restore discipline to this formidable corps, excited to such a degree the animosity of the soldiers, that they boldly demanded his condemnation of the Emperor. Several times Alexander was reduced to the necessity of covering with his imperial purple, the prefect who had become so odious to the praetorians; but even this protection did not long preserve the life of his favorite; the praetorians finally murdered him in the very presence of the Emperor. Ulpian was succeeded in the Prefecture of the Praetorium, by his colleague, Julius Paulus, a man well worthy the office, if extreme aversion for the Christians was at that time a necessary qualification for so important a charge.

Thus the law ever armed with the sword kept guard at the doors of the Church, and when occasion offered, the legists eagerly took advantage of it. A city containing nearly three millions of inhabitants accustomed to scenes of bloodshed, was not likely to be agitated because severity was exercised against a sect, who, according to the expression of Tacitus, had drawn upon themselves the hatred of the whole human race. [6] It was well known that they would not be avenged by their brethren, who envied their fate; nor by the people, who were absurdly prejudiced against them; nor by the emperor, who considered he favored them sufficiently by not proscribing them, and by admitting several to form a portion of his household.

[1] Alexand. vita. pag. 121.
[2] Quin etiam seleratissimi homicidae contra pios jura impia condiderunt. Nam et constitutiones sacrilegae, et disputationes Jurisperitorum legunter injustae. Domitius, de officio Proconsulis libro septimo, rescripta Principum nefaria collegit, ut docerot, quibus poonis affici oporteret eos, qui so oultorea Dei conlitcrentur. *Divin, Instit. lib.* v. *cap* xi.
[3] Dion Cass. Hist, pag 917.
[4] Baronius. Annal. ad ann. 225.
[5] Dion Cass Hist, page 917.
[6] Odio humani generis convicti. Tacit. Annal. lib. xv. cap. xliv.

Chapter Three - Martyrs Under Alexander Severus. Situation and Solicitude of Pope St. Urban. Progress of Christianity in Rome

The calendar of the Church has preserved the memory of several martyrs who suffered during the reign of Alexander. The execution of edicts being suspended, they are but few in number; we find them however in the Martyrologies, the persecuting spirit of the empire having more than once broken down the barriers imposed by the tolerance of the emperor.

St. Hesychius, a soldier, was executed with St. Julius, under Maximinus at Dorostoros in Mysia. No other mention is made of martyrs who suffered at this epoch out of Rome; but in the capital itself, during the first year of the reign of Alexander, we find the names of the saintly priest Callipadius, who was beheaded, Palmatius [1] a personage of elevated rank, and Simplicius a senator, who were massacred with their families; shortly after, Pope Callistus; later, the virgins Martina and Tatiana; and finally, the celebrated martyr whose combats we are going to relate, and who rendered the pontificate of St. Urban forever memorable.

The holy Pope in consequence of numerous acts of violence, was convinced that he would not be permitted to end in peace the ninth year of his courageous episcopacy. The persecutors of the venerable Pontiff were not wanting in pretexts to satisfy their unjust hatred. Without requiring edicts of persecution, the magistrates could easily have recourse to the general laws which condemned to death all those guilty of sacrilege, as well as magicians and disturbers of the public peace. [2] The head of the Christians of Rome and of the empire, was thus liable at any moment to be led before the magistrates upon some charge of this nature. He was twice summoned to the Prsetorium, where he courageously confessed his faith. [3] Thenceforth, it was no longer possible for him to live within the city without exposing his life: he therefore retired to the catacombs of the Appian Way, near the tombs of the martyrs, where recalling to his mind the example of his predecessors, he strengthened his soul for its last combat. While in this mysterious place of concealment, communications were sent him from the Churches of the East and of the West; he directed the twenty-five churches which Rome already counted within her walls; and received with benevolence, the faithful who had re-course to him, or the Pagans, who, touched by grace, earnestly implored to be enlightened by that *Admirable Light,* which the Prince of the Apostles had brought to the Romans. [4] Several priests and deacons assisted the Pontiff and shared his labors and perils. Many of the poor, watched like faithful sentinels along the road which led to the dwelling of the Vicar of Christianity. Being well known by the Christians of Rome, they served as agents between the Church and her chief, and thus concealed from the shrewd emissaries of the Praetorium all traces of the mysterious communications which preserved life throughout the body of the Church.

The documents which certify the intervention of St. Urban in the affairs of the universal Church, are not now extant, but we see, in some of the fragments relating to Pontiffs who preceded or followed him, that during the first three centuries, the papal prerogative was exercised over the Church with as much calmness and authority from the foot of the scaffold, as in later years, when the apostolical letters emanated from the Lateran palace. The *Liber Pontificalis* makes no mention of the decrees attributed afterwards to Urban, on the doubtful authority of Mercator, but it particularly specifies that during the course of his pontificate, [5] the holy Pope consecrated eight bishops, the greater number destined doubtless for an apostolic life and for the foundation of new Churches. At the same time, St. Urban provided for the dignity of divine service in the churches of Borne. There were many Christians at the court of Alexander, in the senate, and among the patricians; it was bat just that a part of the riches of the disciples of Christ, should be devoted to the suitable celebration of the divine mysteries. Aided by liberal contributions from these wealthy Christians, St. Urban replaced the vases of the altar with silver ones, and among other things ordered twenty-five silver patens for the various churches of the city. [6] These patens were very large, for they were destined to receive the bread which each one of the faithful who was to communicate, brought as an offering. Whilst St. Urban was devoting so much attention to the ornaments of material altars, he was exercising his pastoral zeal with still greater ardor in gathering converts to the fold of Christ.

Thirty years before, Tertullian, in addressing the Senate, had exclaimed: "We are but of yesterday; yet already we fill your cities, your islands, your villages, markets, camps, tribes, palaces, and forum; we leave you nothing but your temples." [7] Since that time, numerous recruits had reinforced the Christian ranks. It would be well to enumerate here the different ways in which God in His mercy, led the Gentiles to desire baptism. According to Tertullian, who lived under Alexander Severus, the greater number were attracted by the holiness and purity of life so conspicuous in the Christians; whilst those who witnessed the invincible constancy of the martyrs, were unable to resist the profound impressions made upon their souls. [8] The wonderful prodigies of which the simple faithful were frequently the instruments, such as curing the sick, casting out devils, etc., added much to the opinion already formed by the pagans, respecting the divinity of the Christian religion. [9] Even the oracles frequently confessed the truth of our dogmas, and Tertullian boldly proposed to the Senate, that, in presence of the magistrates, the Pythons, or even the gods, should be interrogated; promising that the rash Christian who ventured to provoke them, should be punished, if the spirit, speaking through these victims of idolatry, did not openly confess the truth and holiness of the God of the Christians. [10] Frequently, the infinite goodness of God, triumphed over the resistance of Pagans, by wonderful visions. We learn this by the express testimony of Tertullian. [11] Later we shall mention numerous conversions of this nature; at present we will simply cite that of Saint Basilides, who was gained to the faith by an apparition of the holy virgin Potaminia, who placed a crown "upon his head, and told him he would soon follow her to martyrdom [12] the learned Arnobius, converted by a similar grace, according to St. Jerome; [13] and many other instances mentioned in the most authentic Acts of the Martyrs. Origen unites with Tertullian in certifying the permanency of these vocations to the faith throughout the third century: "I do not doubt," says this great Christian philosopher, "that Celsus, by the mouth of his Jew, will ridicule me; but that will not prevent my saying that many persons have embraced Christianity, as it were, in spite of themselves, their hearts being so suddenly changed by some spirit which appeared to them, either in broad daylight, or at night, that their former aversion for our doctrine has been converted into such intense love, that they willingly died in its defence. We have witnessed many such cases." [14]

The zeal of the faithful did not permit the all-powerful mercy of the Most High to be the sole agent in these conversions; for it is in the designs of God that the Word of Life, the progress of which, neither man nor hell can restrain, should be spread throughout the world by mortal lips. Not only did the sacred hierarchy plant this fruitful seed; not only did the writings of numerous and eloquent apologists, such as Justin, Athenagoras, Tertullian, frequently prove to the most prejudiced minds, the innocence and happy effects of the Christian doctrine, but on all sides, the love of Christ which consumed so many hearts burning for martyrdom, gave birth to apostles whose eloquence could not be withstood. Without speaking of the innumerable conquests gained in the bosom of families by the sole effect of the powerful example of Christian virtues, how many instances may we not adduce of humble and valiant soldiers, winning to Christ their haughty leaders, who thenceforth considered it a prouder honor to bear on their breasts the proscribed cross, than to command under the Roman eagles? At other times, poor slaves, by their simple and sublime words, suddenly humbled at the foot of the crucifix, the pride of a patrician, or the haughtiness of a stately Roman lady, who, until then had thought of nothing but sensual vanity, or the cruel pleasures of the amphitheatre. And again, Christian virgins, victorious over the world and the flesh, and emulating the purity of angels, seemed to rival those angelic spirits in their zeal for the conquest of souls. But whilst St. Urban guided the Roman Church, none of these spouses of Christ exceeded in love, fidelity, and ardent zeal, the incomparable virgin Cecilia. Charmed with the marvels of Divine grace in this simple and courageous heart, the holy Pontiff, considering her the most precious flower in the garden of Christ, watched over and cherished her with truly paternal tenderness. God did not permit him, however, to know the sublime degree of glory to which Cecilia was destined. St. Urban lived in continual expectation of martyrdom; but he knew not that his sacrifice would be preceded by that of this youthful virgin.

[1] The acts of St. Callistus err, in giving to Palmatius the title of Consul; this qualification should not be taken literally. We frequently find, not only in the acts of the Martyrs and other Saints, but likewise in histories and chronicles which are the foundation of the annals of modern society, that the compilers make many errors with respect to titles, from the fact that they are not familiar with those in use at the time the events took place. This confounding of terms does not detract from the sincerity of the authors, nor from the reliability of the sources whence they derive their facts. Even the most severe critics overlook such trilling errors, which are so frequent in the historical works, written after the fall of the Western Empire.
[2] The process directed against Palmatius and Simplicius, and in consequence of which they obtained the crown of martyrdom, was the result of a search after some Christians, accused of witchcraft, on account of certain omens which had been attributed to them. In cases of this nature, Alexander's governors easily eluded his tolerance towards the Christians. The magistrates knew how to take advantage of an accusation of witchcraft, in the interval of persecution; and as to the crime of sacrilege a simple pi o vocation addressed to a Christian was often sufficient to obtain a reply that could easily be metamorphosed into an insult offered the gods and prove a cause of arrest. Finally, it was an easy matter to excite the people of certain districts to attack the faithful, and then accuse the latter as disturbers of the public peace.
[3] St. Urban merited the title of *Verus Confessor,* which is given him in the *Liber Pontificalis,* by the courage with which he confessed Jesus Christ before

the judges of Rome — twice according to the Acts of St. Cecilia, and seven times according to the Acts of other Martyrs, cited by Henschenius. Tillemont considers this antonomasia of the papal chronicle, a sufficient reason to refuse St. Urban the title of martyr, asserting that the martyrdom of this Pope is only based upon acts which have no authority. If Tillemont had taken the trouble to consult the different editions of the Sacramentary of St. Gregory, which represents the official tradition of the Catholic Church respecting the Saints whom she honors, particularly when they have been Pontiffs, he would have found that St. Urban in the VIII. of the calends of June, is always styled Martyr and Pope.

[4] 1 Pet. xi., 9.

[5] Anast. de Vitis Pontificum Romanorum. *In Urbano.*

[6] Hic fecit ministeria sacrata argentea, et patenas argenteas viginti quinque posuit. *Anast. Ibid.*

[7] Hesterni sumus, et vestra omnia implevimus, urbes, insulas, castella, municipia, conciliabula, castra ipsa, tribus, deourias, palatium, senatum, forum; sola vobis relinquimus templa *Apologeticus. Cap.* xxxvii.

[8] Ad Scapulam. cap. iv.

[9] Apolog. cap. xxxvii.

[10] Apolog. cap. xxiii.

[11] De anima. cap. xlvii.

[12] Euseb. Hist. Eccles. Lib. vi. cap. v.

[13] Appendix ad Chronic. Eusebii.

[14] Contra Cels. Lib. 1. n° 46.

Chapter Four - Saint Cecilia. Family of the Cecilli. The Appian Way In The Third Century

Cecilia was born in Rome, of one of the most illustrious patrician families. The ancient and noble race of the Cecilii, one of the branches of which adopted and rendered illustrious the surname of Metellus, gloried in their descent from Caia Cecilia Tanaquil, wife of Tarquin the elder, one of the most celebrated personages in the regal period. The Romans, to prove their admiration for this matron, had erected in the capitol a statue to her honor. [1] Varro, as Pliny relates, certifies that even in his time the distaff and spindle of Caia Cecilia were carefully preserved in the temple of Sangus, and that, the dress which this princess had woven for Servius Tullius [2] was kept in the temple of Fortune.

This traditional homage paid to a woman who did not forget in her political character the proprieties and occupations of her sex, is one of the characteristic features of ancient Rome, and we shall have occasion to remark to what an exalted degree the qualities and attributes of Caia Cecilia, enter into the type of the Roman wife. Even one of the Fathers of the Church, St. Jerome, eulogizes this mysterious personage, citing her as a model of conjugal modesty among the Gentiles. "The name of the prince to whom she was married," says the holy Doctor, "disappears beneath the shades of antiquity like that of other kings; but the rare virtue which elevated this woman above others of her sex, is so deeply engraven in the memory of all ages that it can never be effaced." [3] Thus the name of Cecilia which Tanaquil added to her Etruscan name, when called to reign over Rome, was respected by all generations in the Eternal City, at the time when it pleased the Almighty to offer a Christian Cecilia to the veneration, not only of the capital, but of the entire world. The illustrious race to which this holy virgin belonged, not only boasted of being allied to Caia Cecilia, but of numerous distinguished men who were its glory. Even in the time of the Republic, it had attained the highest pinnacle of grandeur. Without speaking of the dignities of the Dictatorship, Censorship, and Chief Pontificate, which members of the Cecilii family had successively enjoyed, and of which the annalists and the monuments of Rome still bear witness, its noble name is inscribed upon the Consular archives, eighteen times before the accession of Augustus to the Empire. [4]

The coins struck in Rome by the Cecilii family, are still so numerous that a series of forty-four, all belonging to the Republican period, has been published. [5] The military triumphs awarded to the different members of this house were numerous and splendid, and added to the fame of the ancient Cecilii, the title of Macedonicus, Balearicus, Numidicus, Dalmaticus, Creticus, in memory of brilliant victories over the enemies of Rome. The Cecilii family were often entrusted with the consular fasces by the Emperors, and, during the years which more immediately preceded the memorable epoch that gave birth to the happy virgin who rendered it more illustrious than all the great generals of whom it was so proud, we find in the archives the names of Caecilius Silanus, [6] Cascilius Rufus, [7] Caecilius Simplex, [8] Caecilius Classicus, [9] and Caecilius Balbinus, [10] as having been invested with the magistracy. [11]

Among the females of this illustrious race who are mentioned in history, we find the names of Cecilia, daughter of Metellus Balearicus, of whom Cicero relates several marvellous circumstances; [12] Cecilia, daughter of Metellus Dalmaticus, first married to Aemilius Scaurus and afterwards to the Dictator L. Sylla; and Cecilia, daughter of Q. Metellus Creticus and wife of Crassus, to whose memory, was erected a large and magnificent tomb, which is still the principal monument of the Appian Way. This celebrated edifice is built upon the very ground under which extend the mysterious Crypts that served as a place of concealment for St. Urban, and under the shadow of which the remains of St. Cecilia reposed for six centuries.

Thus were Pagan and Christian Rome mingled, until the latter having conquered by its blood, the divine plan, according to which the city of the seven hills had become mistress of the world — solely to unite all nations under the same spiritual empire — was rendered manifest to all nations and to all ages. Hence that sublime reciprocal relation which, at every step, so forcibly impresses the traveller in Rome, constantly meeting, as he does, with souvenirs of the Ancient city; her traditions and even her proper names applied, continued, and accomplished with astonishing plenitude under the Christian sway.

We cannot resist introducing our readers to a place under the walls of Rome, so intimately connected with incidents relating to St. Cecilia, and so visibly stamped with the elevated predestination of Christianity, that we cannot visit it without being struck by the mysterious connection between the two. This place is the Appian Way, the theatre of decisive events in behalf of the Eternal City. It was once adorned by the immense and costly sepulchral monuments of the Roman families. The ruins of these still cover the ground under which is the sacred labyrinth in whose shades legions of martyrs have slept.

Nothing can equal the grandeur and solemnity of this Way, which, during the reign of Alexander Severus, when the city was still enclosed on that side by the walls of Servius Tullius, commenced at the Capena gate and extended to the Campagna. It derives its name from Appius Claudius, who exercised the functions of Censor in the year of Rome, 442, and who raised it to the dignity of a Military Way. In 594, it was repaired by the consul, Marcus Cornelius Cetegus, and newly embellished by the application of the *Viaria* law of Caius Gracchus; under the empire it was successively improved by Vespasian, Domitian, Nerva, Trajan, Caracalla, Diocletian, and Maximin, as is attested by the inscriptions on the mile stones which have remained to our day.

Traversing the plain, which extends t6ward the south, the Appian Way is undulating like the ground. Sumptuous villas, temples of graceful or severe architecture, and here and there beautiful villages called *pagi,* embellished it throughout its course; but its principal ornament once consisted in the double row of tombs, traces of which may be found at the present day, for more than fourteen miles on either side of the way. The pavement, composed of solid blocks of lava, is magnificent and solid, like all the works of the royal people; it is still indented for miles with the deep ruts formed by the wheels of the Roman chariots, two thousand years ago. The Appian Way, like all the ancient roads, was somewhat narrow, on either side of it were foot-paths, along which the sepulchres were built. The style of these funereal monuments, imposing ruins of which may still be seen, was very varied; some were imitations of temples, built in an elegant and severe style; others were of a circular form, like a tower; many, pyramidal, and a large number, quadrilateral. These sepulchres belonged either to individuals or to entire families; some were intended for the patricians, others for their freedmen. The body of the deceased was frequently placed in a sarcophagus, but sometimes the loculus merely contained the ashes, according to the custom which was introduced towards the end of the Republic, of burning the corpse, a practice which became very general, except in some families who remained faithful to the ancient custom, which was afterwards re-established by Christianity. In addition to the tombs, the Appian Way likewise offered many mysterious columbaria, in which were a number of urns, placed one above the other, and containing the ashes of several generations. The gloom produced by this variety of sepulchres, contrasted strangely with the magnificence and luxury of the structures behind these avenues of death. The Pagans, fully sensible of the sublime lesson of the nothingness of human life, were actuated by a moral sentiment in selecting the public way, as the site of their tombs. [13] But the Christian religion was destined to complete this lesson by excavating under the very ground of the Appian, whole cities of sepulchres, which would not only remind man of his mortality, but elevate his soul by thoughts of immortality and triumph.

Such was the general aspect of this famous Road, which a poet of the first ages of the empire styled the "Queen of Ways;" [14] and if my readers will accompany me through it for several miles, dating from the time of Alexander Severus, we will return to the Capena gate, formerly situated in the valley between the Aventine and Caelian hills, not a mile this side of the present entrance. This latter opens in the enclosure of the walls constructed by Aurelian, thirty years after the events which form the subject of our history.

Issuing from the Capena gate, over which passed one of the might v aqueducts of Rome, [15] the traveller came in sight of the temples of Honor and Virtue, erected by Marcellus after the fall of Syracuse. [16] About a quarter of a mile from the gate, almost opposite the magnificent warm baths of Antoninus Caracalla, the Latin road separated from the Appian and turned towards the left. Near this spot were situated the gardens which still bore the name of the poet Terence. [17] Further on, commenced the interminable series of tombs. We learn from Cicero that the sepulchres of the Scipios, the Calatini, the Servilii and the Metelli, were situated outside the Capena gate, a short distance from the walls; [18] and the discovery made in the last century of the hypogeum of the Scipios confirms this precious information. [19] As yet we have not discovered the tomb of the Metelli, but as we proceed we will find many funereal reminiscences of this family, who seem, as it were, established upon this Way, awaiting the arrival of the noble offspring, to whom was reserved the honor of rendering the name of the Cecilii popular until the end of time. Not far from these famous sepulchres and quite near the Capena gate, was situated the tomb of Horatia, the young Roman maiden, who, during the monarchical period, was killed by her own brother for having wept over the death of her betrothed. Farther on, we find on this same Way, other monuments of the decisive victory which Rome gained over Alba. We learn from Roman history that the tomb of Horatia was constructed of cutstone, [20] which accounts for its having defied the ravages of time.

Another reminiscence of the early days of Rome, strikes the traveller's eyes before he reaches the tomb of the Scipios. The valley of Egeria which extends towards the left, was watered by the fountain of the Nymph who dictated the laws of Numa; it also contained the temple of the Camoenae, and a sacred wood. But it had lost its antique character, and already Juvenal complained that pompous marble had usurped the place of the fresh grass, and concealed the rock from which the waters flowed. [21] The poet also discloses to us another fact which it is very important to mention, namely, that in his time the Egerian fountain, the temple of the Camaenae, and the grove itself were in the possession of the Jews. "The proscribed muses," he says, "have given place to beggars." [22] For a long time, and particularly during the life of Juvenal, the Pagans confounded the Jews with the Christians. This gives us reason to believe that this quarter was inhabited by the disciples of Christ. Nearly all the first Christians were plebeians; they had been chosen from among the children of Jacob by St. Peter himself, who, when the edict of Claudius banished the Jews from Rome, was forced to leave the Capital for a short time; the beggarly Jews, mentioned with such severity by the poet, may, therefore, have been a Christian colony.

This conjecture becomes almost a certainty, if we examine attentively the Appian Way at the very point where we have arrested our steps. Outside, it is covered with Pagan monuments; whilst concealed from every eye, within the* bowels of the earth, commence the sombre galleries of the Christian catacombs. We have not yet reached the Aurelian enclosure, and already a new Appian Way bursts upon us where the heroes of Christ sleep in peace. On either side of this Queen of Ways, near the Capena gate, under the temples, baths, and villas of which imperial Rome is so proud, near the tombs of the Metelli and the Scipios, vast cemeteries extend where repose the generations of martyrs who preceded the reign of Aurelian. These subterraneous passages, which have been explored several times, and are still subjects of investigation, mark the spot where the Appian Way first assumes a Christian character; we meet them in the very commencement of our pilgrimage. It would be difficult to account for their presence so near the walls of Rome, exposed to the view of the whole city, had the neighborhood been peopled solely by Pagans; but the difficulty vanishes, if it be true that the indigent Jews of whom Juvenal speaks, were, in fact, a Christian Community. They lived in this vicinity which, in the topographical inscriptions of Rome, bears the title of *Vicus Camaenarum,* and rented, not only the Egerian fountain, but also the temple of the Canioense and the Sacred Grove. They had every facility to open subterraneous vaults, to excavate galleries, to bury therein the bodies of their dead. After passing under the arch of Drusus, and traversing the ground upon which now stands the rampart built by Aurelian, we find, a few steps to the right, the first mile stone [23] of the Appian Way, the inscription bearing the name of Vespasian and Nerva. We next descend to the valley of the Almo, where the Way is watered by the famous brook, in which the priests of Cybele annually washed the statue of their goddess. To the right, upon a hill, rises the monument of Priscilla, wife of Abascantius. Statius, in

23

his poem "Sylvae," describes the conjugal tenderness of this Roman lady and the inconsolable grief of her husband. "Opposite the city," he says, "at the entrance of the Appian Way, near the spot where Cybele ceases her lamentations, and forgets the brooks of Ida for the Almo of Italy; there, O! Priscilla! thy virtuous spouse has laid thee on a precious couch, wrapped in the luxurious purple of Sidon. The devastating hand of time shall be powerless against thee, so precious are the perfumes exhaled by the sacred marble which contains thy honored remains." [24]

Nevertheless, many centuries ago, the tomb of Priscilla was violated, and the monument which contained it. remained ignored upon the Appian Way, until recently, when the discovery of a mutilated marble showed that this sepulchre was the same which had proved powerless to protect the sarcophagus of Priscilla. We have here another instance of the renovation stamped by Christianity upon everything Roman. At the very moment when the poet was celebrating the obsequies of this Priscilla, who is only eulogized by the learned, another Priscilla, of no less illustrious birth, was living in Rome and a Christian. Mother of the Senator Pudens, and grandmother of the virgins Praxedes and Pudentiana, this noble lady will live in the memory of the Church until the end of time. At her own expense, she caused the vast subterraneous galleries which bear her name to be excavated upon the Salarian Way; hence when the ecclesiastical year brings us to the festival days of those who owe to her the burial ground, where their remains lie mingled with hers, the Church repeats her name with honor in the assembly of the faithful. [25]

> Ponit, et Idaeos jam non reminiscitur amnes.
> Hic te Sidonio velatam molliter ostro
> Eximius conjux (nee enim fumantia busta
> Clamoremque rogi potuit perferre) beato
> Composuit, Priscilla, toro; nil longior aetas
> Carpere, nil aevi poterunt vitiare labores
> Siccatam membris; tantus venerabile marmor
> Spirat odor.
>
> *Stace. Silv.* lib. v. Carm. I

"We find one of the most touching reminiscences of the founder of Christian Rome, directly opposite the tomb which Statius has immortalized. It was here that St. Peter, after the defeat of Simon the magician, yielding to the earnest solicitations of the faithful, was fleeing, notwithstanding his ardent desire for martyrdom, from the city over which he was destined to reign by his blood, when he met our Saviour carrying his cross. "Lord, whither art thou going?" said the Apostle. "To Rome," replied the Redeemer; "there to be crucified anew." [26] Warned by this celestial apparition, the Apostle at once retraced his steps; he revealed the divine oracle to the faithful, and the cross of the disciple was soon elevated in Rome, as that of his Master had been in Jerusalem. The sovereignty of spiritual Rome was at once and forever proclaimed by the effusion of the fisherman's blood. The victory had commenced on the Appian Way, and Catholic piety consecrated, by the erection of a sanctuary, the spot where the Apostle received the glorious command for the combat wherein he was to represent his divine Master.

The Way ascends here by rather a steep acclivity, and the tombs appear more and more crowded together; but the disfigured rums found at the present day, give but a faint idea of their former state. Vast *columbaria* on the left, throw some light upon the ashes of those for whom they were destined. One dates back to the days of Augustus and Tiberius, and is sufficiently large to have contained the ashes of three thousand persons. On the same side, at a little distance, that of the slaves and freedmen of Livia Augusta, [27] still bears traces of former magnificence. But if the surface of the ground gives us little information respecting the illustrious dead with whom it is peopled, the depths of the earth, rendered accessible by the indefatigable exertions of the *fossores* of the primitive Church, present avenues of sepulchres, the glory of which increases with time. Following the acclivity of which we have just spoken, a pilgrim, in the time of Alexander Severus, acquainted with the mysterious entrances to this immense necropolis, would have suddenly found himself in a vast city, silently inhabited by the illustrious dead, who had laid down their lives for Christ — not small cemeteries, like those of the Capena gate, but the colossal work of the Christian Pontiffs of the third century. To the right, the pilgrim would have beheld the crypts, excavated by order of Pope Zephyrinus, and continued by St. Callistus, whose name they boar; to the left, the cemetery of Pretextatus, which dates back to the same epoch, and presents, like that of St. Callistus, several stories, one above the other, of innumerable funereal corridors, intersecting one another in every direction, and numerous chapels where the bodies of the most celebrated martyrs repose. Many of these subterranean sanctuaries are lined with precious marbles, which reflected the light of lamps and torches, during the celebration of the holy mysteries; symbolical, and sometimes historical paintings, on the ceilings, walls, and under the arcade of the principal sepulchres, served as an instruction for the faithful, whilst by their emblematical character, they concealed from the eyes of the profane, the secret of the Christian dogmas.

These immense galleries continue for miles under the Appian Way, and in after years, the different quarters of the City of Martyrs, borrowed their names, from the more illustrious soldiers of Christ, buried near the entrance of their principal avenues. But, for the present, we will use the names of Callistus and Pretextatus, to designate, in a general manner, the two immense regions which extend the full length of the Way, from the acclivity we have described, to the valley, where, in the fourth century, the Basilica of St. Sebastian was built.

The persecutions of Decius and Dioclesian, sent innumerable recruits of martyrs to people these sombre dwellings; even in the pontificate of St. Urban, St. Zephyrinus' body [28] rested in one of the crypts situated on the right of the Way, where St. Callistus prepared the glorious asylum in which the invincible successors of St. Peter were to sleep, and into which we shall soon descend, to confide to the tomb, the precious remains of the noble heroine to whom we consecrate these pages. Saint Callistus was not buried in the retreat he had prepared for himself. Martyred in the trans-Tiberian region, near the church of St. Mary, the Christians, fearing they could not safely transport his body to the Appian Way, buried him in one of the crypts of the Aurelian. On the other side of the hill, behind the row of Pagan tombs which, extends to the right, in the valley formed by the depression of the soil, was a mysterious asylum, known, even in the third century, to the Christians of the entire world. For many years, the bodies of the holy Apostles, Sts. Peter and Paul, rested there. In the pontificate of St. Zephyrinus, they were still in their original tombs; the former at the foot of the Vatican on the Triumphal Way, the latter, on the Ostian, as is certified by Gaius, a priest of Rome, in a conference which he held with the Montanist Proclus, in the early part of this century. [29] But St. Callistus, on account of the sacrilegious orgies of Heliogabalus, had felt obliged to remove the holy relics to a place unknown to the Pagatis. The Appian Way was chosen to receive the first and greatest treasure of Christian Rome.

Heliogabalus, in his sacrilegious madness, threatened to profane these sacred remains, which are, as it were, the title deeds of the power of the Roman Church over all others, since they bear witness that St. Peter bequeathed her his authority with his blood. The worthless cousin of Alexander Severus, had erected upon the Palatine, near the palace of the Caesars, a temple destined to receive the infamous idol which bore his name. Being fully determined that no god but Heliogabalus should be adored in Rome, he not only resolved to transfer to this temple the statue of Cybele, the fire of Vesta, the Ancilia, the Palladium, those antique monuments of Roman worship, to which the Gentiles believed the destinies of the Capital of the World to be attached, but he had likewise declared his intention of collecting there, all the most sacred objects of Christian worship. We gather from a Pagan historian, these details so valuable in explaining the traditions of Christian Rome. [30] Saint Callistus, who was Pope at this time, and who has been immortalized by his active interest in guarding the crypts of the Appian Way, wished to protect from dishonor, the remains of the holy Apostles, and therefore removed them from the place where they had hitherto been venerated by the faithful. [31] He caused a sepulchral chamber to be built, the descent into which was effected by means of a well, and there the first Vicar of Christ, and the Doctor of the Gentiles, reposed each in his own tomb for many years, after which they were restored to their primitive resting place. The place where they rested for that brief interval is called the catacombs, [32] a name afterwards applied more or less correctly to the Christian crypts and cemeteries throughout the different Ways. In leaving this sacred spot, and resuming the course of the Appian, we see before us, towards the left, a vast plain which extends in the direction of the Latin Way. About half a mile distant, upon a graceful hill, and overlooking a *nymphaeum,* which was once deemed to be the site of the grotto and fountain of Egeria, a prostyle temple now rears its portico of four fluted columns of Pentelican marble. This temple, built during the Republican period, and less remarkable than many others which adorned the Roman Ways, merits nevertheless, a passing notice from the Christian traveller. At the present day, we are uncertain to what false divinity it was consecrated; for a long time it was supposed to be the temple of the Camaenae, celebrated by the poets, and mentioned on the topographical monuments of Home, at the identical period when the name of Egeria was given to the fountain in the valley. This opinion is not well supported, and yet, without any better foundation, the edifice bears at present, the name of Bacchus. However this may be, we learn from tradition, that it served as a retreat for the pontiff, St. Urban. This touching reminiscence has been perpetuated by an oratory built under the temple, in the soft, sandy stone, and since consecrated as a church, under the name of St. Urban. The crypts of Pretextatus, branch out through the surrounding ground; the pontiff was, consequently, perfectly secure in his place of concealment, which was at some distance from the public roads, and may, moreover, have belonged to the Christians, as did the temple of the Camaenae, under the very walls of Rome.

A Pope, already a confessor, and soon to be a martyr, seeking refuge in a Pagan temple, is a striking feature of that secret and continual labor, by which Christianity sapped the foundation of the religion of the Gentiles. In connection with this fact, we may mention that the Vatican crypt, which received the bleeding body of the Prince of the Apostles, after his martyrdom, was excavated under a temple of Apollo, [33] near the Circus of Nero. All traces of the temple have disappeared forever; but if the tomb of the Galilean fisherman, unceasingly venerated by the faithful, remains buried under its majestic shadow, the cross upon the cupola of Michael Angelo, towering to the very skies, proclaims that Christ, the conqueror of false gods, reigns no longer *merely* in the bowels of the earth.

Returning to the Appian Way, we find the third mile-stone, near which were placed the Christian beggars, charged with pointing out to the faithful, the retreat of St. Urban. To the left, the sepulchre of Cecilia Metella, rose in graceful majesty. Resting upon the summit of a hill, it overlooked the tombs, temples, and villas with which the plain was covered, and the aqueducts which bore the tribute of lakes and rivers to the city of the Caesars. This magnificent monument is now but a mass of ruins, yet it is still the most noble ornament of the Campagna. Supported upon a quadrilateral dais, and built of travertine, it has the appearance of an elegantly proportioned tower; the upper part is embellished with a frieze decorated with festoons separated by bulls' heads; the whole being crowned by a conical roof, also in travertine. [34] Neither man nor time has effaced the dedicatory inscription, placed under the frieze, and surmounted by several trophies. It bears the simple words:

CAECILIAE

Q. CRETICI. F.

METELLAE CRASSI.

Here, then, reposed Cecilia Metella, the daughter of Quintus Caecilius Metellus Creticus, who was consul under Augustus, in the seventh year of the Christian era. Crassus, the husband of Cecilia, erected this tomb in her honor. This last scion of the house of Crassus, is only known by the monument he erected to his noble spouse. Cecilia herself, has no other history than that transcribed upon the "marble. Still, the Christian who recalls the name and virtues of Cecilia, the spouse of Christ, can scarcely pass with indifference, this tomb, admired even by the profane archeologist, for its severe magnificence. The predestined martyr, in going to the crypts to visit the tombs of her family, and to receive the instructions of St. Urban, must have more than once stopped to gaze at this sepulchre, which contained the remains of one of the females of her ancient and illustrious race; but an humble tomb in the vault of the Appian Way, merited by sufferings endured for Christ, seemed to her far more desirable than the most splendid mausoleum which her opulent family could erect to her memory in that stately Way.

The monument of Cecilia Metella served as a fortress in the thirteenth century, and ever since has been disfigured by a crown of battlements. The large sarcophagus of marble, in which Crassus deposited the body of his wife, was carried away in the sixteenth century, and placed under the *cortile* of the Farnese palace, where it still remains.

Let us now return to the epoch of Alexander Severus, and after casting a last glance at the sepulchre of the Pagan Cecilia, let us ascend the hill, and admire one of the most sumptuous and luxurious villages which embellish the vicinity of the Eternal City. It is called the *Pagus Triopius,* and owes its origin to Herod Atticus, a celebrated rhetorician, who was consul in the year 143 of the Christian era. This wealthy Athenian dedicated the village as a monument to the memory of his wife, Anna Regilla, of the Julia family. In his inconsolable grief at the loss of his spouse, he not only dedicated all her favorite jewels to the Eleusinian divinities, Ceres and Proserpine, distributing them among the most venerated sanctuaries of these goddesses; but he also vowed to them that he would expend upon this region of the Appian Way, all the riches left by his lamented wife. A sacred grove, a temple in honor of the two Ceres, a sepulchral field dedicated to Minerva, and to Nemesis, are the solemn testimonials of the regrets of Herod Atticus, the founder of this *Pagus,* which he called *Triopius,* in honor of Ceres, whose sanctuary at Argos bore this name. [35]

The different Greek inscriptions, representing the dedication of this field of mourning, have been preserved until the present day, and the two principal, in beautiful Pentelican marble, after having ornamented the Borghese Villa at Rome, for two centuries, were, in 1808, transported to Paris, where they have since remained. The quarries of this marble, so famous in the history of Greece, belonged to Herod Atticus, who nearly exhausted them in the construction of the Stadium Panathenaicum. [36] It was not long before numerous dwellings were erected around the monument of Anna Regilla. The Pagus was called the abode of hospitality, — as we find upon one of the inscriptions, and during the reign of Alexander Severus, its population was considerable. A temple of Jupiter was erected upon the part which led to the Appian Way. Later we will revisit these places.

The Appian Way becomes more level after leaving the *Pagus Triopius*. In the distance rises Mt. Albanus with its nine cities, its loftiest summit crowned with the temple of Jupiter Latialis. The ancient Way, so long buried beneath its ruins, has reappeared, thanks to the munificence of the immortal Pius IX. Innumerable monuments have been brought to light, and we of the present day tread the pavement furrowed in olden times by the chariots of the conquerors of the world.

Near the fourth mile-stone, not far from Seneca's villa, a pyramid of barbarian construction attracts the eye; between Rome and Alba there are four others very similar. It is a popular tradition that these monuments were erected to the two Horatii and the three Curiatii. [37] However this may be, Livy, the historian, asserts that these valiant champions were buried in this locality. "Their sepulchres," he says, "are erected on the spot where each one fell, the two Romans in the same tomb, near Alba; the three Albans, nearer Rome, at a little distance from one another, according to the scene of combat. [38]

Thus the traces of this memorable contest which decided the victory of the Romans over the Albans, were not effaced from the Appian soil, and may, perhaps, be recognizable even in our days. But the Rome saved by the blood of the Horatii, lies buried under the ruins heaped up by the ravages of time, and of barbarians; it is but a mutilated corpse of which the fragments are exhumed; whilst the Rome, for which the martyrs of the Appian Way combated, raises its imperishable head and pursues its conquests to regions not even coveted by the boundless ambition of the Caesars.

It is time for us to return to the city where St. Urban and Alexander Severus are reigning, each in his own sphere. Gladly would we have followed the course of the Appian to the village *Tres Tabernae*, for it was there the Apostle Paul, the captive of Jesus Christ, led from the East to the feet of Caesar to whom he had appealed, was met by the Christians of Rome, who had gone out to receive him. [39] But we have explored sufficiently; for already we have passed the places which will be mentioned in our story. Nevertheless before retracing our steps towards Rome, let us admire at the fifth mile-stone, the monument of Quintus Caecilius, the uncle of Cicero's celebrated friend, Pomponius Atticus. [40] This tomb, the ruins of which are still imposing, will recall to our minds the name and race of the Christian heroine whose holy footsteps we have traced on this Queen of Roman Ways, where everything speaks of Cecilia, the glory of her ancestors, and the sublimity of her virtues.

[1] Nieburh. Histoire Romaine. Tom. ii, pag. 99.

[2] Lanam in colo et fuso Tanaquilis, quae cadem Caia Caecilia vocata est, in templo Sangi durasse, prodente se, autor est M. Varro: factamque ab ea togam regiam undulatam in aede Fortunae qua Servius Tullius fuerat usus. *Plin. Nat. Hist lib.* viii. cap. lxxiv.

[3] Notior est marito suo Tanaquilla. Ilium inter mu It a Regum nomina jam abscondit antiquitas. Hano vara inter feminas virtus, altius saeculorum omnium memorise, quam ut ezoidere possit, inlixit. *Adversus Jovinianum.* Lib. i. n° 49.

[4] Muratori. Inscriptiones. Tom. i.

[5] Riccio. Lemonete delle antiche famiglie di Roma. Naples, 1843.

[6] A. U. (In the year of the City, [Rome,]), 759.

[7] A. U. 769.

[8] A. U. 822.

[9] A. U. 854.

[10] A. U. 890.

[11] Muratori. *Ibid.* L'art de verifier les dates.

[12] De divinatione. cap. ii. et xlvi.

[13] Varro speaks thus of the etymology of the word *monumentum:* "Monumenta quae in sepulchris: et ideo secundum viam, quo praetereuntes admoneant et se fuisse, et illos esse mortaleis." *De lingua latina. lib.* v. *cap.* vi.

[14]   Qua limite noto
   Appia longarum teritur regma viarum.
        Stace. Sylv. lib. n. carm. n.

[15] Juvenal. Sat. iii. Martial, lib. iii. Ep. xivii.

[16] Tit. Liv. lib. xxv. cap. xi. lib. xxvii. cap. xxv. lib. xxix. cap. ix.

[17] Sueton. Terentii. cap. v.

[18] An tu egressus porta Capena quum Calatini, Scipiorum, Serviliorum, Metellorum Sepulcra vides, miseros putas illos? *Tuscul.* lib. i. cap. vii.

[19] The sepulchres of the Furii and the Manilii have been discovered nearly opposite the tomb of the Scipios.

[20] Cui soror virgo, quae desponsauni ex Curiatiis fuerat, obvia ante portani Capenam fuit. Horatiae sepulcrum, quo loco corruerat icta, constructum est saxo quadrato. Tit. Liv. lib. i. cap. xxvi.

[21] In vallem Egeriae descendimus, et speluncas,
   Dissimiles veris. Quanto praestantius esset
   Numen aquae, viridi si margine clauderet undas
   Herba, nec ingenuum violarent marmora tophum?
                                                    Juvenal. Satyr, iii.

[22] Hoc sacri fontis nemus, et delubra locantur

Judaeis, quorum cophinus, fcenunique supellex;
Omnis enim populo mercedem pendere jussa est
Arbor, et ejectis mendicat Sylva Camaenis.

Juvenal. Ibidem.

[23] This column has been transported to the terrace of the Capitol.

[24] Est locus ante urbem, qua primum nascitur ingeng
  Appia; quaque Italo gemitus Almone Cybela.

[25] The *Liber Pontificalis* mentions another Priscilla who, at the request of Pope Marcellus in the beginning of the 4th century, assisted in the construction of a cemetery upon the same Salarian Way. This may refer to some enlargements made at this period in the cemetery of Priscilla. But, besides the authority of the ancient Acts which inform us that St. Priscilla, Mother of Pudens, caused a cemetery to be constructed upon this Way, the characteristic style of many of the paintings with which it is adorned, evidently points out that it was built before the 4th century.

[26] S. Ambros. Sermo contra Auxentium. n° 13. Hegesipp. lib. iii. S. Greg. Magn. in Psalm, iv. Paenitentiae.

[27] Nibby. Analisi storico-topografico-antiquaria della carta de' dintorni di Roma. tom. iii. pag. 536.

[28] See the successive "guide books" of the Catacombs, from the 7th to the 10th century. We shall often refer to them.

[29] Trophaea Apostolorum habeo, quae ostendere possum. Si enim procedas via Triumphali, quae ad Vaticanum ducit, aut Ostiensi, corum invenies Trophaea quibus ex utraque parte statutis Romana communitur Ecclesia. *Euseb. Historia Ecclesiast.* lib, ii. cap, xxv.

[30] Ubi primum (Heliogabalus) ingressus est urbem, omissis iis quae in provincia gerebantur, Heliogabalum in Palatino monte juxta aedes imperatorias consecravit, eique templum fecit, studens et Matris typum, et Vestae igneni, et Palladium, et Ancilia, et omnia romanis veneranda in illud transferre templum, et id agens ne quis Romae Deus, nisi Heliogabalus coleretur. Dicebat praeterea Judaeorum et Samaritanorum religiones, et Christianam devotionem illuc transferendam, ut omnium culturarum secretum Heliogabali sacerdotium teneret. *Lampridius. Augusta historia.*

The historian also relates that Heliogabalus gave an exhibition of harnessed elephants on the Vatican plain; and that not having sufficient space for so novel an entertainment, he ordered the sepulchres to be destroyed. The tomb of the prince of the Apostles being subterranean, could not indeed be overturned, but as all access to it might be rendered very impracticable for the faithful, St. Callistus probably found in this extravagant command, an additional motive for removing to a place of security, the remains of St. Peter, those precious relics which were then, and ever will be, the Palladium of Christian Rome.

[31] Panvini de Septem Urbis Ecclesiis. cap. iv. pag. 34. Moretti. Disputatio de translatione corporum SS. Petri et Tauli ad Catacumbas.

[32] Kalendarium Bucherianum. Anastase. *in Cornelio.*

[33] Anastase. *in Petro.*

[34] Canina (L'Architettura Romana, text, 3 part page 217) maintains that the roof of Cecilia Metella's tomb was of a conical form. A simple inspection of the interior vault of the monument, proves this conjecture to be well-founded.

[35] Visconti (Ennio Quirino). Iscrizioni greche Triopee. Rome. 1794. page 5.

[36] Pausanias and Philostratus, cited by Ennio Visconti, page 8.

[37] Nibby. cited by Ennio Visconti, pages 543, 544.

[38] Sepulcra extant quo quisque loco cecidit: duo romana uno loco propius Albam; tria albana Romam versus, sed distantia locis, et ut pugnatum est. *Tit. Liv.* lib. i. cap. xxv.

[39] Act. xxviii. 15.

[40] Cornelius Nepos. *In T. Pomponio Attico.* cap. xxii.

Chapter Five - House in which Cecilia Passed Her Youth. She Consecrates Her Virginity to God. Her Parents Promise Her in Marriage. Valerian and Tiburtius

It is an ancient tradition of Christian Rome that the house in which Cecilia lived until she attained a marriageable age, was built upon the Campus Martius. A Church called St. Cecilia de Domo, [1] was erected at an early period upon the ground formerly occupied by the palace. It was rebuilt in the last century, through the liberality of Benedict XIII., as we will mention in its proper place, and the following inscription was taken from the ancient church, and engraven in mediaeval characters upon an antique cippus:

HAEC EST DOMVS
QVA ORABAT
SANCTA CAECILIA. [2]

The popular title (*del divino amore*) which has been attached to .this church forcibly reminds us that it was once the house of the Cecilii, which was truly a temple of divine love, during the years the virgin passed under its roof.

It is not surprising that the house of a patrician should have been built upon the Campus Martius, although ancient writers give us to understand that this immense tract of ground was destined for military exercises. Many temples and public edifices were erected upon a large portion of it under the Emperors, and Augustus, in his sixth consulate, caused his celebrated mausoleum to be constructed between the Flaminian Way and the left bank of the Tiber, even beyond the locality where we have placed the palace of the Cecilii. This mausoleum was surrounded by groves of trees, designed for the amusement of the people. [3] Later, in the third century, many private dwellings, with gardens attached, being erected upon the plain, the Emperors were thwarted in the project they had conceived, of beautifying this region with an immense and sumptuous portico, the pillars of which should reach to the Milvian Bridge. [4] This field for military exercises, was consequently more and more circumscribed, so that nothing prevents our believing that, during the reign of Alexander Severus, the Cecilii family erected a palace upon ground already covered with public and private edifices, and situated this side of the site where Augustus, two centuries previous, had built his superb mausoleum. We, therefore, implicitly believe the tradition respecting the situation of the Cecilii palace. [5] In this magnificent dwelling, decorated with all the splendor of Roman pomp, surrounded by the trophies and crowns of her ancestors, Cecilia, despising the ostentation and attractions of the age, practised with perfect fidelity, the divine law which Christ came to establish upon earth. History throws no light upon the means used by the Holy Spirit to win her to this celestial doctrine; but we know that from her earliest infancy, she was initiated in the mysteries of Christianity. Probably an aged relative, or faithful nurse, previously illuminated by the true light, instructed the young girl in the principles of that faith, the profession of which, in those days, almost necessarily involved the sacrifice of earthly happiness.

Although Cecilia's parents were Pagans, they do not appear to have opposed the attachment of their daughter to a religion which was daily gaining ground in Rome, and which had followers even in the imperial household. Either through tenderness or indifference, they permitted her to practise her religion, and attend the assemblies of the Christians. During the respite from persecution, a calm which was but the precursor of a storm, Cecilia publicly attended the celebration of the divine mysteries in the churches where the faithful were wont to assemble. She frequented the crypts of the martyrs, where the festivals of those Christian heroes frequently gathered the faithful of Rome; and the poor, who were entrusted with the secret of St. Urban's retreat, knew her well, and promptly delivered all her messages.

The Christians of this period lived in continual expectation of martyrdom; the thought of it seemed a necessary element in all their plans for the future; even as a sailor, who commences a long sea voyage, has ever present to his mind the dangers of a storm. Cecilia did not shrink from this prospect, so formidable to nature. On the contrary, she found rest and consolation in the thought that martyrdom would unite her forever to Christ, who had deigned to choose her from the bosom of a Pagan family, and to reveal himself to her. Whilst awaiting the happy summons, her heart was constantly united to that of her divine Master, with whom she held colloquies day and night. [6] Ravished with the charms of this interior communication, she sought Him at all times in the holy oracles, and the book of the Gospels, hidden under her garments, ever rested on her heart. [7] She derived from this sacred contact, a supernatural courage which elevated her above the weakness of human nature, whilst the vivifying unction of the words which are spirit and life (John vi., verse 64.) was communicated to her. The hand of the celestial spouse could alone claim the privilege of culling this fresh and fragrant flower from among the thorns of the Gentiles, and he inspired the heart of Cecilia with a love worthy of that which he had shown her by dying upon the cross. The virgin fully responded to the advances of her God, and vowed in her heart never to accept a mortal spouse. It is not known whether she received from St. Urban the sacred veil which Pudentiana and Praxedes had worn with honor, and which formed the most beautiful ornament of many Roman virgins. Cecilia may have privately made, in the secrecy of her own heart, the sacrifice of human affections, to consecrate herself to an eternal love. The spouse who had called her to be the bride of heaven, accepted her vows, and awaited in eternity, the day of their union. But where will this young maiden, whose soul is in heaven while her feet still tread the earth, find a protector in this most profane of cities, and in the bosom of a Pagan family? The Spouse she has chosen will defend His bride; He has commanded her guardian angel to appear to her; this celestial messenger has assured Cecilia of his protection; he will shield her from the world and its perils. She will be conscious that he is ever at her side, ready to strike with his avenging arm, the rash mortal who would presume to touch the treasure of heaven.

However, the virgin could not expect to gain without combat the nuptial crown destined for her; and she was soon called upon to merit it by a painful trial. Adorned with every natural grace, faint image of the beauty of her soul, Cecilia was fitted for the most illustrious alliance. Her parents, proud of their daughter, determined to unite her in marriage to some noble patrician. Incapable of understanding the sublime love which consumed the heart of Cecilia, and the ties which bound her to heaven, they sought for her an earthly spouse, and thus compelled the bride of Christ to receive a mortal bridegroom.

Marriages between Christians and Pagans still occurred at this epoch; though they sometimes led into difficult situations, they were often the instruments employed by God, to gain the infidel party to the true faith. The Church, however, conformably to the Apostolic doctrine, [8] strongly disapproved of them; necessity alone could excuse the faithful who contracted them. [9] Cecilia, as we have said, was forced by the imperious will of her parents, notwithstanding her vow of virginity, to marry a young pagan. The wisdom and greatness of God could alone triumph over so painful a situation.

Valerian was the name of the young Roman, destined, according to human views, to receive the hand of Cecilia. His noble birth, handsome person, and generous qualities, seemed to render him worthy such an honor, and he ardently longed for the day, when he would possess the treasure coveted by so many young patricians. The happy bridegroom had a brother, named Tiburtius, whom he loved with that ingenuous and devoted affection which was one of the principal features of his character. It made him happy to think that his "anion with Cecilia would strengthen the tender bonds which united them. The two brothers were not mistaken in their hope; but God alone knew to what an extent the love planted in their hearts by Cecilia, would surpass all earthly affection; and how soon these two brothers and their sister would pass to a region where pure souls are united in the bosom of infinite love.

[1] See the certificate of Urban III., of the Calends of March, given in full by Fonseca. *De Basilica S. Laurentii in Damaso*. Page 252.

[2] *This is the house where Saint Cecilia prayed.* This inscription has been removed to the Sacristy.

[3] Suetonius, in *Augusto*. cap. 100.

[4] Julius Capitolinus and Trebellius Pollion, cited by Canina. *Ibid.* page 439.

[5] We may also add that there was no reason for pointing out in Rome, the house in which Cecilia lived before her marriage, unless an ancient and venerable tradition had been really attached to the place where the church of St. Cecilia de Domo was afterwards built. Rome was sufficiently rich in the possession of the house where St. Cecilia consummated her sacrifice. This incontestable monument sufficed for the piety of the faithful; there was no necessity of gratuitously imagining the existence of a house upon the Campus Martius.

[6] Non diebus, non noctibus, a colloquiis divinis et oratione cessabat. *Acta S, Ceciliae*, edit, of Bosio (1600) and of Laderchi (1723).

[7] This custom of the first Christians, of carrying the Gospel concealed under their garments, was still preserved in the fourth, and fifth centuries. St. Jerome speaks of it as being very frequent among the Christian females, (in Matthaeum, lib. iv. ad caput xxiii. 6.) and St. John Chrysostom says: They wore it suspended around their necks. (Ad populum Antioch. Homil. xix. n° 4.) We find remains of this pious practice among the Irish Catholics, who, during their travels, or while ill, are in the habit of wearing the opening verses of the Gospel of St. John, (verses 1 — 14.) printed upon a sheet of paper. At the present time, when so many emigrate to America, it is probable that scarcely one could be found, who has not this sacred text sewed in his garments.

[8] II. Cor. vi. 14.

[9] We find nevertheless many celebrated examples after the third century; In the fourth, St. Monica married Patricius, a Pagan. In the fifth, St. Clotilda married Clovis.

Chapter Six - Anxiety of Saint Cecilia at Her Approaching Union with Valerian. Celebration of the Marriage. Confidence Reposed in Valerian by Saint Cecilia

Cecilia was not at liberty to refuse the testimonies of affection lavished upon her by Valerian. Full of esteem for the noble qualities of this young Pagan, she could have loved him as a brother; but she was betrothed to him, and the wedding-day was rapidly approaching. Who can conceive the anguish of the young virgin? The irresistible command of her parents, the high spirit of the young man, chilled her blood with fear, and she had no other resource, than to bury deeper in her soul, the chaste secret of that love which reigned supreme in her heart. [1]

She knew that her angel watched over her, but she would soon be forced to contend for herself; it was time to prepare for combat. Under a magnificent dress, embroidered with gold, she wore a hair shirt, seeking thus to mortify her innocent flesh, [2] and bring it into subjection to the spirit, that it might not recoil, when she would be called upon to pay with her blood, the signal honor of being the chosen bride of heaven. Condemned to live in the midst of patrician effeminacy, she took every precaution to deaden by voluntary suffering, that attraction to pleasure which tyrannizes over the children of Eve, and too frequently reveals to an imprudent and negligent soul, the deep corruption of the human heart.

If, following the example of the widow of Bethulia, Cecilia concealed under her garments the instruments of her penance, like David, she also weakened her flesh by rigorous fasts. According to the custom of the first Christians, when they wished to appease heaven, or obtain some signal favor, she abstained from food two, and sometimes three days, only taking in the evening a slight repast necessary to support life. [3] This courageous preparation by means of which she hoped to insure victory, was rendered still more efficacious by her continual and ardent prayers. With heartfelt earnestness she recommended to God the dreaded hour! [4] With tears and sighs she implored the assistance of the celestial spirits who cooperate in our salvation, of the holy Apostles, patrons and founders of Christian Rome, of the blessed inhabitants of heaven who protect our combats. [5] The favor which Cecilia so fervently solicited, was granted; but her celestial spouse was pleased to try his noble bride, that her virtue might be strengthened and purified. Was she not soon, in return for so much suffering, to enter into the possession of eternal happiness? Moreover, the approaching conflict which was to crown her with so much glory, was but the prelude to those combats in the midst of which, she would require a manly courage, not yet sufficiently developed in her heart by divine love.

The day finally arrives when Valerian is to receive the hand of Cecilia. [6] The palace of the Cecilii is in a state of commotion. The heart of the young man bounds with happiness, and the two families, proud of being united in their children, look forward to the hope of a posterity worthy their ancestors. Cecilia [7] is led forward, attired in the nuptial dress of the patrician ladies. The purity of her soul is well represented by her simple [8] white woolen tunic, trimmed with bands, [9] and fastened with a white woollen girdle. [10] This modest apparel, the last trace of the ancient gravity of Roman customs, was, at the same time, a glorious reminiscence in the Cecilii family; the plain robe of the bride being a memento of that woven by the royal matron, Caia Cecilia. [11] The hair of the virgin, according to custom, was divided into six tresses, [12] which was at once an imitation of the Vestal headdress, [13] and a touching symbol of Cecilia's consecration. [14] A flame-colored veil concealed from profane eyes her maiden beauty, on which the angels gazed with admiration. At this solemn moment, the virgin's heart was firm and calm; she confided in the protection of her guardian angel. For the first time, she was compelled to endure the celebration of Pagan ceremonies. The wine and milk were offered in her presence, [15] but she turned away her eyes. The cake, symbol of alliance, was broken, [16] and Cecilia's timid hand, adorned with the invisible ring of the spouse of Christ, was placed in that of Valerian. All was accomplished in the eyes of man, and the virgin, over whom heaven was watching, had taken another step towards danger. According to an ancient custom, the bride was conducted to the dwelling of her husband, at sunset. [17] The house of Valerian was situated in the trans-Tiberian region, near the Salutaris Way, a short distance from the Cestius Bridge, which connects the island of the Tiber to the Janiculum district. [18] This mansion, the last earthly dwelling of Cecilia, was destined soon to surpass in glory, the palaces, baths, and temples, which surrounded it, [19] and of which the antiquaries of the present day can scarcely find a trace. A sanctuary, consecrated by the blood of a virgin, it was to survive all the disasters of Rome, and to proclaim through the course of ages, the fidelity of her who dwelt for a short period beneath its roof. Nuptial torches preceded the retinue which accompanied Cecilia to the dwelling of her husband. The crowd extolled the charms of the young virgin, but she conversed in her heart, with that Almighty God who preserved the three children in the fiery furnace, and saved Daniel from the lion's fury. These memorials of the ancient covenant, so frequently carved upon the crypts which Cecilia had piously visited, animated her courage, as they had strengthened that of the martyrs. At length, the bridal party arrived at the palace. Under the portico, decorated with white tapestry, embroidered with festoons of flowers and leaves, [20] Valerian awaited Cecilia. According to the ancient custom, the bridegroom saluted his bride with this question: "Who art thou?" The bride replied, "Where thou art Caius, I will be Caia." [21] The allusion was doubly touching at the marriage of one of the daughters of the Cecilii family, this formula being another reminiscence of Caia Cecilia, who was venerated by the Romans, as the type of woman, in her domestic relations. The Christian Cecilia found a more accomplished model in the portrait drawn by the Holy Ghost, of the strong woman, and Valerian was soon to comprehend the truth of this divine oracle, so fully accomplished in his spouse. "Strength and beauty are her clothing, and she shall laugh in the latter day. She hath opened her mouth to wisdom, and the law of clemency is on her tongue. Her husband rose up, and he praised her." (Proverbs, xxxi. 25—28.) Cecilia then crossed the threshold of the door. [22] We have reason to believe, that, being a Christian, she was not compelled to conform to the superstitious ceremonies observed by the Romans, at the entrance of a bride under the conjugal roof. Those which followed were more congenial to a Christian. Water was presented to the bride, as an emblem of the purity with which she should be adorned; [23] a key was placed in her hands, as a symbol of the interior administration, henceforth confided to her care; [24] and finally she seated herself for a moment upon a fleece, [25] to remind her that she must not shrink from domestic labor. The bridal party then passed into the *Triclinium,* where the wedding supper was served. During the banquet, an epithalamium was sung, celebrating the union of Valerian and Cecilia, and a band of musicians made the hall re-echo with the harmony of their instruments. [26] During these profane concerts, Cecilia also sang in the depth of her heart, and her melody was united to that of the angels. She repeated that verse of the Psalmist, so well adapted to her situation: "May my heart and my senses remain always pure, O, my God! and may my chastity be preserved inviolable." [27] The Church has faithfully preserved these words of the virgin. They are recited each year, on the day of her triumph; and to honor the sublime concert, in which she sang with the celestial spirits, and which surpassed all the melodies of earth, she has been styled "Queen of Harmony."

After the banquet, matrons guided Cecilia's trembling steps to the door of the nuptial chamber, [28] decorated with all the effeminacy of Roman luxury, and rendered still more imposing by its silence and obscurity. [29] Valerian followed the virgin. When they were alone, Cecilia, strengthened by divine grace, addressed her husband these gentle and touching words: "My generous friend, I have a secret to confide to thee; swear that thou wilt respect it." [30] Valerian vehemently protested that he would preserve the secret of his bride, and that nothing should ever force him to reveal it. "Listen, then," resumed Cecilia, "I am under the care of an angel whom God has appointed protector of my virginity. If thou shouldest violate it, his fury will be enkindled against thee, and thou wilt fall a victim to his vengeance. If on the other hand, thou wilt respect it, he will favor thee with his love, and obtain for thee many blessings." [31]

Astonished and agitated, the young man, who was unconsciously controlled by grace, replied respectfully: "Cecilia, if thou wishest me to believe thee, let me see this angel. When I have seen him, if I recognize him as one of God's angels, I will comply with thy request; but if thou lovest another man, know that I will destroy both him and thee with my sword." [32]

Cecilia continued with ineffable authority: "Valerian, if thou wilt follow my advice, if thou wilt consent to be purified by the waters of the fountain of eternal life, if thou wilt believe in the only true and living God who reigns in heaven, thou shalt see my guardian angel." [33] "And who will purify me that I may see thy Angel?" exclaimed Valerian. [34] "There is a venerable old man," replied Cecilia, "who purifies mortals, after which they may see the Angel of God." [35] "Where shall I find this venerable old man?" cried Valerian. "Go out of the city by the Appian Way," replied Cecilia, "as far as the third mile-stone, there thou wilt find some poor beggars who ask alms of the passers-by. These poor creatures are objects of my constant solicitude, and my secret is known to them. When you approach them, give them my blessing, and say to them, Cecilia sends me to you and begs you will conduct me to the

38

holy old man Urban; I have a private message to deliver to him. When introduced into the presence of the holy man, repeat to him what I have just told thee; he will purify thee and clothe thee in new and white garments. On thy return to this apartment, thou wilt see the holy Angel, who will then be thy friend, and obtain for thee all thou desirest." [36]

[1] Parentum enim tanta vis et sponsi circa illam erat exaestuans, ut non posset amorem sui cordis ostendere, et quod Christum solum diligeret indiciis evidentibus aperire. *Acta S. Caeciliae.*
[2] Caecilia vero subtus ad carnam cilicio induta, desuper auro textis vestibus tegebatur. *Acta S. Caeciliae.*
[3] Biduanis ac triduanis jejuniis orans. *Ibid.*
[4] Cominendabat Domino quod tiniebat. *Ibid.*
[5] Invitabit Angelos precibus, lacrymis interpellabat Apostolos, et sancta agmina omnia Christo famulantia exorabat, ut suis eam deprecationibus adjuvarant, suam Domino pudicitiam commendantes. *Acta S. Caeciliae.*
[6] Venit dies in quo thalamus collocatus est. *Ibid.*
[7] Claustra panditi, januae:
Virgo adest. Viden' ut faces
Splendidas quatiunt comas?
Catull. in nuptias Julias et Manlii. Carm. lxi
[8] Plinii Nat. Histor. lib. viii. cap. lxxiv.
[9] Segmenta et longos habitus et flammea sumit.
Juvenal Sat. ii, v. 24.
[10] Festus upon the word *Cingulus.*
[11] Caia Caecilia prima texuit rectam tunicam, quales cum toga pura tirones induuntur, novaeque nuptae. *Plin, Nat. Hist.* lib. viii. cap. lxxiv.
[12] Festus on the word Senis.
[13] The Romans permitted brides, on the day of their marriage, the privilege of dressing the hair like the Vestals, as a last homage to their virginity.
[14] Tollite, o pueri, faces;
Flammeum video venire. — *Catull. Carm.* lxi.
Timidum nuptae leviter tectura pudorem
Lutea demissos velarunt flammea vultus.
Lucan. Pharsal. ii. v. 360.
We find the use of this veil, called *flammeum,* even in the marriages of Christians, until the fourth century, as is attested by St. Ambrose, (de Virginitate, cap. xv.) who calls it the nuptial *flammeum.* Among the Pagans, the bride wore it to express the stability she intended maintaining in the conjugal state, because this flame-colored veil was the distinctive badge of the Flaminian women to whom divorce was prohibited by law.
[15] Servius, in Georg. i. v. 244. Macrobe. Saturn, iii. 11.
[16] Servius, in Georg. i. v. 31. Pline. xvii. 3.
[17] Vesper adest, juvenes, consurgite, vesper olynipo
Exspectata diu vix tandem lumina tollit.
Jam veniet virgo, jam dicetur Hynienoeus.
39

Catull. Carm. lxii.

[18] The ancient topographical monuments of Rome describe in the trans-Tiberian region, a district which they designate under the name of *Statuae Valerianae*. This denomination, which is not explained by any of the archaeologists, probably refers to some monument of the Valerian family.

[19] See in Canina (Roma antica. pages 533, 605) a detailed account of the monuments of the 14th Region of Rome, situated beyond the Tiber.

[20] Necte coronam
Postibus, et densos per limina tende corymbos.

Juvenal. Sat. vi. v. 51, 52.

Ornentur postes, et grandi janua lauro.

Ibid. v. 79.

[21] *Ubi ta Caius, ego Caïa.* Valère-Maxime. *De nominum ratione.* Festus, on the words *Gaïa, Recta,* and *Regilla.* Alexander ab Alexandre *Genialium dierum.* ii. 5.

[22] Transfer omine cum bono
Limen aureolos pedes,
Rasilemdue subi forem.

Catull. Carm. lxi.

[23] Festus, on the word Aquae.
[24] Festus, on the word Clavis.
[25] Festus, on the word Pellis.
[26] Ite, concinite in modum:
Io Hymen Hymenaee io,
Io Hymen Hymenoee.

Catull. Ibid.

[27] Cantantibus organis, Caecilia in corde suo soli Domino de cantabat dicens: Fiat cor meum et corpus meuni immaculatum ut non confundar. *Acta S. Caeciliae.*

[28] Vos bonae senibus viris
Cognitae bene feminae,
Collocate puellulam.   *Catull. Carm.* lxi.

[29] Sed cum haec agerentur, venit nox in qua suscepit una cum sponso suo cubiculi secreta silentia. *Ibid.*

[30] O dulcissime et amantissime juvenis, est mysterium quod tibi confiteor, si modo tu juratus asseras tota te illud observantia custodire. *Ibid.*

[31] Angelum Dei habec amatorem qui nimio zelo corpus meum custodit; hic si vel leviter senserit quod tu me polluto amore contingas, statim circa te suum furorem exagitat, et amittis florem tuae gratissimae juventutis; si autem cognoverit quod me sincero corde et immaculato amore diligas, et virginitatem meam integram illibatamque custodias, ita te quoque diligit sicut me, et ostendit tibi gratiam suam. *Acta S. Caeciliae.*

[32] Si vis et credam sermonibus tuis, ostende mihi ipsum Angelum et si approbavero quod vere Angelus Dei sit, faciam quod hortaris; si autem virum alterum diligis, et te et ilium gladio feriam. *Ibid.*

[33] Si consiliis meis acquiescas, et permittas te purificari fonte perenni, et credas unum Deum esse in coelis vivum et verum, poteris eum videre. *Ibid.*

[34] Et quis erit qui me purificet, ut ego angelum videam? *Ibid.*

[35] Est senior qui novit purificare homines, ut mereantur videre Angelum Dei. *Acta S. Caeciliae.*

[36] Vade in tertium milliarium ab urbe, via quae Appia nuncupatur; illic invenies pauperes a transeuntibus alimoniae petentes auxilium; de his enim mihi semper cura fuit, et optime hujus mei secreti sunt conscii: hos tu dum videris, dabis eis benedictionem meam, dicens: Caecilia me misit ad vos, ut ostendatis mihi sanctum senem Urbanum; quoniam ad ipsum habeo ejus secreta mandata, quae perferam. Hunc tu, dum videris, indica ei omnia verba mea, et dum te purificaverit, induet te vestimentis novis et candidis, cum quibus, mox ut ingressus fueris istud cubiculum, videbis angelum sanctum etiam tui amatorem effectum, et omnia quae ab ipso poposceris, impetrabis. *Ibid.*

Chapter Seven - Valerian Repairs to Pope Saint Urban. He is Baptized. His Return. Arrival of Tiburtius

Urged by an unknown power, the young Roman, a moment ago so full of fire, quitted without an effort the virgin whose gentle accents had softened his heart, and before day-break reached Urban, having found everything as Cecilia had predicted. He related to the Pontiff his interview with his bride in the nuptial chamber, which at once explained his presence. The venerable old man, overjoyed at the glad tidings, fell upon his knees, and raising his hands to heaven, his eyes moistened with tears, exclaimed: "Lord Jesus Christ, author of chaste resolves, receive the fruit of the divine seed Thou hast sown in the heart of Cecilia. Good Shepherd, Cecilia, thy servant, like an innocent lamb, [1] has fulfilled the mission Thou hast confided to her. In a moment, she has transformed her husband from an impetuous lion, into a gentle lamb. If Valerian did not already believe lie would not be here. Oh, Lord! open the ear of his heart to Thy words, that he may acknowledge Thee, his Creator, and that he may forever renounce the devil, his pomps, and his idols." [2]

Urban remained a long time in prayer; Valerian was deeply touched. Suddenly, a venerable old man, with garments white as snow, appeared before them, holding in his hand a book, written in characters of gold. It was the great Apostle of the Gentiles, St. Paul, the second pillar of the Roman Church. At this imposing sight, Valerian, half dead with terror, fell prostrate upon the ground. The august old man kindly assisted him to rise, saying, "Bead this book and believe. Thou wilt then be worthy of being purified, and of contemplating the Angel whom Cecilia promised thou shouldst see." [3]

Valerian raised his eyes, and without pronouncing the words, commenced to read the following passage: "One Lord, one faith, one baptism; one God and Father of all, who is above all, and through all, and in us all." [4] When tie had finished reading, the old man said to him: "Believest thou this?" Valerian energetically exclaimed: "There is nothing more true under heaven; nothing which should be more firmly believed." [5] As he ceased speaking, the old man disappeared and left Valerian alone with the Pontiff. St. Urban at once conducted the young man to the fountain of salvation, and after admitting him to the most august mysteries of the faith of Christ, told him to return to his bride.

Cecilia had conquered, and the first trophy of her victory, was the heart of Valerian, offered to the Saviour of mankind. During the absence of her husband, she had not left the nuptial chamber, still re-echoing with the sublime converse of the preceding night, and redolent with the celestial perfume of virginity. She had unceasingly prayed for the consummation of the great work, her words had commenced, and she awaited with confidence the return of a husband who would henceforth be dearer to her than ever.

Valerian, habited in the white garment of the neophytes [6] which he had just assumed, [7] reached the door of the chamber, and glancing respectfully around the room, beheld Cecilia prostrate in prayer, and, by her side, the Angel of the Lord, his face resplendent as lightning, his wings brilliant with the most gorgeous colors. The blessed spirit held in his hand, two crowns interwoven with roses and lilies, [8] one of which he placed upon the head of Cecilia, and the other upon that of Valerian, whilst with the musical accents of heaven, he said. "Merit to preserve these crowns, by the purity of your hearts, and the sanctity of your bodies. I bring them fresh from the garden of Heaven. These flowers will never fade, nor lose their celestial fragrance; but no one can see them, who has not endeared himself to Heaven, as you have done, by virginal purity. And now, Valerian, as a reward for thy acquiescence in the chaste desires of Cecilia, Christ the Son of God, has sent me to thee, to receive any request thou dost wish to make him." [9]

The young man, overcome with gratitude, threw himself at the feet of the divine messenger, and thus expressed his desires: "Nothing in life is more precious to me than the affection of my brother, and now that I am rescued from peril, it would be a bitter trial to leave this beloved brother exposed to danger. I will, therefore, reduce my requests to one; I beseech Christ to deliver my brother, Tiburtius, as he has delivered me, and to perfect us both in the confession of His name." [10] The angel, turning towards Valerian, his face radiant with that heavenly joy which the celestial spirits experience when a sinner is converted to God, replied, "Since thou hast asked a favor which Christ is much more eager to grant, than thou to desire it, thou shalt gain the heart of thy brother as Cecilia has won thine, and both shall receive the palm of martyrdom." [11]

As he concluded these words, the angel ascended to heaven, leaving Cecilia and her husband transported with happiness. Cecilia glorified the Master of hearts, who had so brilliantly displayed the riches of His mercy. She trembled with joy in seeing that Valerian's crown was, like her own, intertwined with roses and lilies, as a proof that he also would receive the honor of martyrdom. Tiburtius was to share the palm with his brother, but the happy prediction had not been extended to her. She was destined then to survive the brothers, and assist them in their combat; beyond this the decrees of heaven had not been revealed. Valerian and Cecilia spent the ensuing hours in pious conversation, encouraging each other to merit the crowns which the Angel had placed upon their brows. The neophyte, filled with the divine love which participation in the sacred mysteries had kindled in his heart, spoke with the fervor of a recent convert; Cecilia, initiated from her infancy in the doctrine of salvation, expressed herself with the experience and authority of a tried Christian. In the midst of this holy conversation, Tiburtius, impatient to see his brother, entered, and interrupted a colloquy worthy of angels. Saluting Cecilia, the wife of his beloved brother, he respectfully approached and imprinted upon her forehead a fraternal kiss; [12] but what was his surprise in perceiving the most delightful perfume issuing from her hair. "Cecilia!" cried he, "whence comes this delicious odor of roses and lilies, at this season of the year? Were I to hold in my hand a bouquet of the most fragrant flowers, their perfume would not equal that which I now inhale. It is so marvellous that it seems to renew my whole being." [13] "It is I, O Tibertius," replied Valerian, [14] "who have obtained for thee the favor of enjoying this sweet odor, and if thou wilt only believe, thou wilt also see the flowers whence it comes. Thou wilt then know Him whose blood is crimson as roses, whose flesh is white as lilies. Cecilia and I wear crowns which thy eyes cannot yet behold. The flowers of which they are composed, are brilliant as purple, and spotless as snow." [15] "Is this all a dream, Valerian, or art thou speaking the truth?" cried Tiburtius. "Until now," replied Valerian, "our whole life has been a dream. At last we have discovered the truth, and there is no deceit in us; the gods we adored are but devils." "How dost thou know this?" asked Tiburtius. Valerian answered: "The Angel of God instructed me, and thou canst also see this blessed spirit if thou wilt consent to be purified from the stain of idolatry." "How long," demanded Tiburtius, "must I wait for this purification which will render me worthy of beholding the Angel of God?" "A very short time," replied Valerian; "only swear to me that thou dost renounce the idols and acknowledge there is one only God, who dwells in heaven." "I cannot understand," cried Tiburtius, "why thou dost exact of me this promise."

[1] Hughes of Saint-Cher, commenting these words of Isaias: *"Leo et ovis simul morabuntur,"* ingeniously applies them to St. Cecilia, who, like an innocent Lamb, dwelt with Valerian, figured by the Lion. The allusion is equally clear in St. Urban's words. This renders inexplicable the change which these words have undergone in one of the Anthems of St. Cecilia's office, where, since the ninth century we read *apis,* instead of *ovis.* It is evident that the text is modified by this reading, and that the thread of the discourse is broken. The Ambrosian Missal, in which the words of St. Urban form the Offertory of St. Cecilia's Mass, has preserved the lesson *ovis,* as we read it in the Acts of the Saint. St. Bernard likewise read it so, as we see by a very pointed allusion, in his life of Saint Malachy.

[2] Domine Jesu Christe, seminator casti consilii, suscipe seminum fructus quos in Caecilia seminasti. Domine Jesu Christe, Pastor bone, Caecilia famula tua, quasi ovis argumentosa tibi deservit; nam sponsum, quern quasi leonem ferocem accepit, ad te Domine, quasi agnum mansuetissimum destinavit; iste hue, nisi crederit, non venisset: aperi ergo Domine cordis ejus januarn sermonibus tuis, ut te Creatorem suum esse cognoscens, renuntiet Diabolo, et pompis ejus, et idolis ejus. *Acta S. Caeceliae.*

[3] Lege hujus libri textum, et crede, ut purificari merearis, et videre angelum, cujus tibi aspectum Caecilia virgo devotissima repromisit. *Ibid.*

[4] Unus Dominus, una fides, unum baptisma, unus Deus, et Pater omnium, qui super omnia, et in omnibus nobis est. *Acta S. Caeciliae.*

[5] Cumque hoc infra se legisset, dicit ei senior: Credis ita esse, an adhuc dubitas? Tunc Valerianus voce magna clamavit dicens: Non est aliud, quod verius possit credi sub coelo. *Ibid.*

[6] It should not be a matter of surprise that Valerian wore his white dress through the streets of Rome. Garments of this color were not unusual in a city, peopled by men of every nation, some of whom continually wore white.

[7] Veniens igitur Valerianus indutus candidis vestimentis. *Ibid.*

[8] Caeciliam intra cubiculum orantem invenit, et stantem juxta eam Angelum Domini pennis fulgentibus alas habentem, et flameo aspectu radientem, duas coronas habentem in manibus coruscantes rosis, et liliis albescentes. *Acta S. Ceciliae.*

[9] Istas coronas immaculato corde, et mundo corpore custodite, quia de paradiso Dei eas ad vos attuli, et hoc vobis signum erit, numquam marcidum aspectus sui adhibent floreni, nunquani sui minunt suavitatem odoris, nec ab alio videri poteruunt, nisi ab eis quibus ita castitas placuerit sicut vobis probata est placuisse. Et quia tu, Valeriane, consensisti consilio castitatis, misit me Christus Filius Dei ad te, ut quam volueris, petitionee insinues. *Ibid.*

[10] Nihil mihi in ista vita dulcius extitit, quam unicus mei fratris affectus, et impium mihi est, ut me liberato, germanum meum in periculo perditionis aspiciam; hoc solum omnibus petitionibus meis antepono, et deprecor, ut fratrem meum Tiburtium, sicut me, liberare dignetur, et faciat nos ambos in sui nominis confessione perfectos. *Acta S. Caeciliae.*

[11] Audiens haec angelus laetissimo vultu dixit ad eum: Quoniam hoc petisti, quod melius quam te Christum implere delectat, sicut te per famulam suam Caecilium lucratus est Christus; ita per te quoque tuum lucrabitur fratrem, et cum eodem ad martyrii palmam pervenies. *Ibid.*

[12] Illis epulantibus in Christo, atque in sedificatione sancta sermocinantibns, Tiburtius Valeriani frater advenit, et ingressus est quasi ad cognatam suam, osculatus est caput sancta? Caeciliae, et ait, etc. *Acta S. Caeciliae.*

[13] Miror hoc tempore roseus hic odor et liliorum unde respiret; nam si tenerem ipsas rosas, aut ipsa lilia in manibus meis, nec sic potuernnt odoramenta mihi tantae suavitatis intundere; confiteor vobis, ita sum refectus, ut putem me totum subito renovatum. *Ibid.*

[14] It is almost useless to observe that Valerian, under this figurative language, referred to the mystery of the Blessed Eucharist, which was concealed from the Pagans, and revealed to the Catechumens only a few days before their baptism.

[15] Odorem quidem meruisti, me interpellate, suscipere, modo te credente promereberis etiam ipso roseo aspectu gaudere, et intelligere cujus in rosis sanguis florescit, et in liliis cujus corpus albescit; coronas enim habemus, quas tui oculi videre non praevalent, floreo rubore, et niveo candore vernantes. *Acta S. Caeciliae.*

Chapter Eight - Interview of Tiburtius with St. Cecilia and Valerian. His Conversion and Baptism

Cecilia had maintained perfect silence during the dialogue between the brothers: the ardent zeal of Valerian had left her no time to speak, and besides, it was but proper that he should be the first to address his brother. But the virgin, who had been nourished from her childhood in the evangelical doctrine, understood much better than her husband, how to convert a Gentile from the errors of idolatry. Recalling the arguments employed against idols, by the ancient prophets, the Christian apologists, and the martyrs, Cecilia thus spoke:

"I am astonished, Tiburtius, that thou hast not already understood that statues of clay, wood, stone, brass, or any other metal, cannot be gods. How can any one esteem as gods, vain idols, upon which spiders spin their webs, and birds build their nests? [1] Statues, composed of materials drawn from the earth by the hand of malefactors, condemned to the mines. Tell me, Tiburtius, is there any difference between a corpse and an idol? A corpse has all its members, yet it possesses neither breath, voice, nor feeling. An idol also has all its members, but those members are incapable of action, and, consequently, far inferior to those of a dead man. At least, during his life, the eyes, ears, mouth, nose, feet, and hands of the man, fulfilled their office; but the idol began with death, and remained dead; it never lived, nor even had the power to live." [2]

Tiburtius, suddenly impressed with the emptiness of the idols before which he had offered incense, exclaimed: "Yes, it is so, and he who does not understand it, is upon a level with the brutes." [3] Cecilia, overcome with joy at this reply, pressed to her heart the pagan who already commenced to see the light. "I recognize thee as my brother!" she exclaimed. "The love of Christ has made Valerian my husband; the contempt thou dost profess for idols, makes me truly thy sister. The moment has arrived when thou wilt believe; go then, with thy brother, and receive the sacrament of regeneration. Thou shalt then see the angel, and obtain forgiveness for all thy sins." [4]

Tiburtius then turned to Valerian "who is the man to whom thou wilt conduct me?" "A great personage," replied Valerian; "he is called Urban; he is a venerable old man, with white hair, an angelic countenance, and whose conversation is full of truth and wisdom." "Can it be," said Tiburtius, "the Urban whom the Christians call their Pope? I have heard that he has already been twice condemned, and that he is concealed in some subterranean vaults, I know not where. If he be discovered, he will be cast to the flames, and if we are found with him, we will share his fate. Thus in recompense for seeking a divinity concealed in Heaven, we will suffer upon earth cruel torments." [5]

Although Tiburtius had learned to despise the idols, he did not yet contemn the sufferings of this world. Cecilia came to his assistance. "If this life were the only one," said she, "if there were no other, we would be reasonable in fearing to lose it; but if there be another life which will never end, should we dread losing that which is transitory, when at the price of this sacrifice, we shall win that which will last forever?"

Such language was very novel to a young man educated in the Roman society of the III. century, a society, remarkable alike for the most humiliating superstitious, a corruption of morals worthy of Heliogabalus, and all the aberrations of sceptical philosophy; he therefore replied to the young virgin. "I have never heard such a doctrine; can there be another life after this!" "But," answered Cecilia, "is the life we possess in this world, worthy the name? After having been the sport of every suffering, both of soul and body, it terminates in death which puts an end to its pleasures, and its pains. When it ceases, we can scarcely believe it has ever existed; for that which is gone forever, is as nothing. As to the second life which succeeds the first, it has endless joys for the just, eternal torments for the wicked." "But who has lived this life?" asked Tiburtius, "who has returned to tell us what passes there? Upon whose testimony can we believe it?" Then Cecilia, rising with the majesty of an Apostle, uttered these forcible words: [7] "The Creator of heaven and earth and of all they contain, engendered a Son out of His own substance, before all beings, and by His divine virtue produced the Holy Ghost; the Son, that through Him, He might create all things; the Holy Ghost, that He might vivify them. All that exists, the Son of God, engendered by the Father, has created; all that is created, the Holy Ghost, who proceeds from the Father, [8] has animated." [9]

"But how is this, Cecilia P cried Tiburtius; "a moment ago thou did'st say we should believe in one only God, who is in heaven, and now thou speakest of three Gods." Cecilia replied: "There is but one God in His majesty, and if thou wouldst understand how He exists in the Holy Trinity, listen to this comparison. A man possesses wisdom; by wisdom we mean genius, memory, and understanding; genius, which discerns truths; memory, which retains them; and understanding, which examines them. Do we then believe the same man possesses three different kinds of wisdom, or do we not rather say that he exercises his wisdom by three separate faculties? How then can we hesitate to acknowledge a majestic Trinity in the essential unity of the omnipotent God?" [10]

Tiburtius, dazzled by the brilliancy of so august a mystery, exclaimed: "O, Cecilia! a human tongue could not give such enlightened explanations; the angel of God speaks by thy mouth!" Such was the lively gratitude with which this young man welcomed the divine light that was beginning to dawn upon his soul. He did not venture again to address the virgin, the interpreter of heaven; but turning towards his brother Valerian, he said: "I willingly confess, the mystery of one only God no longer arrests me; I desire but one thing, to hear the continuation of this discourse which will satisfy all my doubts." "Thou should'st apply to me, Tiburtius," said Cecilia, "thy brother, newly clothed in his baptismal robe, is unable to answer all thy questions. But I have been instructed from my cradle in the wisdom of Christ; thou wilt find me ready to 'solve all the difficulties thou may'st wish to propose." [11] "Well," answered Tiburtius, "I wish to know who has told you of that other life of which you both speak?"

The virgin, resuming her discourse with divine enthusiasm, continued: "The Father sent His only Son from heaven to earth to be conceived in the womb of a virgin. This divine Son, from the summit of a mountain, proclaimed these words; "Come ye all to me." At once, people of every age and condition hastened to Him. He then said to them; 'Do penance for the sins of which you have been guilty; for the kingdom of God which will put an end to the kingdom of men is at hand. God will admit into this kingdom those who have believed, and will confer the highest honors upon those who have been most holy. The wicked shall be punished with eternal torments; they shall be devoured by fire, but shall never be consumed. The just shall be surrounded with an eternal splendor of glory, and endless delights shall be their portion. Seek no longer, children of men, the fleeting joys of this life; but ensure for yourselves the eternal felicity of the life to come. The former is short, the latter will last forever.' The nations did not at first believe in this oracle; they asked: 'Who has entered into this life and returned to certify to us the truth of what thou sayest?' The Son of God replied: 'If I raise from the dead, those whom you yourselves have buried, will you still refuse to believe the truth? If you will not believe my words, at least believe my miracles.' [12] To prove the truth of His words, He, in presence of the people, raised to life persons who had been buried three or four days, and whose bodies had already become putrefied. He walked upon the sea, commanded the wind, stilled tempests. He restored sight to the blind, speech to the dumb, hearing to the deaf, the use of their limbs to the lame and paralytic; he put the devils to flight, and delivered the possessed.

"The impious were irritated at these miracles, because the people left them to attach themselves to Him, and threw their garments under His feet, exclaiming: 'Blessed is He who cometh in the name of the Lord.' Men, called Pharisees, jealous of his success, betrayed Him to the governor, Pilate, saying that He was a magician and a man guilty of every crime. They excited a tumultuous sedition, in the midst of which they crucified Him. Knowing that

His death would effect the salvation of the world, He permitted Himself to be taken, insulted, scourged, and put to death. He knew that His passion alone could chain the devil, and confine the "unclean spirits in their place of punishment. He, therefore, who had never committed sin, was loaded with chains, in order that the human race might be delivered from the bonds of sin. He who is forever blessed was cursed, that we might be freed from malediction. He suffered Himself to be the sport of the wicked, to snatch us from the illusions of the devil whose playthings we were. He was crowned with a crown of thorns, to deliver us from the capital punishment which the thorns of our sins had merited. He tasted the gall presented Him, in older to expiate the sensuality of our first parents, by which sin had entered into the world. In His thirst they gave Him vinegar to drink, and He willingly accepted it, for it was His wish to drain the chalice we had merited. He was stripped of His garments, that He might cover with a robe of dazzling whiteness, the nudity produced in our first parents by the serpent's perfidy. He was nailed to the tree of the Cross to take away the prevarication which had come by a tree. He permitted death to approach Him, that it might be overthrown in the struggle; and that, as it had reigned by the serpent, it might become with the serpent, the captive of Christ. Finally, when the elements contemplated their Creator, elevated upon the cross, they were seized with fear; the earth quaked, the rocks were rent, the sun was obscured, and darkness covered the whole world. A bloody cloud intercepted the pale rays of the moon, and the stars disappeared from the heavens. The graves were opened, and many bodies of the saints that had slept, arose, to attest that the Saviour had descended into hell, that He had snatched the devil's sceptre from his hands, and that in dying he had conquered death, which henceforth should be chained under the feet of those who should believe in Him.

"Now thou seest why we rejoice when we are ill-treated for His sake, and why we glory in persecution. It should be thus, since we know that this perishable and miserable life will be followed by the eternal life, which the Son of God promised to His Apostles, after His resurrection, before ascending to heaven. The testimony of three persons is sufficient to satisfy a wise man, but Christ, after His resurrection, appeared not only to His twelve apostles, but to more than five hundred persons, that there might not be the slightest pretext for doubting so astonishing a prodigy. His disciples who were sent by Him to preach these marvels throughout the entire world, supported their doctrine by the most evident miracles. In his name, they cured all kinds of diseases, cast out devils, and raised the dead to life. I think, Tiburtius, I have now fully answered thy questions; reflect if it be not well to contemn the present life, and seek with ardor and courage that which will follow. He who believes in the Son of God, and observes His commandments, will not die when his perishable body is placed in the tomb; he will be received by the holy angels, and conducted to Paradise. But death and hell combine to distract man with a thousand useless cares, and to engage his thoughts with a multitude of imaginary wants. Sometimes he is intimidated by an approaching misfortune; at others, seized with a desire of wealth; again, he is fascinated with sensual beauty, or lured by intemperance; in fine, by inducing man to abandon himself to the free gratification of his carnal appetite, death successfully produces such a total forgetfulness of the future, that his soul, when separated from the body, is found entirely void of merit, loaded only with the overpowering weight of sin. I feel, Tiburtius, that I have merely touched upon a few points of this grand subject; if thou wishest me to continue, I am at thy service." [13] But the young Pagan had understood everything, and the rapid discourse of Cecilia had completely changed his soul. His tears flowed abundantly, and his heart was rent with sighs. His soul had not been hardened by the vices which spring from the love of pleasure or of wealth. "If ever," he cried, throwing himself at Cecilia's feet, "my heart or my thoughts cling to this life, I consent not to enjoy that which will follow. Let the giddy and thoughtless revel if they will, in the senseless pleasures of the present; until now I have lived without an object: it shall not be so henceforth." [14] After having made this promise to the virgin, Tiburtius turned to Valerian. "My dear brother," he exclaimed, "take pity on me; delay no longer; every detention alarms me, and I can no longer support the weight which overpowers me. I beseech thee to conduct me immediately to the man of God, that he may purify me, and render me a participant of that life, the desire of which already consumes my heart." [15] But two days had elapsed since the marriage of Cecilia, when Tiburtius received the grace of baptism, and thus, Christian virginity reaped its glorious fruit. "The faithful wife," as St. Paul had said, "sanctified the unbelieving husband," [16] who by the merit of his faith, obtained the conversion of his brother. Valerian and Tiburtius took leave of Cecilia, whose presence in this once Pagan house, had been the pledge of so many favors, and hastily set out in search of Urban. With what joy the angels must have gazed upon these two brothers, wending their steps toward the Appian Way, one clothed in his baptismal robe, the other panting like a hart for the waters of the fountain. [17]

When they reached the Pontiff, they related all that had occurred since the neophyte's return to his bride, and the holy old man rendered thanks to God for having reserved such glorious triumphs for his faithful servant. He received Tiburtius with joy, and the young man soon descended into the pool of salvation, whence he returned, purified, relieved of his burden, breathing with delight the pure air of the new life which he had so ardently longed to embrace. Valerian returned to Cecilia, after accomplishing the seven days, during which, according to custom, he wore the white robes. The Pontiff retained Tiburtius during these seven days, and, by the unction of the Holy Ghost, consecrated him a soldier of Christ. The young man was completely changed; the symbolical palms and crowns which he had seen engraved upon the martyrs' tombs, excited new ardor in his soul; he may, perhaps, have had some presentiment that the day was not far distant when his own mortal

49

remains, and those of Valerian, would be buried by Cecilia under the funereal arches where he had received the mystery of his regeneration. In awaiting this glorious consummation, the angels of God frequently visited and conversed with him. If he breathed a desire to heaven, these celestial messengers hastened to obtain it for *him* whom they already considered their brother. [18]

Cecilia and Valerian admired the marvels of divine grace in the heart of Tiburtius, and the bonds which united the three friends were strengthened each day. The influence of this holy house was sensibly felt throughout Borne, and the Christians rejoiced in the honor reflected upon their faith by the noble example of virtue, daily given by this patrician family, which esteemed itself so happy in having become a part of the family of Christ. Cecilia, however, by the influence of her character, and the masculine eloquence of her words, seemed to be the presiding spirit. She was no longer the timid virgin, abandoned by her parents to an idolatrous husband; henceforth, armed for every kind of struggle, ready for every combat, and shrinking from no act of devotedness, she was one of the most solid supports of the Church of Rome.

Having become the dispensatrix of a large fortune, she was enabled to satisfy her ardent love for the poor of Christ. She, nevertheless, without detriment to her humility, or to Christian modesty, continued to wear the dress and ornaments suitable to her rank. [19] Superior to the vanities of her sex, trampling underfoot the world and its pomp, sighing day and night for the moment when her celestial Spouse would deliver her from this body of death, Cecilia could not be ranked among the Christian women, who, slaves to dress and fashion, merited the invectives of Tertullian. "I do not know," he had said to them, "if hands accustomed to bracelets, can support chains; if feet adorned with anklets, can support the pressure of manacles. I fear that heads covered with a network of pearls and precious stones, will scarcely leave room for the sword." [20] In fact, Christian women ought never to lose sight of the moment when they might be summoned to confess their faith in Jesus Christ. Cecilia ardently sighed for it; she longed to divest herself of the world's livery, to be clothed with a nuptial robe purpled with her blood. In the meantime, she continued to mortify her innocent body, by a rough hair shirt which she concealed under her rich, luxurious garments.

[1] The Pagans surrounded the heads of their divinities with a *nimbus* to protect them from being injured by the weather, or by the birds of which Cecilia speaks. The nimbus, found in Egypt and among the Etruscans, at a later period, was considered a mark of veneration to the statue which it adorned; but Tibullus and Horace speak of the nimbus in its original signification. Cecilia's invective is an additional proof of the antiquity of our acts.

[2] *Acta S. Caeciliae.*

[3] Tunc cum omni alacritate Tiburtius ait: Qui ita non credit pecus est. *Ibid.*

[4] Haec dicente Tiburtio, Sancta Caecilia osculato est pectus ejus, et dixit: hodie meum te fateor vere esse cognatum; sicut enim mihi amor Domini fratrem tuum conjugem fecit, ita te mihi cognatum contemptus faciet idolorum: unde quia paratus es ad credendum, vade cum fratre tuo ut purificationem accipias, per duam merearis angelicos vultus aspicere, et omnium tuarum veniam invenire culparum. *Ibid.*

[6] Tunc dicit fratri suo Tiburtius: Obsecro, frater, ut dicas mihi ad quem me ducturus es? Respondit Valerianus: Ad magnum virum, Urbanum nomine, in quo est aspectus angelicus, et veneranda canities, sermo verus, et sapientia conditus. Dicit ei Tiburtius: Tu ilium Urbanum dicis, quem Papam suum Christiani nominant? Hunc ego audivi jam secundo damnatum, et iterum pro ipsa re qua damnatus est latebram sui praecavere fovendo; iste si inventus fuerit, sine dubio atrocibus dabitur flammis, et, ut dici solet, centenas exolvet, et nos simul cremabimur, si ad ilium fuerimus inventi, et dum quaerimus divinitatem in coelis latentem, incurrimus furorem exurentem in terris. *Acta S. Caeciliae.*

[7] Tunc beata Caecilia erigens se stetit, et cum magna constantia dixit. *Acta S. Caeciliae.*

[8] St. Cecilia speaks twice of the Holy Ghost as proceeding from the Father, without saying that He also proceeds from the Son. Such was the language of the primitive Church, which rarely insisted upon the procession of the Holy Ghost with respect to the Son. This is not the proper place to explain the reasons which rendered the confessions of the Church less explicit, upon this dogma, during the early ages. These words of the Saint, are an additional proof of the antiquity of our history.

[9] Caeli, terraeque, maris, et omnium volucrum, repentium, pecudumque creator ex se ipso antequam ista omnia faceret, genuit Filium, et protulit ex virtute sua Spiritum sanctum; Filium ut crearet omnia; Spiritum, ut vivificaret universa; omnia autem quae sunt, Filius ex Patrie genitus condidit; universa autem quaxondita sunt, ex Patrie procedens Spiritus sanctus animavit. *Acta S. Caeciliae.*

[10] Unus est Deus in majestate aua, quem ita in sancta Trinitate dividimus, ut in uno hoinine dicimus esse sapientiam, quam sapientiam dicimus habere ingenium, memoriam et intellectum: nam ingenio adinveninius quod nos didicimus: memoria tenemus quod docemur; intellectu advertimus quicquid vel videre nobis contigerit, vel audire; quid modo faciemus? Numquid non ista tria una sapientia in homine possidet? Si ergo homo in una sapientia trium possidet numerum, quomodo non Deus omnipotens in una Deitate suae Trinitatis obtinet majestatem? *Acta S. Caeciliae.*

[11] De his mecum loquere, quia tyrocinii tempus fratrem tuum tibi prohibet dare responsum: me antem, quam ab ipsis incunabulis Christi sapientia docuit, ad quamcumque causam quaerere volueris, imparatam habere non poteris. *Ibid.*

[12] It is easy to perceive that St. Cecilia, in her oratorical discourse, announces evangelical facts in a general way, not literally conformable to the New Testament. Our Saviour did not address the whole human race, but only the Jewish nation. We must acknowledge, however, that in speaking to the Jews, He came for all, and intended that His law should be preached to all. If Cecilia had spoken in a less general manner, Tiburtius would not have understood the explanation

51

she gave him. Thus the Jews, as a nation, did not make to our Saviour the objection of which Cecilia speaks, but the Gentiles, to whom the Apostles preached, frequently alleged it. It is likewise true that at the time of the advent of the Messiah, materialism had made considerable progress among the Jews. The Sadducees, in particular, professed the grossest sensualism, and the number of carnal Jews far exceeded that of the spiritual.

[13] *Acta S. Caeciliae.*

[14] Si de ista vita ulterius, vel mente tractavero, vel cogitavero, vel cogitatione quaesiere, in illa vita non inveniar; habeant stulti lucrum labentis temporis, ego qui usque hodie sine causa vixi, jam non sit sine causa quod vivo. *Acta S. Caeciliae.*

[15] Miserere mei, frater charissime, et rumpe moras, quarum nexus patior; dilationes timeo, pondus ferre non possum: obsecro te, perdue me ad hominem Dei, ut me purificans ilius vitae participem faciat. *Ibid.*

[16] Cor. vii. 14.

[17] Ps. xli. 1.

[18] Tantam deinceps gratiam consecutus est Domini, ut et Angelos Domini videret quotidie, et omnium quae poposcisset a Domino protinus eveniret effectus. *Acta sanctae Caeciliae.*

[19] Several portraits may be seen in the Catacombs, of female martyrs richly attired; these frescoes date back to the third century. Two figures in the cemetery of Priscilla in the Salarian Way, have been reproduced by Agincourt. (Histoire de l'Art par les monuments. Peinture. Planche viii) The invectives of Tertullian in his work *De cultu faeminarum*, likewise attests the custom sanctioned by the example of many Christian ladies, of wearing the garments used before their baptism. The bearing of this remark will be apparent in the continuation of our history.

[20] Ceterum nescio an manus spatalio circumdari solita in duritiam catenae stupescere sustineat. Nescio an crus periscelio laetatum in nervum se patiatur arctari. Timeo cervicem, ne margaritarum et smaragdorum laqueis occupata, locum spatae non det. *De cultu faemnarum.* Cap. xiii.

Chapter Nine - Alexander Severus Leaves Rome — Violence Exercised Against the Christians Valerian and Tiburtius are Summoned Before the Prefect of Rome — Interrogatory of Tiburtius

It was now spring, and, according to custom, the Roman army was about to commence its summer campaign. Whether the war undertaken by Alexander against the Persians broke out this year, [1] or whether his arms were directed against other enemies, certain it is that he absented himself from Borne with so much solemnity, that the medals of his reign have left a memorial of it to posterity. The Prefect [2] of Rome at this time, was Turcius Almachius, a man well known by the hatred he bore the Christians. As we have before stated, antipathy against the new religion was so violently fermenting in the hearts of the first magistrates of the empire, that they could scarcely support the tolerance, imposed upon them by the personal conduct of the Emperor. The moment was therefore most favorable to persecute the odious sect, and Alexander's character gave little reason to fear his serious displeasure. The ancient edicts were still in force, and the prince was not a man to acknowledge in favor of the Christians, a patronage rejected by the laws of the empire. Besides, there would be sufficient time to throw the blame upon the Christians themselves, since the presence and progress of these enemies of the human race were naturally calculated to rouse the passions of the people, and thus occasion a sedition which would render it the magistrate's duty to punish those, who, if not its authors, were at least the eternal pretext for disturbance.

Almachius first directed his violence against the great body of Christians who belonged to the plebian order. The carnage was very great, the more so as the prefect did not fear their opposition. Not satisfied with mangling their bodies by every species of torture, Almachius also resolved that they should not be interred. [3] The first Christians were most zealous in burying their brother martyrs, and many among them obtained the crown of martyrdom in accomplishing this pious duty.

The city of the glorious dead already extended its vast and gloomy ways all around the ramparts of Rome, of which it formed the invisible bulwark. Nevertheless its avenues, although crossed in every direction, were not yet sufficiently large for the numerous soldiers of Christ who were to be immolated in the terrible persecutions of Maximinus, Decius, and Diocletian. There reposed in peace, [4] that valorous phalanx of soldiers whose blood had cemented the edifice of the church; but the tempest roused by Almachius would have rendered it necessary to compress still more the already crowded ranks of this silent dwelling, had not Urban's predecessor, St. Callistus, foreseen in his pastoral zeal this necessity, and excavated that vast cemetery of the Appian Way, to which as we have previously stated, his name is attached. [5] The Christians who devoted themselves to the touching and perilous ministry of burying the martyrs, frequently purchased with gold the remains of their brothers. They lovingly re-united the limbs separated by the sword, and gathered the blood with sponges which they afterwards pressed into vials or *ampullae;* and to preserve for Christian posterity the full testimonials of the martyrs' victory, they sought diligently even for the instruments of torture. New Rome was destined to repose upon this superhuman foundation, that the hand of God, and not that of man, might be evident in the astonishing transformation which was soon to take place.

Valerian and Tiburtius distinguished themselves among all the Christians of Rome by their zeal in gathering the bodies of the martyrs. They spent their wealth in preparing places of interment for these generous athletes, poor according to the flesh, but already kings in the palaces of heaven. Eager to testify their respect for these precious remains, they anointed them with the richest perfumes,* whilst at the same time by abundant alms they provided for those families, who, by the loss of their principal members, had been deprived of the means of subsistance.

The two brothers were soon denounced to the prefect, both for their donations to the lower classes, and for their transgression of the law, forbidding the interment of the martyrs. They were consequently arrested and led before the tribunal of Almachius. The prefect had no intention of condemning the two patricians whom he had summoned before him; he merely wished to intimidate them, and obtain satisfaction for their having publicly violated his orders.

"How is it possible!" he said to them, "that you, scions of a noble family, can have so far degenerated from your blood as to associate yourselves with the most superstitious of sects? I hear that you are squandering your fortune upon people of the basest extraction, and that you even go so far as to bury with honor the bodies of wretches who have been punished for their crimes. Must we conclude that they are your accomplices, and that this is the motive which induces you to give them honorable burial?"

It is easily seen by the prefect's language that he had acted without the emperor's orders in his violent proceedings against the Christians; he invoked no edict, preferring to impute to imaginary crimes the cruel death which so many of the faithful had suffered by his orders. The younger of the brothers was the first to answer. "Would to heaven!" cried Tiburtius, "that those whom you call our accomplices, would deign to admit us among the number of their servants. They have had the happiness of despising that which appears something, and is nevertheless nothing; in dying, they have obtained that which is not apparent, and yet is the only reality. May we imitate their holy lives, and walk one day in their footsteps!"

Almachius, completely disconcerted by this courageous reply, endeavored to interrupt the young patrician by remarking the striking resemblance between the two brothers. "Tell me, Tiburtius," he asked, "which is the older of you two?" Tiburtius replied, "my brother is not older than I, nor am I younger than he; the One Holy, Eternal God has made us equals by His grace." [7] "Well," resumed Almachius," tell me what is that which appears something, and is nothing?" "Every thing in this world," Tiburtius warmly replied, "every thing which leads souls to eternal death, the inevitable end of the happiness of this life." "Now tell me," continued Almachius, "what is that which is not apparent, and yet is the only reality?" "It is," answered Tiburtius, "a future life of happiness for the just and of eternal torments for the wicked. Both rapidly approach, and yet, through a fatal self-delusion, we turn away the eyes of our heart that we may not see this inevitable future. Our bodily eyes are fixed upon present objects, and we seek to deceive our conscience by branding virtue with the epithets that belong only to evil, while we embellish evil with the qualities which pertain solely to virtue."

Almachius interrupted the young man: "I am convinced," said he, "the sentiments which you express do not proceed from the spirit which animates you." "You are right," replied Tiburtius, "I do not speak according to that spirit of the world which once animated me; but according to the spirit of Him whom I have received into the inmost recesses of my soul, — the Lord Jesus Christ." [8] "Do you know what you are saying?" angrily retorted the prefect, indignant at hearing the young man pronounce that sacred name which attested the profession of Christianity in him who uttered it with so much love. "Do you know what you are asking?" said Tiburtius. "Young man," replied Almachius, "your enthusiasm blinds you!" Tiburtius answered: "I have learned, I know, and I believe that all I have spoken, is truth." "But I do not understand it," retorted the prefect, and I cannot enter into this order of ideas." "That is because," answered the young man, borrowing the words of the Apostle, "the sensual man perceiveth not the things that are of the Spirit of God. [9] But the spiritual man judge th all things; and he himself is judged of no man." [10] Almachius smiled with vexation, concealing his mortification at the insult which he had received; [11] but not wishing that the young man should compromise himself further, he sent him away, and commanded Valerian to be brought forward.

[1] We are rather inclined to agree with Pagi and F. Blanchini that in this year, 230, Alexander was engaged in an expedition against the Persians; however this may be, the monuments of the epoch prove that there was an expedition to the East, and a victorious return. Mezzabarba refers to this year the three following medals; the first, upon which the prince is designated: IMP. CAES. A L E X A N D. A U G., presents a sun rising tin the east. The two others represent — one, Alexander, holding a laurel branch and a standard; the other, the victorious Emperor, surrounded by soldiers, and borne on a triumphal chariot. Ekkel is not so positive as Mezzabarba, regarding the precise dates of these medals, but he formally admits that Alexander may have gone to the East in 230. This concession, joined to the positive assertion of the authors mentioned above, is sufficient to render our history perfectly clear.
[2] The Prefect of Rome, *Praefectus Urbis,* exercised a purely civil magistracy, and should not be confounded with the Prefect of the Praetorium.
[3] Turcius Almachius Urbis Praefectus Sanctos Domini fortiter laniabat, et inhumata jubebat eorum corpora derelinqui. *Acta Sanctae Caeciliae.*
[4] *In pace.* These two words, so frequently engraven on the tombs of the martyrs, express the repose to which the first Christians aspired after their combats. They are taken from the words of Ecclesiasticus. (xliv. 14). Corpora ipsorum, in pace sepulta sunt. Which the Roman church still chants in the office of martyrs.
[5] Fecit aliud caemeterium Via Appia, ubi multi Sacerdotes et Martyres requiescunt, quod appellatur usque in hodiernum diem Caemeterium Callisti. *Anastas. in Calixto.*
[6] If the Christians expended little in incense which the Pagans used so freely in their sacrifices, they compensated for this, as Tertullian says, by the value they

set on perfumes, using them profusely in the burial of martyrs. "Thura plane non emimus. Si Arabiae queruntur, scient Sabaei pluris et carioris suas merces Christianis sepeliendis profligari, quam diis fumigandis." *Apologet.* Cap. xlii.

[7] nec hic major, nec ego minor, quia unus est Deus sanctus aeternus, qui nos sua gratia coaequavit. *Acta S. Caeciliae.*

[8] Verum dicis, quia non mente mea loquor, quam in saeculo habebam, sed ejus quem in visceribus meae mentis accepi, hoo est Dominum Jesum Christum. *Acta S. Caeciliae.*

[9] 1 Cor. ii. 14.

[10] 1 Cor. ii. 15.

[11] Tunc ridens Praefectus jussit amoveri Tiburtium et applicari Valerianum. *Acta S. Caecilae.*

Chapter Ten - Interrogatory of Valerian. The Two Brothers are Condemned to Death

"Valerian," said the prefect, "your brother's head is evidently crazed; you, I hope, will be able to give me a sensible reply." "There is one only physician," answered Valerian, "who has deigned to take charge of my brother's head and of mine. He is Christ, the Son of the living God." [1] "Come," said Almachius. "speak with wisdom." "Your ear is false," replied Valerian, "you cannot understand our language."

The prefect restrained himself, and refusing to accept the spontaneous confession of Christianity which the two brothers were eager to make before his tribunal, he endeavored to defend the Pagan sensualism to which the Caesars were indebted for the passive submission of their people. "It is you who are in error," he said, "and more than any one. You leave necessary and useful things to pursue folly. You disdain pleasures, reject happiness, despise all that constitutes the charm of existence; in a word, you have no attraction but for that which is opposed to the comforts and luxuries of life." Valerian calmly replied, "I have seen, during the winter, men traversing the country with songs and merriment, abandoning themselves to every kind of pleasure. At the same time, I have seen peasants in the field, industriously ploughing the ground, planting the vine, inserting rose bushes upon the eglantine; others grafting fruit trees, or thinning the underbush, which might injure their plantations; all, in fine, energetically devoting themselves to the culture of the earth. The men of pleasure, after looking at the peasants, commenced to deride their painful work." "Miserable creatures!" they exclaimed, "abandon this superfluous labor; come, rejoice with us, and share our amusements. Why fatigue yourselves with painful toil? "Why spend your lives in such tiresome occupations?" They accompanied these words with shouts of laughter, clapping of hands, and cruel insults.

"Spring followed the cold and rainy season, and behold! the fields cultivated with so much care, were covered with luxuriant foliage; the bushes perfumed the air with their exquisite roses, the grapes hung in festoons from the vines, and the trees groaned under the weight of their luscious fruits. The peasants, whose labor had appeared so senseless, were filled with joy, but the frivolous young men who had boasted of their wisdom, were reduced to a frightful famine, and regretting too late their effeminate sloth, said one to the other, L Look at those people whom we ridiculed. Their industry seemed to us a disgrace; we shuddered at their mode of life, and thought it contemptible. Their very persons we considered vile, their society despicable. The result has proved that they were wise, and we, miserable, proud, and foolish. We would not labor, we would not even assist them in their work; in the midst of our pleasures we scorned and ridiculed them; and now, behold them surrounded with flowers, crowned with glory." [2] Thus the young patrician, whose grave and gentle character offered a striking contrast to the impetuous nature of his brother, imitated the language of Solomon, and condemned the vanities of the world, in the very bosom of the proudest and most voluptuous of cities. Almachius had listened to his discourse without interrupting him. Resuming the conversation in his turn, he said: "You have spoken eloquently, I acknowledge; but I do not see that you have answered my question." "Permit me to finish," replied Valerian, "you have treated us as fools, because we bestow our riches upon the poor, receive strangers with hospitality, succor widows and orphans, and give the bodies of the martyrs honorable burial. According to your doctrine, our folly consists in refusing to indulge in voluptuous pleasures, and in disdaining to avail ourselves of the prerogatives of our birth. A time will come when we shall reap the fruit of our privations. We shall then rejoice, but those who now revel in enjoyment, will weep. The present time is given us to sow seed; now, those who sow in joy in this life, will reap sighs and tears in the next; whilst those, who in this life, sow fleeting tears, shall reap in the future, an abundant harvest of endless happiness."

"And so," replied the prefect, "we and our invincible princes, will have tears and mourning for our portion, whilst you will possess eternal felicity?"

"And who are you and your princes?" cried Valerian; "you are but mortals, born upon the day appointed for you, and destined to die when your hour shall come. Moreover, you will have to render to God, a rigorous account of the sovereign power which he has placed in your hands." [3]

The interrogatory had already exceeded the prefect's designs. In endeavoring to justify his tyranny against the faithful, he had involved himself in unexpected embarrassments. Two patricians had appeared at his bar, and through his imprudence, had given vent to expressions insulting to the imperial dignity; moreover the two brothers had solemnly professed Christianity in the very sanctuary of the law. Almachius hoped to extricate himself from this difficult situation by making to them a proposition, which, should they accept it, would justify him in releasing them without delay. He therefore said: "Enough of these long, useless discourses. Offer libations to the gods, and you shall retire without undergoing any punishment."

There was no question either of burning incense to the idols, or of taking part in a sacrifice; a simple libation, scarcely perceptible to those present, would release the two brothers, and shield the magistrate's dignity. Valerian and Tiburtius replied in the same breath: "Every day we offer sacrifice to God, but not to idols." [4] "To what God?" enquired the prefect, "do you pay homage?" "Is there then any other," answered the brothers, "that you should ask such a question in regard to God? Is there more than one?" [5] "But at least tell me the name of this one God, of whom you speak." "The name of God, neither you nor any mortal can discover, even had you wings and could mount to the highest clouds." [6] "Jupiter, then, is not the name of a god?" "You are mistaken, Almachius," said Valerian, "Jupiter is the name of a corrupter, a libertine. Your own authors represent him as a homicide, a man guilty of every vice, and you dare to call him a God! I am astonished at your audacity, for the name of God can only belong to a being who has nothing in common with sin, and who possesses every virtue." [7] "And so," replied Almachius, "the entire universe is in error; you and your brother alone know the true God."

Valerian's heart was agitated with noble and holy pride at these words of the prefect, and proclaiming before this haughty magistrate, the immense progress of Christianity which Tertullian had so lately announced to the Roman Senate, in his apology, he exclaimed: "Do not deceive yourself, Almachius! The Christians, followers of this holy doctrine are already innumerable in the empire. You Pagans will soon form the minority; you are like the planks which float upon the sea after a shipwreck, and which have no other destination than to be burned." [8]

Almachius, irritated at Valerian's generous boldness, ordered him to be scourged with rods; he still hesitated to condemn him to death. The lictors immediately stripped the young man, who expressed his joy at suffering for the name of Christ, by these courageous words: "The happy moment has at last arrived for which I have so ardently longed; this day is more delightful to me than all the festivals of the world." [9] During the infliction of the cruel punishment, a herald made the following proclamation: [10] "Beware of blaspheming the gods and goddesses." Meanwhile, in clear and powerful tones, that were distinctly heard amid the noise occasioned by the strokes of the whip, Valerian addressed the multitude: "Citizens of Rome," he cried, "let not the view of these torments prevent you from confessing the truth; be firm in your faith; believe in the Lord, who alone is holy. Destroy the gods of wood and stone to which Almachius burns his incense; crush them into dust, and know that they who adore them will be eternally tormented." [11]

Almachius was agitated by this scene. What would be the issue of this trial which he had so imprudently undertaken? Instead of two young men whom he had hoped to intimidate, he found himself confronted by two courageous

Christians, who were worthy of being compared to the most heroic of the martyrs whom he had recently condemned to death. Should he release these men after a trivial punishment, when they had insulted the divinities of the empire, and defied the magistrate on his bench? or should he declare them guilty of death? A perfidious counsel addressed to his cupidity, settled his doubts; his assessor, Tarquinius, whispered to him: "Condemn them to death; the occasion is a favorable one. If you delay, they will continue to distribute their riches to the poor, and when they shall finally suffer capital punishment, there will be nothing left for you to confiscate."

Almachius understood this language. He was personally interested in confiscated property, and therefore resolved that his prey should not escape. The two brothers were again brought before him; Valerian, his body mangled by the whips, and Tiburtius, piously jealous that his brother had been preferred to him in the honor of suffering for Christ. The sentence was immediately pronounced: the two brothers were to be conducted to the *Pagus Triopius* on the Appian Way, near the fourth mile-stone. [12] At the end of the route, there was a temple of Jupiter which served as an entrance to the Pagus. [13] Here Valerian and Tiburtius were to be invited to burn incense before the idols, and in case of their refusal, were to be beheaded.

[1] Cui Praefectus dixit: Valeriana, quoniam non est sani capitis frater tuus, saltem credo quod tu mihi poteris dare sapienter responsum. Valerianus dixit: Unas est medicus, qui fratris mei caput et meum sua Sapientia fovet, qui est Christus Filiua Dei vivi. *Acta S. Caecilae.*

[2] *Acta S. Caeciliae.*

[3] Quid enim vos estis? aut quid principes vestri? homunciones estis, tempore vestro nati, tempore vestro expleto morituri; tantam Deo reddituri rationem, quantum summae vobis tradidit potestatls. *Acta S. Caeciliae.*

[4] Nos non diis sed Deo quotidie sacrificium exhibemus. *Acta S. Caeciliae.*

[5] Et quis est Dcus alias, ut de Deo nos interroges? Est alius praeter unum? *Ibid.*

[6] Nomen Dei non invenies etiamsi pennis volare possis. *Ibid.*

[7] Erras Praefecte; Jovis nomen non est hominis corruptoris, atque stupratoris? Homicidam ilium vestri auctores commemorant, et criminosum illum literae vestrae demonstrant; hunc tu Deum dicis? miror qua fronte locutus sis; cum Deus dici non possit, nisi unus qui est ab omni peccato alienus, et omnibus virtutibus plenus. Acta S. Caeciliae.

[8] Innumerabilis multitudo Christianitatis est, quae sanctitatem suscepit; sed magis vos pauci estis, qui sicut astulae de naufragio remansistis ad nihil aliud, nisi ut igni tradamini. *Ibid.*

[9] Ecce bora, quam sitienter optavi; ecce dies omni mihi festivitate jucundior. *Ibid.*

[10] Deos, Deasque blasphemare noli. *Acta S. Caeciliae.*

This proclamation, made by a public crier during the chastisement of a culprit, is prescribed in the Code, and in the *Pandect,* where it is based upon an edict of Gordian, and a sentence of Ulpian, both of the 3d century. Many examples are to

59

be found among the ancient authors. Spartianus, in his *Historiae Augustae,* quotes the proclamation made during the scourging of a plebian who had dared to embrace Severus, the proconsul of Africa. *Legatum populi Romani homo plebius temere amplecti noli.* Lampridus relates that under the reign of Alexander Severus, a herald proclaimed the following words during the chastisement of a court intriguer: *Fumo punitur qui vendidit fumum.*

[11] Gives Romani, videte ne vos a veritate ista mea tormenta revocent, sed state viriliter credentes in Sancto Domino, et Deos quos colit Almachius lapideos et ligneos in calcem convertite, hoc scientes, scquia interna tribulatione erunt omnes qui colunt eos. *Acta S. Caeciliae.*

[12] According to the law of the XII. tables, executions took place outside the city, and not within its walls. Many examples of the application of this law can be found in ancient authors and in the acts of the martyrs. This custom was also observed among the Jews. St. Paul, in his Epistle to the Hebrews xii., 11-14, remarks that our Saviour was crucified outside the city gates, and he explains the mystery of this circumstance of the Passion. We find no difficulty in asserting that the *Pagus Triopius* to which our martyrs were conducted was upon the Appian Way; their being buried here give us reason to draw this conclusion. The martyrs of Rome were generally buried in the Crypts of the Way upon which they died, the faithful who buried them having thus less risk to run. We have already remarked this with regard to Pope St. Callistus. We designate the Pagus Triopius as the theatre of the martyrdom of Valerian and Tiburtius, because this Pagus, although described on one of its inscriptions as situated at the third milestone, in reality did but commence there, and extended to the fourth mile-stone.

[13] Tunc Assessor Praefecti Tarquinius clam dixit Praefecto: invenisti occasionem, tolle eos, nam si moram feceris, et de die in diem protraxeris, omnes facilitates suas pauperibus erogabunt, et, punitis eis, tu nihil invenies. *Acta S. Caeciliae.*

Chapter Eleven - Conversion of Maximus, Notary of Almachius. Cecilia's Interview with Her Husband and Brother. Martyrdom of Saints Valerian and Tiburtius

As soon as the sentence was pronounced, Valerian and Tiburtius were hurried forth to the place of execution, without being allowed a moment's time to bid farewell to her, who was the cherished bride of the one and the beloved sister of the other. Cecilia had not been present at the trial of the two confessors, but her ardent prayers had assisted them when before the judges, where they had proved themselves worthy of her and of their baptism. God, however, whose holy will it was that she should survive them, was preparing for her at this very moment a consoling interview with her friends. Maximus, the notary of Almachius, was chosen to accompany the martyrs to their place of execution. It was his duty to render an account to the prefect of the issue of this terrible drama. His orders were to release Valerian and Tiburtius if they sacrificed to the gods; or to record their execution if they persisted in the profession of Christianity. At the sight of these two patricians, walking so cheerfully to execution, and conversing together with tenderness and tranquil joy, Maximus could not restrain his tears, and turning towards them, he exclaimed: "O, noble and brilliant flowers of the Roman youth! O, brothers, united by such tender love! You persist in despising the gods, and at the very moment when you lose every thing, you hasten to death as to a banquet." [1] Tiburtius replied: "If we were not certain that the life which succeeds this will last forever, do you think we would be so joyful at this hour?" "And what is that other life?" asked Maximus. "As the body is clothed with garments," replied Tiburtius, "so is the soul clothed with the body; and as the body is stripped of its garments, so will the soul be divested of the body. The body, which is formed of the earth, will return to the earth; it will be reduced to dust, to rise again like the phoenix, [2] As to the soul, if it be pure, it will be transported to the delights of Paradise, there to await in the enjoyment of inebriating happiness, the resurrection of its body." [3]

This unexpected conversation made a deep impression upon Maximus; it was the first time he had heard any thing contrary to those principles of materialism which were then so prevalent among the Pagans. He was pleased with the new light revealed to him. "If I were certain of this future life of which you speak," said he, "I feel that like you, I would despise the present life." Then Valerian filled with the holy ardor which the Holy Ghost had communicated to him, thus addressed Maximus. "Since you only require proof of the truth we have announced to you, receive the promise I now make you. At the moment when it will please our Lord to grant us the grace to shed our blood for the confession of His name, He will deign to open your eyes and permit you to see the glory into which we shall enter. The only condition to this favor is, that you repent of your past sins." "I accept," said Maximus, "and call down upon myself the thunderbolts of heaven, if from that moment I do not confess as the only true God, Him who reserves for us a life beyond the grave. Now therefore you have but to show me the vision which you have promised. [4]

By this reply, Maximus offered himself to be enrolled among the militia of Jesus Christ; but the two brothers were unwilling to die before having seen him regenerated in the baptismal waters. They therefore said to him: "Persuade our executioners to conduct us to your house; they can guard us there, without losing sight of us for a moment. We ask but a day's delay. We will then send for him who will purify you, and this very night you shall see what we have promised you."

Maximus did not hesitate to comply. The present life, with its fears and hopes, was already nothing in his eyes. He led the martyrs, with their accompanying escort, to his house, where Valerian and Tiburtius at once commenced to explain to him the Christian doctrine. The notary's family and the soldiers were present; grace touched their hearts; they were convinced by the powerful words of the two apostles, and declared themselves believers in Jesus Christ. Cecilia had been informed by Valerian of all that was passing. Her fervent prayers had doubtless contributed in obtaining so great an effusion of graces; but it was necessary to consummate the divine work in these men so rapidly converted to the faith of Christ. Cecilia prepared every thing with prudent zeal; at nightfall, she entered the house of Maximus, accompanied by several priests. [5] Human language cannot describe the sweetness of the interview which God in His goodness had prepared for the two spouses. The prophetic roses of Valerian's crown were soon to expand in the sun of eternity; while those which decked Cecilia's brow, were yet to exhale their perfume upon earth for a few days longer. It must have been sweet for these favored servants of God to converse together upon His holy designs in their regard, and to recall the many graces which He had bestowed upon them, from the mysterious interview in the nuptial chamber, to the present moment, when the palm of martyrdom was already within Valerian's reach. Tiburtius, the angels' favorite, and Cecilia's second conquest, shared, we may presume, their parting interview, and bade farewell to Cecilia with all the tenderness of his affectionate nature. But the two brothers and the virgin did not forget the abundant harvest which they had so happily met on the road to martyrdom; it was time to gather it into the granaries of the heavenly Father. In presence of Cecilia, of her husband, and of her brother, amidst hymns of thanksgiving to God, Maximus, with his family and the soldiers, solemnly professed the Christian faith, and the priests poured upon their heads the regenerating waters of baptism. The house of Almachius' notary had become a temple, and those who dwelt in it during these few hours stolen from heaven, seemed animated by one heart and one soul.

The rising sun ushered in the day of the martyrdom of Valerian and Tiburtius — the XVIII of the calends of May. A solemn silence succeeded to the transports which faith had awakened in every heart. It was interrupted by Cecilia, who gave the signal for departure, quoting the words of St. Paul: "arise, soldiers of Christ! cast off the works of darkness, and put on the armor of light. You have fought a good fight, you have finished your course; you have kept the faith. For the rest there is laid up for you a crown of justice, which the Lord, the just judge, will render to you, and to all who love His coming." [6] Animated by these words, the martyr band resumed its march. The two confessors were conducted by the new Christian, Maximus, and escorted by the soldiers whose brows were still moistened with baptismal dew. The Acts do not mention whether Cecilia followed her husband and brother to the place of their triumph. She may have returned to Rome, to await the hour when she would be reunited to these cherished souls; or she may have preferred accompanying the confessors and remaining with them until their souls had taken flight to heaven. What had Cecilia to dread upon earth? In preservation of her virginity, she had braved the anger of a Pagan husband, and in a few days she was to defy upon his tribunal, the formidable representative of Roman power.

The martyrs, with their pious escort, wended their steps towards the Appian Way, through which they were obliged to pass in order to reach the *Pagus Triopius*. The remembrance of Peter, meeting in this same place our Saviour carrying His cross, redoubled the brothers' courage. Both to the right and to the left, stretched the vast and silent galleries of the Christian Crypts, so that the martyrs, as they passed to execution, saluted the hallowed spot where they were so soon to rest. They probably arrested their steps for a moment, to gaze thoughtfully at the mysterious valley, which contained the tombs of the Apostles, whom they were so soon to join in the kingdom of everlasting joy.

Directly opposite, was St. Urban's retreat, where they had so lately learned the secret of that glorious immortality, to gain which they were about to sacrifice without regret, the joys of this present life. Towards the summit of the last hill, they passed near the tomb of Metella;, the name of Cecilia, which the inscription bore, reminded Valerian of that spouse whom heaven had given him, and to whom he owed much more than earthly happiness. He was only preceding her by a few days, and soon their souls would be forever united in their true country. The fury of Almachius gave them every reason to suppose that the virgin's hour was fast approaching. The martyrs finally arrived at the *Pagus*, which, although called *hospitable* upon one of the inscriptions of Anna Regilla, had nothing to offer the Christians but the sword or apostasy. The priests of Jupiter were waiting with the incense. They commanded Tiburtius and Valerian to pay homage to the idol. The brothers refused, and, throwing themselves upon their knees, offered their necks to the executioners. [7] The Christian soldiers could not draw their swords upon the martyrs. Others, however, offered to supply their place, and the two noble youths received at once, death and the crown of life. At this moment, heaven was opened to the eyes of Maximus, who gazed for an instant upon the happiness of the saints. The zealous faithful secured the bodies of these two heroes of the Faith, and brought them to Cecilia. She herself buried the dear and holy remains in the cemetery of Pretextatus, near the second mile-stone. She anointed them with the richest perfumes; raised over them the triumphal stone, engraven with the palm and crown, symbols of their glorious victory, and she accompanied this pious duty with tears of mingled hope and sorrow. Not far from their tombs, she was soon to rest her heaven-crowned brow, and twine her palm with that of her husband.

[1] O Juventutis fios purpureus, o gernianus fraternitatis afectus, quem vos impia definitione volentes amittere, ad interitum vestrum quasi ad epulas festinatis? *Acta S. Caeciliae.*
[2] The ancients admitted the existence of this fabulous bird, and the first Christians considered it a symbol of the resurrection of the body. Tiburtius speaks here in the language of St. Clement of Rome, (Epis. ad Corinthios, i. n°25.) Tertul-

lian, (De resurrectione carnis, cap. xii.) St. Ambrose, (Hexaemeron, lib. v. cap. xxiii.) St. Cyril of Jerusalem, (Cateches xviii., cap. xxiii.) and St. Epiphanius, (Ancorat. cap. lxxxv.)

[3] Sicut vestitur vestimentis corpus, ita vestitur anima corpore, et sicut spoliatur vestimentis corpus, ita spoliatur anima corpore; corpus quidem, quod terrenum semen per libidinem dedit, terreno ventri reddetur, ut in pulverem redactum, sicut Phoenix, futuri luminis aspectu resurgat; anima vero ad Paradisi delicias, si sancta sit, perferetur, ut in deliciis affluens tempus suae resurrectionis expectet. *Acta S. Caeciliae.*

[4] Tunc Maximus devotabat so dicens: Fulmineis ignibus consumar, si ex hac hora non ilium solum Deum confitear, qui alteram vitam fecit isti vitae succedere; hoc tantum vos, quod promisistis ostendite. *Acta S. Caeciliae.*

[5] Tunc sancta Caecilia venit ad eos nocte cum sacerdotibus. *Ibid.*

[6] Igitur cum aurora noctis finem daret, facto magno silentio, sancta Caecilia dixit eis: Eia milites Christi, abjicite opera tenebrarum, et induimini arma lucis; certamen bonum certastis, cursum consummastis, fidem servastis; ite ad coronam vitae, quam dabit vobis Justus judex; non solum autem vobis, sed et omnibus qui diligunt adventum ejus. *Acta S. Caeciliae.*

[7] Venientibus ergo Sanctis offeruntur thura, et recusant; recusantes ponunt genua, feriuntur gladio, projiciunt corpus mortule, et gaudium suscipiunt sempiternum. *Acta S. Caeciliae.*

Chapter Twelve - Martyrdom of St. Maximus — Almachius Sends for Cecilia, And Urges Her to Sacrifice to the Idols — She Refuses and Converts the Envoys of the Prefect the Virgin Appears Before the Tribunal of Almachius

The happy witnesses of the martyrdom of Valerian and Tiburtius returned to Rome, filled with admiration at the courage of those who had initiated them into the secrets of eternal life, and ardently desiring to follow them as soon as possible. Maximus, burning with divine love, unceasingly repeated that he had caught a glimpse of heaven. He affirmed on oath, that, at the moment when the martyrs were struck by the sword, he had seen the angels of God, resplendent as suns, and had beheld the souls of Valerian and Tiburtius leave their bodies, like brides adorned for a nuptial festival. The angels received them, and bore them to heaven upon their wings. [1] While saying these words, he shed tears of joy. Many Pagans, after listening to him, were converted, renouncing their idols, and believed in the one only God, Creator of all things.

The news of his notary's conversion soon reached Almachius. He was doubly irritated, because this courageous example had been followed not only by the household of Maximus, but also by many other persons. The notary's fate was soon decided. He was not beheaded as the two patricians had been; the

64

Prefect caused him to be beaten to death with whips loaded with lead, which was the punishment of persons of inferior rank. The martyr courageously rendered up his soul to God, and Cecilia buried him with her own hands. She chose a sepulchre near those of her husband and brother, and ordered that a phoenix should be sculptured on the tombstone, [2] in remembrance of the allusion made by Tiburtius to this marvellous bird, when explaining to Maximus the resurrection of the body.

Meanwhile, Almachius had ordered the confiscation of all property belonging to Valerian and Tiburtius. In so doing, he had acted conformably to the Roman law. By his orders, search was made for their goods. But the charitable and prudent

Cecilia had already distributed them to the poor, thus sending all her treasures before her, on the eve of her departure for her celestial country.

Cecilia was so well known in Rome by her noble birth, her husband's death, and that of his brother, had been accompanied by so many remarkable circumstances, and her profession of Catholicity was so public, that the Prefect of Rome felt it was absolutely necessary to require her to sacrifice to the gods of the Empire. Nevertheless, he at first showed some hesitation. He would have been glad to pause in his cruel course, and to avoid shedding the blood of this noble lady, admired by all who approached her for her beauty, modesty, and singular virtue. Hoping to avoid the publicity of a trial, which *might* end tragically, and which would certainly compromise still more the responsibility of a magistrate acting in the Emperor's absence and without his orders, he sent officers of justice to the virgin's dwelling with the proposal that she should privately sacrifice to the gods, trusting to obtain from her a compliance with his wishes, sufficient to shield his honor as a judge, without obliging him to summon her before his public tribunal.

The officers entered Cecilia's dwelling, and laid before her the prefect's proposition. The virgin easily perceived the emotion which they experienced in gazing upon her gentle and dignified countenance. Respect, deference, and evident embarrassment in fulfilling their mission, were apparent in their words, and even in their attitude.

Cecilia replied to their proposal with heavenly calmness: "Citizens and brothers," said she, "hear me. You are the magistrate's officers, and in the depths of your hearts you despise his impious conduct. I am only too happy to suffer all kinds of torments for the confession of Jesus Christ, for I have not the slightest attachment to this life; but I pity you, who, still in the flower of your youth, are condemned to obey the orders of an unjust judge." [3] The officers of Almachius could scarcely refrain from weeping at these words, so distressing did it seem to see this young, noble, and talented patrician lady actually longing for death; they besought her not to sacrifice so many advantages. [4]

The virgin interrupted them: "To die for Christ is not to sacrifice one's youth, but to renew it; it is giving vile dross for gold; exchanging a mean and

65

miserable dwelling for a magnificent palace; relinquishing a perishable thing, and receiving in return an immortal gift. If any one should offer you to-day a large amount of gold, upon the sole condition that you should give in return the same weight of a baser metal, would you not show the greatest eagerness in making so advantageous an exchange? Would you not urge your parents, associates, and friends to share your good fortune? If any one should try to induce you, even with tears, not to accept such an offer, would you not consider him insane? And yet, the result of all this eagerness would simply be the exchanging of a vile metal for an equal weight of another, more precious it is true, but still a mere metal. Jesus Christ, our God, is not satisfied with giving weight for weight; He returns a hundred fold for all offered him, and adds to it eternal life." [5]

The officers, completely conquered by this discourse, were unable to conceal their emotion. In the enthusiasm of her zeal, Cecilia mounted upon a marble stand, and in an inspired voice exclaimed: "Do you believe what I have told you?" Their reply was unanimous. "Yes, we believe that Christ, the Son of God, who possesses such a servant, is the true God." [6] "Go, then," Cecilia resumed, "and tell the miserable Almachius that I ask a delay; that I beg he will defer my martyrdom for a short period. Then return here and you will find him who will render you participants of eternal life." [7] The officers, already Christians in their hearts, carried Cecilia's message to the prefect, who, by a dispensation of Divine Providence, deferred summoning the virgin before his tribunal. Cecilia immediately sent a message to Pope Urban, informing him of her approaching martyrdom, and of the new conversions which she had effected. Besides the officers of Almachius, a number of persons of every age, sex, and condition, principally from the trans-Tiberian region, touched by divine grace, ardently desired baptism.

St. Urban was desirous of coming himself to reap so rich a harvest, and to bless the heroic virgin, who would in a few days extend to him from heaven, the palm of martyrdom. The presence of the holy pontiff was a great happiness for Cecilia. The baptism was celebrated with much splendor; more than four hundred persons received the grace of regeneration. Cecilia, desirous of preventing the confiscation of her goods, employed the last hours of her life in making over to one of the converts, named Gordian, all claims to her house, that it might henceforth serve as an assembly for the Christians, and increase the number of the Roman Churches. [8]

Notwithstanding the danger, St. Urban remained under Cecilia's roof for several days, during which time, her house was a centre whence the rays of divine grace were diffused throughout Rome, for the advancement of the Church, and the destruction of the empire of Satan. At length Cecilia was summoned before Almachius. The virgin thus called upon to confess her faith, appeared before the judge with holy assurance. Although in presence of the man whose hands had been imbrued in the blood of her husband and of her brother, in the midst of a praetorium decorated with the impure and sacrilegious images of the heathen divinities, the bride of Christ had never appeared more dignified and modest. Wholly absorbed in Him to whom she had given her heart, and who had at length called her to celebrate the heavenly nuptials, Cecilia looked with contempt upon the perishable things of earth.

Her mission was accomplished. The martyrs whom she had formed, had preceded her to heaven; others would soon follow her. One earnest protestation against the brutal force which sought to deter men in their search after the eternal good; one last courageous avowal of her faith, and she would receive the palm of martyrdom.

[1] Maximus juratus asserebat, dicens: Vidi Angelos Dei fulgentes sicut sol, in hora qua verberati sunt gladio, et egredientes aninias eorum de corporibus, quasi virgines do thalamo: quas in gremio suo suscipientes Angeli, remigio alarum suarum ferebant ad coelos. *Acta S. Caeciliae.*

[2] Quam sancta Caecilia juxta Valerianum et Tibnrtium sepeliit in novo sarcophago, et jussit ut in sarcophago ejus sculperetur phoenix ad indicium fidei ejus, qui resurrectionem se inventurum, phoenicis exemplo, ex toto corde suscepit. *Acta S. Caeciliae.*

This passage of the Acts is of great importance in confirming the use of the Phoenix, as a symbol, upon Christian tombs. Mamachi (*Origines Christianae*, torn. iii. p. 93.) had remarked it, but neither he nor any other Christian archaeologist, had been able to mention any other analogous fact. They limited themselves to the notice of the Phoenix found upon the mosaics or paintings, subsequent to the peace of the Church, where the fabulous bird is represented upon a palm tree, with a circle of rays around its head. Nevertheless, the Phoenix is engraved upon many of the sepulchral monuments of the Catacombs, where it has been frequently mistaken for a dove. There is, however, a distinction to be remarked. Both birds hold a branch in their beak, but the dove holds an olive branch, and the Phoenix a palm. The bird with the palm, when well-designed, is identical with the Phoenix upon the Egyptian medals; moreover, an irresistable monument corroborates this statement; upon the principal gate of St. Paul's Church, we find a bird, precisely like those we have remarked in the Catacombs, holding a palm branch in its beak. Above the head, the word Fenix is written. The Chevalier de Rossi, who has kindly furnished us with this information respecting the frequent use of this symbol, will give, in his valuable collection of the Christian inscriptions of Rome, a marble of the Catacombs, never before given to the public, upon which this bird is engraven, not only with the palm, but also with the nimbus of the 4th century.

[3] Audite me cives et fratres, vos ministri estis judicis vestri, et videtur vobis, quod ab ejus impietate alieni esse mereamini; mihi quidem gloriosum est, et valde optabile omnia, pro Christi confessione perferre tormenta, quia cum hac vita numquam dignata sum habere amicitias; sed de vestra satis doleo juventute, quam sine sollicitudine gerentes, faeitis quidquid vobis fuerit ab injusto judice imperatum. *Acta S. Caeciliae.*

[4] Tunc illi dabant voces et fletus, quod tarn elegans puella, et tam sapiens et nobilis, libenter optaret occidi, et rogabant earn dicentes ne tale decus amitteret, ne tantam pulchritudinem versaret in mortem. *Ibid.*

[5] *Acta S. Caeciliae.*

[6] Et his clictis ascendit super lapidem, qui erat juxta pedes ejus, et dixit omnibus: Creditis haec quae dixi? At illi dixerunt: Credimus Christum Filium Dei verum Deum esse, qui talem possidet famulam. *Ibid.*

[7] Iie ergo et dicite infelici Almachio, quod ego inducias petara, ut non urgeat passionem meam, et hic intra domum meam faciem venire, qui vos omnes faciat vitae aeternae participes. *Ibid.*

[8] Inter quos unus clarissimus vir erat nomine Gordianus, hic sub defensione sui nominis domum sanctae Coeciliae suo nomine titulavit, ut in occulto ex illa die, ex qua baptism a Christi ibi celebratum est, Ecclesia Dominica fieret. *Acta S. Caeciliae.*

Chapter Thirteen - Interrogatory of St. Cecilia

Almachius shuddered in presence of so noble and gentle a victim, and feigning not to recognize the daughter of the Cecilii, thus boldly addressed her:

"Young woman, what is thy name?" [1]

"Men call me Cecilia," replied the virgin, but my most beautiful name is that of Christian." [2]

"What is thy rank?" "A citizen of Rome, of an illustrious and noble race." [3] "My question refers to thy religion; we know the nobility of thy family."

"Your interrogation was not very precise, since it requires two answers," [4] replied Cecilia.

"Whence comes this assurance in my presence?"

"From a pure conscience and sincere faith." [5]

"Art thou ignorant of the extent of my power?"

"And do you know who is my protector and my spouse?" [6]

"Who is he?" "The Lord Jesus Christ." [7]

"Thou wert the bride of Valerian; this I know." The virgin could not unfold the mysteries of heaven to profane ears. She took no notice, therefore, of the prefect's remark, but reverting to the insolent manner in which he had boasted of his power: "Prefect," she said, "you spoke of power; you have not the least idea of what it is: but if you question me upon the subject, I can demonstrate the truth to you." [8]

"Well, speak," replied Almachius, "I would like to hear thy ideas.

"You only listen to what pleases you," said Cecilia; "however, attend. The power of man is like a bladder inflated with wind. Let but a needle pierce the bladder, it will immediately collapse." [9]

"Thou did'st commence with insult," replied the prefect, "and wilt thou continue in the same strain?"

"Insults," replied the virgin, "consist in alleging things which have no foundation. Prove that what I have said is false, and I will acknowledge that I have insulted you; otherwise your reproach is injurious." [10]

Almachius changed the subject. "Knowest thou not that our masters, the invincible emperors, [11] have ordered that those who confess themselves Christians are to be punished; whereas, those who consent to deny the name of Christ are to be acquitted?"

"Your emperors are in error as well as your excellency. The law which you quote simply proves that you are cruel and we innocent. If the name of Christian were a crime, it would be our part to deny it, and yours to force us by torments to confess it." [12]

"But," said the prefect, "the emperors have enacted this law through motives of clemency, that they might provide you with a means of saving your lives."

"Can there be any thing more unjust, than your conduct towards the Christians!" replied the virgin. "You use tortures to force criminals to acknowledge the time, the place, and the accomplices of their guilt; whereas, our crime is that we bear the name of Christian, and if we do but deny that name, we obtain your favor. But we know the greatness of this name, and we cannot deny it. Better die and be happy, than live and be miserable. You wish us to pronounce a lie; but in speaking the truth, we inflict a much greater and more cruel torture upon you than that which you make us suffer. [13]

"Cease this audacity" said Almachius, "and choose either to sacrifice to the gods, or to deny the name of Christian, and thou shalt go in peace."

"What a humiliating position for a magistrate!" said Cecilia, with a smile of compassion. M He wishes me to deny the title which proves my innocence, and to pollute my lips with a lie. He consents to spare me, but his clemency is a refinement of cruelty. If you believe the accusation brought against me, why endeavor to force me to deny it? If you desire to release me, why do you not inquire into the truth of the charge?" [14]

"Here are the accusers," replied Almachius, "they declare that thou art a Christian. Simply deny it, and the accusation is worthless; but if thou wilt persist in not denying it, thou wilt see thy folly when thy sentence is pronounced."

"The accusation is my triumph," said Cecilia, "the punishment will be my victory. Do not tax me with folly, rather reproach yourself for believing you could induce me to deny Christ." [15]

"Unhappy woman!" exclaimed Almachius, "knowest thou not that the power of life and death is placed in my hands by the authority of the invincible princes? How darest thou address me with so much pride?"

"Pride is one thing, firmness another," replied the virgin. "I spoke with firmness, not with pride, for it is a vice we detest. If you are not afraid of hearing the truth, I will prove to you that what you have said is false?" [16]

""Well," said the prefect, "what did I say that is false?"

"You told an untruth when you said that the princes had conferred upon you the power of life and death."

"I told a lie in saying that?" said Almachius with astonishment.

"Yes," replied Cecilia," "and if you permit me, I will prove to you that your lie is self-evident."

"Explain thyself," said the prefect quite disconcerted.

"Did you not say that your princes have conferred upon you the power of life and death? You well know that you have only the power of death. You can take away life from those who enjoy it, but you cannot restore it to the dead. Say, then, that the emperors have made of you a minister of death, and nothing more; if you add anything else, you do not speak the truth." [17]

The prefect concealing his "mortification at this affront, said with feigned moderation: "Cease this audacity, and sacrifice to the gods! "As he spoke he pointed to the statues that filled the Praetorium.

"You certainly have lost the use of your eyes," replied Cecilia, "I, and all who have good sight, can only see in the gods of which you speak, pieces of stone, brass, or lead." [18]

"As a philosopher, I bore thy insults when they were directed only against me," said Almachius, "but I will not suffer an insult against the gods."

"Since you first opened your mouth," replied the virgin, with severe irony, "you have not uttered a word that I have not proved to be either unjust or unreasonable. That nothing maybe wanting, behold you convicted of having lost your sight. You call gods, these objects which we all see are but useless stones. Touch them yourself, and you will feel what they are. Why thus expose yourself to the ridicule of the people? Every one knows that God is in heaven. These stone statues would be of more service if they were cast into a furnace and converted into lime. They decay in their idleness, and are incapable of either protecting themselves from the flames, or of delivering you from them. Christ alone can save from death, and deliver the guilty from eternal fire." [19]

These were the last words which Cecilia pronounced before the judge. In her animated replies, she had avenged the dignity of man, so unworthily violated by idolatry and Pagan tyranny; she had branded the gross materialism which had so long enslaved the world, redeemed by the blood of a God. Nothing remained but to suffer the glorious death for which she so ardently longed.

But though Almachius could hardly avoid pronouncing sentence against one who had openly insulted the officers of justice, the religion of the gods, and the majesty of the empire, he dreaded commanding the execution of a noble patrician lady, who added to innumerable charms, the gift of winning the hearts of all who approached her. Moreover, he feared the Emperor's reproaches on his return, for so odious a spectacle in the very heart of Home could scarcely fail to excite murmurs among the patricians. Alexander would learn that the insults offered to the Empire and the gods, had sprung from the imprudence of the prefect, who, without any imperial mandate, had arrested the Christians. His violence against the faithful of the lower class had led not only distinguished noblemen to his bar, but even the daughter of the Cecilii. Almachius would not have exposed himself to such serious embarrassments, had he been aware of the sacred bonds which unites all the disciples of Christ, "in whom," says St. Paul, "there is neither Scythian nor Roman, nor free man, nor slave, but Christ is all and in all."

[1] Quod tibi nomon est, puella? Acta S. Caeciliae.

[2] Caecilia, sed apud homines; quod autem illustrius est Christiana sum. *Ibid.*

[3] Civis Romana, illustris et nobilis. *Acta S. Caeciliae.*

[4] Interrogatio tua stultum sumpsit exordium, quae duas responsiones una putat inquisitione concludi. *Ibid.*

[5] De conscientia bona et fide non ficta. *Ibid.*

[6] Et tu ignoras cujus sponsa sim ego? *Ibid.*

[7] Domini Jesu Christi. *Ibid.*

[8] Tu, Praefecte, te ipsum ignoras, cujus sis potestatis; nam si me interroges de tua potestate, verissimis tibi assertionibus manifesto. *Ibid.*

[9] Qualiter delectaris, taliter judicaris, tamen audi: potestas hominis sic est quasi uter vento repletus, quem si una acus pupugerit, omnis rigor cervicis ejus follescit, et quidquid rigidum in se habere cernitur incurvatur. *Acta S. Caeciliae.*

[10] Injuria non dicitur, nisi quod verbis fallentibus irrogatur; aut injuriam doce, si false locuta sum, aut te ipsum corripe calumniam inferentem. *Ibid.*

[11] We will explain elsewhere the reason why Almachius invoked the emperors rather than the Emperor Alexander Severus, who reigned alone. The reader has probably already divined it.

[12] Sic imperatores vestri errant, sicut et Nobilitas vestra; sententia enim, quam ab eis prolatam esse testaris, vos saevientes, et nos innocentes ostendit; si enim malum esset hoc nomen, nos negaremus, vos vero ad conntendum suppliciis urgeretis. *Ibid.*

[13] *Acta S. Caeciliae.*

[14] O judicem necessitate confusum, vult ut negem me innocentem, ut ipse faciat nocentem; parcit et saevit, dissimulat et advertit; si vis damnare, cur hortaris negare? Si vis absolvere, quare non vis inquirere? *Ibid.*

[15] Horum mihi accusatio votiva est, et tua poena victoria; noli me ut dementem arguere, sed te ipsum increpa, quia Christum me aestimas denegare. *Acta S. Caeciliae.*

[16] Aliud est esse superbum, et aliud esse constantem; ego constanter locuta sum et non superbe, quia superbiam et nos fortiter execramur; tu autem si verum audire non times, iterum te docebo falsissime et nunc esse locutum. *Ibid.*

[17] Dixisti principes tuos, et vivificandi, et mortificandi copiam tribuisse licentiae, cum solem mortificandi scias tibi traditam potestatem; vitam enim viventibus tollere potes, mortuis dare non potes: die ergo, quia Imperatores tui, mortis ministrum te esse voluerunt; nam si quid plus dixeris, videberis frustra mentitus. *Acta S. Caeciliae.*

[18] Nescio ubi tu oculos amiseris, nam quos tu Deos dicis, ego, et omnes qui oculos sanos habemus, saxa videmus esse, et aeramentum, et plumbum. *Ibid.*

[19] Ex eo quod os aperuisti, non fuit sermo quern non probarem injustum, stultum, et vanum; sed ne quid deeset, puto etiam exterioribus oculis te ccecum ostendis, ut quod omnes lapidem videmus esse, saxum inutile, hoc tu Deum esse testaris. Do, si jubes, consilium: mitte manum tuam, et tangendo disce saxum hoc esse, si videndo non nosti; nefas est enim ut totus populus de te risum habeat, cum omnes sciant Deum in caelis esse; istas autem figuras saxeas per ignem melius in calcem posse converti, quae modo sui otio pereunt, et neque tibi pereunti, neque sibi, si in ignem mittantur, poterunt subvenire. Solus Christus eripit de morte, et do igno ipse valet liberare. *Acta S. Caeciliae.*

Chapter Fourteen - Martyrdom of St. Cecilia

Desirous that Cecilia should be executed without publicity or tumult, Almachius commanded that she should be taken home, and confined in the bath-room of her palace, called by the Romans, the *Caldarium* [1]

This was to be kept intensely heated, until the suffocating atmosphere had deprived her of life.

This cowardly expedient, however, failed. Cecilia joyfully entered the place of her martyrdom, and remained there the rest of the day, and the ensuing night, without the fiery atmosphere she breathed, producing even the slightest moisture upon her skin. A celestial dew, like that which refreshed the three children in the Babylonian furnace, delightfully tempered the air of the heated apartment, so that the remark made in later years of the intrepid Archdeacon Lawrence, could well have been applied to the virgin, viz.: that the fire of divine love which consumed him interiorly, destroyed the strength of the material fire which surrounded him exteriorly. [2] Vainly did the ministers of Almachius increase the fire by heaping wood upon the furnace; vainly did the heated apertures send forth volumes of boiling vapor into the apartment. The power of God protected His servant, who calmly waited until it should please her Divine Spouse to admit her, by some other kind of death, into His eternal kingdom. [3]

Almachius, on hearing of this prodigy, was much disconcerted. He had hoped to avoid shedding the blood of a Roman lady; but he had gone too far to recede, and there was no alternative but to send a lictor to behead the saintly virgin. The officer presented himself before her, armed with a sword. Cecilia hailed him with joy as the bearer of her nuptial crown. She offered her neck to the executioner with an eagerness that might be expected from one who had already triumphed over all that could terrify or seduce human nature. The lictor vigorously brandished his sword, but his arm was so unsteady, that although he struck her three times, he could not succeed in severing the head from the body. Terrified, he withdrew from the room, leaving the virgin stretched upon the ground, bathed in her blood. The law forbade the executioner, who, after three attempts, had not dispatched his victim, to venture upon a fourth trial. [4]

The doors of the bath-room had remained open after the lictor's departure; and the crowd of Christians who were awaiting the consummation of the sacrifice, respectfully entered the room. A sublime and lamentable spectacle met their eyes. Cecilia, in the agonies of death, still smiled upon the poor whom she loved, and the neophytes, who had been converted by her. With eagerness, they gathered up with linen cloths, the blood which was flowing from her virginal wounds; [5] all endeavored by every means to testify their veneration and love. From one moment to the next, they expected to see her sever the last link which held her captive, and yield up her beautiful soul to God. The crown is suspended above Cecilia's head; she has only to stretch forth her hand to grasp it, and yet she lingers. The faithful were ignorant of the delay which she had asked and obtained from heaven.

During three entire days, they surrounded her bloody couch, wavering between hope and fear, and filled with respect for the will of God, so mysteriously manifested in His servant. Cecilia unceasingly exhorted them to remain firm in the faith. From time to time, she made the poor approach her; she lavished upon them the most touching marks of her affection, and desired that the remainder of her fortune should be divided among them. [6] The officers whose duty it was to confiscate her property, had not presented themselves. They knew that the executioner had missed his victim; and, moreover, this palace, stained with blood, must have been as terrible to the Pagans as it was august in the eyes of the faithful, who venerated it as the glorious arena where Cecilia had won her crown.

For one moment, the crowd subsided. The dying virgin was about to receive the visit of Saint Urban, who, as we have said, had been concealed in the palace for several days. Until the present moment, prudence had prevented the venerable old man from approaching the martyr, who was awaiting his visit, before taking her flight to heaven. She wished to receive the blessing of the Father of the faithful, and to consign to his hands the only inheritance which she left. The Pontiff entered the bath-room, and was deeply moved at beholding his beloved daughter extended like a lamb offered in sacrifice, upon the altar, inundated with her blood.

Cecilia gazed at him with ineffable sweetness and joy. "Father," she said, "I asked this delay of three days, from our Lord, that I might place in the hands of your Beatitude, [7] my last treasure, the poor whom I feed and who will miss me. I also bequeath to you this house in which I have lived, that you may consecrate it as a church, and that it may become the temple of the Lord forever. [8]

After these words, the virgin thought only of preparing her soul to meet its Spouse. She thanked Christ, that He had deigned to associate her to the glory of the athletes, and had crowned her with a wreath composed of the roses of martyrdom, twined with the lilies of virginity. The heavens were already

73

opened to her eyes, and a moment of faintness announced that her last hour was approaching. She was lying upon her right side, in an attitude of virginal modesty. At the last moment, her arms fell by her side, and, turning her face against the ground so that none could witness the last secret communings of her departing soul with the divine object of all her love, she tranquilly expired. [9]

So great a martyr could be buried by none but the most august hands. Saint Urban, assisted by the deacons, presided at her funeral ceremonies. They laid her in a cypress coffin, in the same attitude in which she had expired, clothed in the rich robe of silk and gold, which she had worn at the time of her martyrdom; and placed at her feet the linen cloths and veils with which the faithful had collected her precious blood.

The following night, her holy body was carried to the Appian Way, to the cemetery of Saint Callistus, near the third mile-stone. Valerian, Tiburtius and Maximus, were buried at a short distance from the spot, but the entrance to their tombs was upon the left of the Appian Way.

To honor the apostalate which Cecilia had exercised, Saint Urban desired that she should be buried in the enclosure prepared by Saint Callistus for the Pontiffs, [10] and in which he had interred his predecessor, Saint Zephyrinus. This well merited, but unusual distinction, joined to the desire of burying the virgin at the spot where the cemetery of Saint Callistus turned towards that of Pretextatus, in order to place her near her husband, accounts for the fact of all traces of her sepulchre having been lost, until it was discovered by means of a revelation. Thus the goodness of God restored to the Roman Church the treasure which she believed had been stolen from her sacred Crypts by the hands of strangers.

[1] The Roman baths were divided into several halls. The first was the *frigidarium*, where cold baths were taken; the second, *tepidarium*, where the water was tepid; and the third, called *caldarium*, or *calidarium*, or sometimes *sudatorium*, was reserved for vapor baths. Reservoirs of boiling water sent whirlwinds of vapor through this hall; and a furnace, called *laconicum*, the flames of which were circulated by means of pipes laid under the floor, and imbedded in the thick walls, increased the temperature to a burning heat. The vaulted ceiling was generally built of stucco, and was of hemispherical form. It was closed by a brass shield, which was worked by means of a chain, and served as a valve when the intensity of the heat became suffocating. A description of the *caldarium* may be found in Vitruvius, lib. x. cap x.

The punishment to which Almachius condemned St. Cecilia, is not without a parallel in history. This method of inflicting death, without shedding blood, was employed by Constantine, in the execution of the Empress Fausta. Zosimus relates that by the Emperor's orders, the princess was enclosed in a bath, heated to suffocation, and that she was taken out dead. We find another example in Rome of a martyrdom inflicted under circumstances analogous to those that attended the death of St. Cecilia. It is that of the brothers Sts. John and Paul, unde Julian the Apostate. This prince, not wishing to publish edicts against the Christians, adopted a less dangerous and more efficacious system of persecution. The two Christians, after professing their faith before the Roman Prefect, Terentianus, were reconducted to their own palace, where they were secretly beheaded by the executioners who afterwards buried them.

[2] Superari charitas Christi flamma non potuit, et segnior fuit ignis qui foris ussit quam qui intus accendit. *Sermo in Natali S. Laurentii.*

[3] Cumque fuisset in calore balnei inclusa, et subter incendia nimia lignorum pabula ministrarent die integra et nocte tota, quasi in frigido loco illibata perstitit sanitate, ita ut nec una pars membrorum ejus saltem sudoris signo lassaretur. *Acta S. Caeciliae.*

[4] Hoc cum audisset Almachius, misit qui eam in ipso balneo decollaret; quam cum spiculator tertio ictu percussisset, caput ejus amputare non potuit: sic autem seminecem earn cruentus carnifex dereliquit; nam apud veteres lex erat eis imposita, ut si in tribus percussionibus non decollaretur, amplius percutere non audebat. *Acta S. Caecilae.*

[5] Cujus sanguinem omnes bibulis linteaminibus populi, qui per eam crediderant, extergebant. *Ibid.*

[6] Per triduum autem quod supervixit, non cessavit, quos nutrierat et quos docuerat in fide Domini confortare, quibus et divisit universa quae habuit. *Acta S. Caeciliae.*

[7] Respecting the antiquity of this title given to the Roman Pontiff, many examples may be found in letters addressed to the Pope from the East and the West throughout the fourth century. Such uniformity at this time, proves that the custom dated still farther back. Among other letters, may be seen those from the Orientals to Saint Julius, those of Saint Athanasius and the Bishops of Egypt to the same Pontiff, those of Saint Jerome and of Aurelius of Carthage to Saint Damasus, etc.

[8] Sancto Urbano Papae dixit: A dime triduanas mihi propose! inducias, ut et istos tuse Beatitudini traderem quos nutrivi, et banc domum meam in aeternum Eoclesiae nomini consocrares. *Acta S. Caeciliae.*

[9] These details respecting Cecilia's dying position are not mentioned in the Acts: they are gathered from a more striking source, as we shall mention later.

[10] Tunc sanctus Urbanus Papa corpus ejus auferens cum Diaconibus, nocte sepelivit eam inter collegas suos Episcopos, et Martyres, ubi sancti Confessores sunt collocati. *Acta S. Caeciliae.*

Chapter Fifteen - Martyrdom of St. Urban. Pontificate of St. Pontinus. Death of Alexander Severus

Scarcely a month elapsed before Urban was summoned to the tribunal of Almachius. The Pontiff had been discovered with two priests and three deacons in a grotto where he had been concealed; for it had been impossible for him to remain long in Cecilia's palace. The prefect's officers, disconcerted at not finding in the palace the treasures they expected, and ignorant of Cecilia's donations to the poor, accused Urban of having received immense sums to secure them from confiscation. Cupidity rendered the search more active, and the Pontiff was finally discovered and arrested.

"Is this," said Almachius, "that Urban, that seducer, who has already been twice condemned, and whom the Christians have made their Pope?" [1]

"Yes," replied the holy Pontiff, "It is I who have seduced men from the paths of iniquity, and have led them into the way of truth." [2]

"Is that the way of truth," retorted Almachius, "in which the gods are not honored, nor the princes obeyed?" [3]

"No," said Urban, "I do not honor your gods any more than I fear your princes. Do what you have to do." [4]

The venerable old man was cast into prison with his companions, and during the night, some Christians, who had bribed with gold the jailor, Anolinus, came to visit him, and to give him proofs of their filial veneration.

St. Urban, accompanied by his priests and deacons, appeared a second time before the prefect. Almachius at first manifested a little moderation, the result of the uneasiness which he experienced at having so violently persecuted the Christians. "Cease your obstinacy," he said, "and sacrifice, to the gods. Already five thousand men have perished in consequence of your seductions. [5] You are responsible for them."

"They have not perished as you imagine, wretched man," replied Urban, "but have ascended gloriously to the kingdom of heaven."

"Yes," said the prefect, "it was this vain hope which so woefully seduced Cecilia, her husband, and her brother-in-law; it was this hope which made them count as nothing the brilliant existence that awaited them on earth. At their death, they left you immense treasures — you must restore them." [6]

By these words, the judge betrayed his cupidity. Urban, disdaining to answer the accusation, contented himself with saying: "Foolish man! rather render homage to your Creator; for those of whom you speak, gave up their lives, after distributing their fortunes to the poor." [7]

"Cease this audacity if you wish to live; otherwise you shall perish."

"None can perish," said Urban, "but those who by their faith or works, displease the Creator."

The prefect then addressed the two priests: "And are you of the same opinion?"

"All the counsels of our Father are wise," they replied; "but wisdom will not enter into a perverted soul." [8]

"I see," replied Almachius, you are worse than your master, decrepit and foolish as he is. Are you not ashamed, miserable wretches, to persevere in your insolence, after so many condemnations?" [9]

He then commanded them to be scourged with loaded whips. The order was executed in his presence, and the two confessors, during the blows, repeated: "Lord! we thank Thee."

Almachius, enraged at their constancy, cried out in a voice trembling with passion:

"They must be protected by some enchantment, or they could not still resist our orders."

"It is you," said Urban, "who have become like your gods; for you have ears and hear not; eyes and see not." [10]

"What! do you dare to insult the gods!" cried the prefect; "your head shall be the forfeit of your audacity; I swear it by the gods and goddesses."

"If you wish to judge for yourself how much respect the gods merit, read their history. As to our God, He has created all things, and He strengthens us by these words: 'Fear not those who kill the body, for they cannot kill the soul.'"

"I understand," said Almachius, "you are old, and for this reason you look upon death as a rest; you are jealous of these young men; you persuade them to sacrifice their lives, because your own is nearly at an end."

One of the priests, indignant at this outrage, interrupted the prefect: "Your words are evident falsehoods," he said. "Our Father, from his youth, has always regarded Jesus Christ as his life, and death as a gain. More than once he confessed Christ, and exposed his life for the flock confided to his care." [11]

Almachius ordered the old man and his companions to be re-conducted to prison. Here they were again visited by the Christians, and the jailor, Anolinus, was so impressed by the veneration and homage paid to the venerable old man, that he was converted to the faith, baptized by St. Urban, and soon after paid with his life the honor of being enrolled among the soldiers of Christ.

A short time after, the martyrs were again summoned before Almachius, who ordered that they should be conducted to the Pagus Triopius, where he hoped they would consent to offer incense to the idol of Jupiter. [12] A critic of our day, has remarked with some reason, that the prefect's motive in choosing a Pagus of the Appian Way for the holy Pontiffs trial, was to give greater publicity to his apostasy, if he abjured Christianity so near the place where he had exercised his ministry; or more solemnity to his execution, should he refuse to sacrifice to the gods, in a region so frequented by the Christians. [13]

The Confessors rejected with horror the proposal that they should offer incense to the idols, and were, in consequence, so cruelly beaten, that Lucian, one of the deacons, expired under the blows of the executioner. Finally, on the eighth of the calends of June, three days later, Almachius sent the confessors to a temple of Diana, [14] ordering the soldiers to behead them if they refused to offer sacrifice. On the way, Urban thus exhorted his companions: "It is the Lord who calls us; He who has said: c Come to me, all ye that labor and are burdened, and I will refresh you.' Until now, we have known the Lord only as in a glass, and as an enigma; behold the moment when we go to see Him face to face. [15]

When they entered the temple, the martyrs said to the executioners: "Finish your work. It is useless to propose to us an action which you know we scorn." They insisted, however; and upon the martyrs' refusal, led them out of the temple and beheaded them. Fabian, Callistus, and Ammonius, three Christian tribunes, who had visited the Pontiff* in prison, caused the bodies of the martyrs to be carried to the cemetery of Pretextatus. [16]

A more honorable sepulture was reserved for St. Urban, in return for that which in his paternal tenderness he had prepared for Cecilia. Marmenia, the wife of the prefect's Vicar, had embraced Christianity immediately after the martyrdom of St. Urban. Having learned through the priest, Fortunatus, who had baptized her, the place where the bodies of St. Urban and his companions had been deposited, she caused these sacred remains to be removed to her villa, which was situated upon the left side of the Appian Way, near a villa built by Vespasian, above the cemetery of Pretextatus, not far from the tombs of Valerian, Tiburtius and Maximus. She ordered a crypt to be excavated, in which she placed a sepulchre, closed by a slab of precious marble, the interior of the tomb being also lined with marble. Here, Marmenia placed the bodies of St. Urban and his companions, after anointing them with perfumes. This crypt was afterwards enlarged, and converted into a vast cubiculum, solidly built, and of quadrangular dimensions. [17] In one of the manuscripts of the Acts of St. Urban, this cubiculum is described as being situated in the upper story of the Catacombs. [18]

St. Urban had occupied the Holy See eight years, eleven months and twelve days. He was succeeded by Pontianus, who governed in peace for several years. The return of Alexander Severus restored tranquillity to the Church of Rome; at least the violence of Alrnachius does not seem to have been prolonged beyond this epoch. The impressions of the Emperor when he was made acquainted with the prefect's conduct, are not known. The historians of Alexander were little interested in the Christians, and, moreover, they generally passed over in silence facts which merely referred to the magistrates. It is to be supposed that this prince, who detested cruelty, blamed the excesses of the prefect, but it does not appear that he expressed in any other way his displeasure at the judicial murder of Cecilia and the two patricians. However this may have been, the system followed under the reign of Alexander with regard to the sovereign Pontiffs, was soon carried out in the case of Pontianus. This saintly Pope had to suffer persecution on account of his ministry; he was not condemned to death, like his predecessors, Sts. Urban and Callistus, but an order emanating from the imperial court, exiled him to the isle of Buccinia, [19] one of the wildest on the southern coast of Sardinia.

Alexander did not long survive this act of injustice. How frequently we see in history, and even in our own day, the judgments of God visited upon princes who seemed personally favorable to His church, but who, forgetful of the future, and of justice, neglected to break the chains which others had forged for the Spouse of Christ. These princes thought that in lightening her fetters, they had fulfilled their duty. They did not foresee that, after their death, those chains would be riveted more firmly than ever upon that Church which they ought not only to have loved and venerated as Christians, but to have protected and delivered as kings.

Alexander had scarcely entered upon the thirteenth year of his reign, and the twenty sixth of his age, when he was assassinated at Mayence by his own soldiers, leaving the empire to Julius Verus Maximinus, one of the chiefs of his army. This man is suspected of having been the author of the sedition in which the unfortunate prince and his Mother, Julia Mammaea, lost their lives.

[1] Nonne iste est Urbanus seductor, qui jam semel et iterum damnatus est, quem Christiani sibi Papam fecerunt? *Laderchi Acta S. Urbani.*

[2] Ego seduco homines, ut viam iniquitatis relinquant, et ad viam veritatis deveniant. *Ibid.*

[3] O via veritatis, quae nec Deos colit, nec Principes ob temporat. *Ibid.*

[4] nec Deos tuos colo, nec principes tuos timeo; fac quod facturus es. *Acta S. Urbani.*

[5] The Acts of St. Urban, from which we gather these details, have not, doubtless, the same authority as those of St. Cecilia, but there is a tone of candor and truth throughout them which does not permit us to reject them with disdain, as many critics have done. The most serious objection to them occurs in this passage, as it is incredible that 5000 persons should have been martyred for the faith in Rome, in so short a time, and by the orders of a prefect. But this can be easily explained as being an error of the copyist. The manuscripts frequently passed through so many hands that mistakes might easily be made in figures, and it certainly seems unjust to reject the whole account merely for a fault which can be so easily explained.

[6] Hac vana spe inducta Caecilia cum sponso suo et cognato, omnem gloriam perdiderunt, et immensum tibi dimiserunt thesaurum, quern te nunc exhibere oportet. *Ada S. Urbani.*

[7] Stulte, agnosce creatorem pro quo illi sua omnia pauperisms erogantes, mori exoptaverunt. *Ibid.*

[8] Patris nostri monita per omnia sunt salubria, sed inmalevolam animam non intrat sapiential *Ibid.*

[9] Ut video deteriores effecti estis quam delirus senex magister vester; sed miseri non erubescitis, qui toties damnati praescriptionibus in impudentia perduratis. *Ibid.*

[10] Immo tu miser Diis tuis similis es effectus, aures habens, et non audiens, oculos, et non videns. *Acta S. Urbani.*

[11] Manifesto mentiris; patri enim nostro, et in juventute Christus vivere fuit, et mori lucrum; multeties quippe pro eo Confessor effectus, animam suam pro ejus ovibus posuit. *Ibid.*

[12] Ducite eos ad templum juxta Pagum, et vol sacrificent Deo magno Jovi, vel multiplicibus macerentur suppliciis. *Acta S. Urbani.*

[13] Riccy. Dell' antico pago Lemonio. Rome, 1802, page 104.

[14] The Acts of St. Urban do not specify the locality of this temple; it may have been in the interior of the city. Had it been on the Nomentana road, as we conjectured in our first edition, in consequence of some remarks, in the martyrology attributed to St. Jerome, it is probable the Acts would not have omitted to mention the circumstance.

[15] Ecce nos Dominus vocat inquiens: Venite ad me omnes quilaboratis et onerati estis, et ego reficiam vos. Hactenus eum vide mus quasi per speculum, et in aenigmate; prcesto autem est, ut videamus eum facie ad faciem. *Acta S. Urbani.*

[16] *Acta S. Urbani.*

[17] Levaverunt inde cum magno honore glebas almas, et adduxerunt eas in domum Marmeniae, quae erat extra palatium Vespasiani Augusti, sita prope columnas, in qua sepulcrum B. Marmenia miro jussit modo poni: quod etiam marmoreis tabulis ex omni parte conglutinans contexit parietem, in quo recondiderunt cum aromatibus corpus Beatissimi Urbani et Mamiliani Presbyteri, et desuper sacrum tumulum miro lapide operiri curaverunt: super quod ingens antrum fabricari fecerunt, quadratum et firmissimae fabricae, etc. *Acta S. Urbani.*

[18] Corpus autem B. Urbani Papae et Martyris, ibidem in superiori caemaculo condiderunt. *Acta SS, Mali, ad dium* xxv. page 13. This circumstance is also found in an ancient manuscript of the Vatican Basilica from which Laderchi has extracted abridged Acts of St. Urban.

[19] Anastas. *in Pontiano.*

Chapter Sixteen - Zeal of the Romans Pontiffs in Collecting the Acts of the Martyrs. The Memory of St. Cecilia Preserved in the Church of Rome. Her Basilica

Maximinus, upon his accession to the imperial throne, manifested a bitter hostility against the Christians. The persecution, which had been suspended since the reign of Septimus Severus, was renewed with the greatest violence. The new Emperor directed his decrees in a special manner against the heads of the Church [1] and singled out the Pontiff of Rome as his first victim. An order was immediately dispatched to the island of Buccina, commanding the execution of the courageous pastor whose absence had been so severely felt by the Roman Church. Pontianus had occupied the Holy See, two months and seven days. His body was afterwards transported to Rome and buried in the cemetery of St. Callistus. [2] Anterus succeeded Pontianus upon the apostolic chair; but lie had scarcely governed the Church one month when he was beheaded by order of Maximinus, and thus obtained the crown of martyrdom. A fact, connected with the short pontificate of Anterus, is of some importance in relation to the history of Cecilia. In the first ages, under the persecution of

Domitian, the great Pontiff, St. Clement, wishing to preserve for future ages an account of the triumphs of the Martyrs, had appointed seven notaries whose duty it was to commit to writing all the circumstances, accompanying the generous sacrifice of these athletes of the faith. Each notary was appointed overseer of two of the fourteen regions of Rome. [3] The glorious memoirs they had the charge of collecting, must have considerably increased both in number and importance, during the persecutions of Trajan, Antoninus, Marcus Aurelius, and Severus. We have seen what sublime pages were furnished to the collection, through the tyranny of Almachius, in the reign of Alexander Severus. The holy Pope Anterus made a compilation of the acts collected by the Notaries of the Church, in order to preserve them in the Archives of the Apostolic See. A fresco painted on the ceiling of a cubiculum in the cemetery of Sts. Nereus and Achilles, joining that of St. Callistus, seems to have been designed for the purpose of handing down to posterity the remembrance of this wise measure of Anterus. A venerable old man is represented seated upon an estrade, between two ministers, who are standing on either side. His hands are raised in the act of blessing three other persons, one of whom is kneeling, the other two in an attitude of profound veneration. They have just placed at his feet a round box filled with rolls of parchment. Boxes containing similar rolls of parchment, are very frequently seen in the wall paintings of the Roman cemeteries. The learned archaeologist, F. Bianchini, whose opinion is of great weight, thinks that this fresco was designed as a memento of the holy Pope's [4] zeal in collecting the Acts of the Martyrs; however this may be, the fresco painting is of an elegant and correct style, and was most probably executed in the third century.

The Christians of this period, who were so interested in preserving mementos of all that related to faith, must have been anxious to perpetuate the remembrance of the holy pontiffs zeal in gathering the Acts of the Martyrs; the more so, as he received the palm of martyrdom in reward for the labor by which he laid the foundation of the Archives of the Church. Anterus was denounced before the prefect as one who honored the memory of the enemies of the empire and of the gods, and he expiated with his blood, the crime of having generously opposed the policy of the Caesars. [5] His body was buried in the Cemetery of Callistus.

The pious Fabian, successor of Anterus, was not less zealous for the glory of God. He commanded that the seven notaries should each be assisted by a sub-deacon, who should aid him in compiling the Acts of the Martyrs. [6] The same desire of rendering homage to these noble victims, among whom he himself was ranked after a pontificate of fourteen years, led him to undertake the great works in the cemeteries. [7] He caused several additional galleries to be excavated, and many new frescos to be painted. It was but natural he should wish that one of these frescos should represent the zeal shown by his predecessor in transmitting to posterity the remembrance of the trials, endured by the innumerable heroes who slept in these gloomy vaults.

The age in which Cecilia lived, was prolific in reliable historians, who faithfully gathered such precious reminiscences, and the Supreme Pontiff did not feel that he was lowering his dignity by carefully superintending the compilation of the Acts, so that even the slightest circumstance might not be omitted. Moreover, it was a discipline established in the church from the time of the first persecutions, to write the circumstances attending the combats of the martyrs, and, notwithstanding the immense losses we have sustained by the ravages of time, and by other accidents, the authentic Acts which are still extant throughout all parts, both of the Eastern and Western Church, suffice to prove that the intentions of Popes Clement, Anterus, and Fabian, were understood and carried out throughout Christendom.

We will particularly quote the following words of the deacon, Pontius, in the life of his bishop, St. Cyprian, written at the death of this great martyr, twenty-eight years after the death of St. Cecilia: "Such was," says this author, "the veneration of our ancestors for the martyrs, whether baptized or catechumens, that they have committed to writing nearly all the details respecting the sufferings they endured, so that these accounts have been transmitted to us, who were not then even born." [8]

If such was the case in a simple province of the Church, the measures organized by the sovereign Pontiff, in the centre of Christianity, must have resulted in the most authentic and imposing Acts concerning the martyrs. Add to this, that many Acts which have been transmitted to us, refer to persons of secondary importance, and yet the most precise account is given of every circumstance attending the martyrdom; the interrogations, the replies, the torments, the miracles, and the sepultures. The noble birth of Cecilia, Valerian and Tiburtius; the impression which such a tragedy must naturally have created among the Gentiles, as well as among the Christians, rendered the compilation of their Acts an easy matter. Even in the absence of the notaries of the Church, the faithful would have retained for along time, the greater part of the details. We cannot, therefore, doubt that the Acts of St. Cecilia were written at a time when there was every facility of authenticating the facts. Divine Providence, who wished to give Rome a Christian Cecilia in place of that matron of ancient times, whose fame was not destined to survive the Capitol, took care that the memory of our Saint should be preserved and become more glorious from age to age.

After the persecution of Maximin, the Church was called to suffer those of Decius, Valerian, Gallienus, Aurelian, and finally the most terrible of all, that of Diocletian. The number of martyrs increased to a frightful extent, but none of these new and illustrious names eclipsed that of Cecilia. In the fourth century, when the Diptych of the Canon of the Mass was closed to be opened but once more, Cecilia's name was retained therein, and the greatest honor which the Church can bestow, was thus secured to her forever.

From her throne in heaven, she hears her name daily pronounced in the silent prayers which accompany the celebration of the Holy Sacrifice; and her blood, once shed for Christ, is presented before the throne of God with that of the Spotless Lamb, to whom she is forever united, amidst the roses and lilies of paradise.

Thus after the persecutions, the Roman Church awarded to Cecilia an honor granted to but few of those who had been her glory during those times of trial. Out of the thirty Popes, martyrs, six only were commemorated on the immortal Diptych; the daughter of the Cecilii was preferred to so many heroes. The Virgin Agnes, her rival in the love of Christ, precedes her upon this triumphal list; the pious widow Anastasia follows her; all three daughters of the Roman Church. In the sixth century, St. Gregory added the names of the two Virgin Martyrs of Catania and Syracuse, Agatha and Lucy; but thrcnigh liturgical courtesy, he gave the precedence to the two Roman Virgins. [9]

The tenth of the Calends of December (22 Nov.) was appointed for the feast of St. Cecilia in the earliest ages, as we find in the Martyrology attributed to St. Jerome. [10] The holy martyrs, Valerian, Tiburtius, and Maximus, continued to be venerated on the eighteenth of the Calends of May (14 April), and St. Urban on the eighth of the Calends of June (25 May), the respective anniversaries of their martyrdom. That of Cecilia took place between these two epochs. But the feasts of the Ascension and of Pentecost were celebrated at this season, and sometimes fell on the anniversary of the holy Virgin's death. It was therefore resolved to honor her memory on another day, that nothing might interfere with the solemnity of her festival. It is impossible to determine why the Church selected the 22d of November [11] Probably the rebuilding of Cecilia's house, under a form more appropriate for a church, or its dedication in the fourth or fifth century, may have been the occasion of transferring the feast of its holy Patroness to a day so much later than that of her martyrdom. The importance and solemnity of St. Cecilia's feast at Rome in the fifth century, are attested by the sacramentary of St. Gelasius, which was drawn up at this period. The feast is preceded by a preparatory Vigil. [12] St. Cecilia shares with St. Lawrence this honor, which St. Sebastian and St. Agnes, although so famous in the Archives of the mother Church, do not seem to have obtained. It is true that the feast of St. Cecilia no longer enjoys this distinction; but this testimony of the veneration of earlier times towards the Saint is sufficient to show how vividly the memory of her virtues was retained among the Christians even at the end of the fifth century, when her acts were compiled for the last time.

The Church which was erected beyond the Tiber under the name of St. Cecilia, likewise bore witness to the magnificent reminiscences we have retraced. It is well known that when the churches erected in honor of the Roman Martyrs, in the capital of Christendom, did not contain their relics, or were not built at the entrance of the cemeteries where the bodies of their patrons reposed, they served to mark the places sanctified by the martyr's life and sufferings. This custom was not observed merely in Rome, it was established as a point of discipline in the African church by the fourteenth can-

on of the fourth council of Carthage, in 398, [13] which canon is even inserted in the digest of ecclesiastical laws.f Later, this discipline was modified; but
it was still kept up in Rome for many centuries. This accounts for the small
number of churches dedicated to St. Peter, although he was patron of the
city. Four churches only were dedicated to him, and these are all monuments
of his life; the Vatican, which preserves his body; that of St. Peter ad Vincula,
where his chains are kept; the Mamertine Prison, or St. Peter in Carcere,
which is built over the dungeon where he was confined with St. Paul; and
finally, St. Peter in Montorio, upon the ground where it is presumed he was
crucified. The body of our glorious martyr reposed many centuries in the
cemetery of Callistus, out of the city, upon the Appian Way. In order to explain the origin of the trans-Tiberian Church, which bore the name of St. Cecilia, we must naturally refer to the house which Cecilia confided at her death
to the Pontiff Urban. The bathroom where she suffered martyrdom is still
visible, and the memory of St. Ceoilia so intimately associated with this
Church could never be lost in Rome." [15]

The first mention we find of the Church of St. Cecilia in the official documents which have reached us, dates back to the year 499. Among the signa-
tures of a council held in Rome in that year, under Pope Symmachus, are
those of Boniface and Marcian, who sign themselves priests of St. Cecilia's
Church. [16]

But even before this time, many epigraphical monuments prove the existence of this church, and the veneration paid in it to the Roman Virgin. An inscription, unfortunately mutilated, which was still to be seen in the last century, in the pavement of the Church, contained a consular date, which could
scarcely be later than the year 464. The following is the inscription, for the
restoration of which we are indebted to the science and friendship of M. le
Chevalier de Rossi:

*Apol*LONIAE H. P. BONITATIS EXIMIAE *et mirae verecun*DIAE ET VLTRA AE-
TATIS ANNOS *filiae* (N. N.) *cubi*CVLARIS *sanctae martyri*S CAE *ciliae q. vix.
ann.* XII. MENSE. I. DIEB. XIII. *de saecvlo re*CESSiT XVIIII KAL SEPT. RIO COSS.
*parentes miseri fv*NERIS ACERVITATE PERCVLSI *titulum*...CI IVSSERVNT. [17]

We learn by this epitaph that a private individual, exercising the functions
of *cubicularis*, or guardian of St. Cecilia's Church, had buried his daughter in
this place, under the date of a consul whose name terminates with these two
syllables; RI VS. The writing of this inscription being evidently of the V. century, and the VI. presenting no consul whose name terminates with the given
syllables, we must seek in the V. the person designated. Now, here we find
several consulates which might answer our purpose. The most recent is that
of Eusticus *Olybrius* in the year 461. In preferring this one to others of more
ancient date, we confirm the opinion that from the year 464, under the pon-

tificate of St. Hilarius, the Church of St. Cecilia was sufficiently important to require the services of *cubiculares.*

In the last century, there still existed in the pavement, a number of inscriptions, either whole or in fragments, which would be very useful now in tracing the historyof this venerable Sanctuary.

Later, we will mention under what circumstances these valuable records of antiquity were destroyed. But we must mention *one* slab found in the pavement of the portico, the inscriptions on which, relating to a young girl named Thecla, might, according to the opinion of our learned friend, be referred to the IV. century.

[1] Euseb.

[2] Amastas. *in Pontiano.*

[3] Hic fecit septem Regiones dividi Notariis fidelibus Ecclesiae, qui gesta martyrum sollicite et curiose unusquisque per Regionem suam diligenter perquirerent. *Anastas in Clemente.*

[4] Anastasii Bibliothecarii de vitis Pontificum, *in Antero notae historicae.* Tom. i. p. 184.

[5] Hic gesta Martyrum diligenter a Notarus exquisivit, et in Ecclesia recondidit. Propter quod a Maximo Praefecto martyrio coronatus est. *Anastas, in Antero.*

[6] Fecit septem subdiaconos qui septem Notariis imminerent, ut gesta Martyrum in integro colligerent. *Anastas. in Fabiano.*

[7] Multas fabricas per caemeteria fieri praecepit. *Ibid.*

[8] Cum majores nostri plebeiis et catechumenis martyrium consecutis tantum honoris pro martyrii ipsius veneratione dederint, de passionibus eorum multa, aut prope dixerim pene cuneta conscripserunt, ut ad nostram quoque notitiam qui nondum nati fuimus pervenirent. *Pontius diaconus, in vita Cacilii Cypriani.*

[9] Many liturgists maintain that St. Gregory at the same time inserted in the canon the names of all the female Saints fonnd therein. The only author who speaks of the addition made by St. Gregory to the Diptych contained in the prayer, Nobis quoqne peccatoribus, is St. Adhelmar of Sherbum, whose words are very clear, and who speaks but of Saints Agatha and Lucy as having been added to the others. Vid. S. Adhelmi Episcopi Saxonum occidentalium de Virginitate, cap. xxiii. Bibblioth, vet. Patrum, tome xiii., page 44. The author, speaking of St. Cecilia and Agnes, gives no reason to suppose that their names had been recently added, which he distinctly states of the two Sicilian martyrs.

[10] Florentini, Martyrologium S. Hieronymi. *X. Kal. Decembris.*

[11] It is remarkable that the Roman Martyrology of the 22d of November, neither mentions the death (Natalis) nor the burial (Depositio) of St. Cecilia. We simply read Romae, sanctae Caeciliae, Virginis et Martyris, quae sponsum suum Valerianum, etc. The 23d thus mentions the feast of St. Clement, Natalis sancti Clementis Papae. On the 14th of April, Saints Tiburtius, Valerian, and Maximus, are announced by the Natalis, as well as St. Urban on the 25th of May.

[12] Muratori. *Liturgia Romana vetus,* tome i. *Sacramentarium Gelasianum,* page 672.

[13] Et onmino nulla memoria Martyrum probabiliter acceptctur, nisi aut ibi corpus, aut aliquoe oertffl reliquiae shit, aut ubi origo alicujus hnbitationis, vol possessions, vol passionis, fidelissima origine traditur. Labbe. Concilia, tome ii, page 1218.

[14] De consecratione. Distinct, i, can. xxvi. *Placuit ut altaria.*

[15] Among the Churches of Rome, erected like that of St. Cecilia, upon the ground formerly occupied by the dwellings of their patrons, we will cite those of St. Praxedes, of St. Boniface, now St. Alexis, upon the Aventine; of Saints John and Paul; of St. Eusebius; of St. Prisca; of St. Bibiana, etc.

[16] Labbe. Concil. Tome iv, page 1316.

[17] This inscription has been inaccurately given by Maffei, *Museum Verononse,* page 291, No. 6.

Chapter Seventeen - Compilation of the Acts of Saint Cecilia, in the V. Century, In Their Present Form. Motives of This Compilation. Canon of Pope St. Gelasius upon the Use of the Acts of the Martyrs

As we have already stated, we cannot assign an earlier date than the V. century, to the definitive compilation of the Acts of our Saint. The defective Latin of this document, does not permit us to place it at an earlier date; and, besides, the use immediately made of it, by all the Churches of the West, is a positive proof that it was not written at a later period.

These Acts must be classed among those which were compiled from ancient memorials, after the close of the persecutions. The author wished to unite in a simple narrative, the different circumstances of St. Cecilia's life, which he had been enabled to gather, either from the Acts collected by the Notaries of the Church; or from other records which must have been abundant in a city where the holy Martyr was so highly venerated; or, finally, from oral traditions and metaphorical monuments. His story begins -at the preparation for the marriage of Cecilia and Tiburtius, and ends with the Virgin's death and burial. It is very evident that the author endeavored to make his work uniform throughout, and that he blended in his recital all the documents which were at his disposal. His language is naive, and his style such as is remarked in the series of Acts of the Martyrs, which begins at the IV. century; numerous examples of which are published in the collection of Dom Bainart. In these compositions, the Latin language is so altered that it is easy to see it was on the eve of ceasing to be the vulgar tongue. Our Acts, however, are not written in the barbarous style, used in the Papal Chronicle, known under the name of the Catalogue of Felix IV., and which stops at the year 534. [1]

Besides we must not suppose that during the two centuries preceding the reign of Constantine, the Latin language was written and spoken in Rome with the purity and accuracy found among the classics of this period, the tradition of which St. Ambrose, St. Jerome, and St. Augustin, made every effort to preserve. The greater part of the Christian inscriptions in the Catacombs, even those on profane monuments, previous to the IV. century, prove that the language of the masters of the world was far from being universally spoken and written correctly, even in the capital of the empire.

The neglect of the rules of grammar and of rhetoric, which characterizes the decline of a nation, is very visible in the Acts of the martyrs compiled at this period; in fact, the writers seem to have affected unusual carelessness of style. The transpositions of phrase disappear, the language becomes more simple; the biblical narrations are imitated with minute exactness, and more or less success; the expressions used in the *Italic* version of the Holy Scriptures are introduced with eagerness, and frequently impart animation to the recital. Such is the literary character of the Acts of St. Cecilia. If the narrative be found very interesting, the credit is not due to the style in which it is related; although the tone of candor which reigns throughout, is a powerful proof of the sincerity of the author, and even in those passages which are evidently written for effect, we can easily trace the original Acts. These rhetorical attempts merely prove that the genius of the compiler was not equal to the conception of a drama, so sublime and so touching, as the one to which he has consecrated his feeble talent. We may assuredly affirm that the admirable discourse of St. Cecilia to Tiburtius was not composed by the narrator, who has given it to us in his rude and inelegant diction which almost conceals its original beauty.

We shall have many occasions in the course of our story, to demonstrate the accuracy of our historian, and to defend his narrative from the imputations cast upon it by the Jansenists. Let it suffice to observe here, that the author wrote under the eyes of his fellow citizens; that he was not relating the life of an obscure person, about whom he could have invented many circumstances without being liable to contradiction; finally, that his recital was almost universally accepted throughout the Churches of the West. The presumption consequently would be in his favor, even had we not the most distinct and evident proofs of his veracity. The Acts of St. Cecilia, like those of many others, were composed to be read from the Ambon, in the church dedicated to the Saint, on the day of her feast. This public reading being intended to increase the solemnity, it was necessary to make a complete and uniform narration of everything contained in the documents of the Roman Church, relating to the martyr. Hence the monotonous style, and the oratorical velleities of the compiler, who precedes his narrative with a prelude of generalities, in the style of the exordiums found in many of the Acts collected by Dom Ruinart.

This custom of solemnly reading the Acts of the Martyrs, on their festivals, has been preserved until the present day in our Legends of the Breviary. In the fifth century it was in full force, and very dear to the faithful. St. Augustin,

Bishop of Hippo, frequently alluded to it in his Sermons de Sanctis; [2] and we have still a Canon of one of the Councils of the African Church, expressly confirming this custom. It was likewise in vigor in the Gallican Church at the same epoch, as we learn from a sermon of St. Cesarius of Aries, in which he complains of the abuse of the permission given to invalids, to sit during the reading of the *Holy Passions of the Martyrs.* [3] Rome, so rich in memorials, and so zealous in demonstrations of piety towards the martyrs, could not be outdone by the other Churches. Each of its Basilicas had, as it were, its own martyr, and honored him with special veneration; the Romans must have desired to have the Acts of each glorious patron, that they might be read on the solemnity of his feast. But Diocletian having particularly ordered the destruction of ecclesiastical books, many Acts compiled by the notaries, were destroyed. Later accounts of the deeds of certain martyrs were not written with sufficient discernment. Moreover, many Acts, at different epochs, had been compiled by heretics, with the intention of insinuating their errors by means of these documents. Towards the close of the fifth century, the Holy See found it necessary to take measures for guarding the faith of the Church from the danger to which it was exposed. As all the Acts of the Martyrs, whether genuine or apocryphal, were supposed to be authorized by the Church, they were all read with equal avidity by the unsuspecting faithful, and hence many inconveniencies might arise. The examination of all the Acts extant was a labor requiring time, hence no alternative was left but that of a temporary prohibition of all. A council held by Pope, St. Gelasius, about 495, drew up the famous canon which contains the catalogue of the books considered orthodox by the Roman Church. [4] It is couched in the following terms: "We likewise receive the Acts of the holy Martyrs with the brilliant description of their torments and the marvellous triumph of their confessions. What Catholic could doubt their truth? Who does not know that the martyrs in their combats suffered the most dreadful torments, and supported fearful trials, not by their own strength, but with the grace and assistance of God." [5]

Thus the canon of St. Gelasius confirmed the existence of the Acts of the Martyrs, and appealed to catholic opinion respecting the truth of their accounts; it approved and recommended the use of them, and signalized them as being glorious proofs of the wonderful power of God. But as these acts were not of equal authority, and as it was important that they should not be indiscriminately used in the Roman Liturgy, such use being the most solemn confirmation which they could receive from the Holy See, the Pontiff adds the following general order: "According to ancient custom and the dictates of prudence, it is not our practice to read the Acts of the Martyrs in the Holy Roman Church. The reasons for this conduct are manifold. The authors of some of these Acts are completely unknown; others have been written by unbelievers, or by illiterate men, who have introduced superfluous things without that perspicuity which the subject requires. As examples, we may cite the Acts of Quiricus, Julitte, George, whose Passions, it is said, have been compiled by heretics. Therefore the Holy Roman Church has prohibited the use of them, lest the contrary practice should offer some slight ground for criticism." [6]

This extreme reserve with which the Roman Church prohibited the public reading of these Acts, applied even to those, which, as historical monuments, were considered the most certain; it is, therefore, no argument against the authenticity of any particular Acts. There is no question of literary criticism, but of ecclesiastical policy.

But we have said that the Acts of St. Cecilia were compiled in the fifth century, for the purpose of being publicly read in the Church of the martyr, and that the custom was universal throughout Rome. In order to reconcile this apparent contradiction, it is only necessary to remember that in the language of the ecclesiastical Acts of Rome during the pontificate of St. Gelasius, and long after, when referring to liturgical customs, the Holy Roman Church signified the Patriarchal Church of Lateran, See of the supreme Pontiff, or the Church of St. Peter on the Vatican. This fact is established by Dom Mabellon, who interpreted in this sense the Canon of St. Gelasius, [7] and by the learned Moretti who develops this Thesis in speaking of the Acts of St. Callistus. [8] Since this celebrated decree recognizes the importance of the Acts of the Martyrs, and does not invalidate their historical truth, except in the case of those which it expressly condemns, as for instance, in the case of the Acts of Quiricus, Julitte, and George, it evidently was not intended to prohibit the reading of the Passions of Martyrs in the private churches of Borne.

This conclusion is rendered still more clear by the direct testimony of a venerable memorial of the Roman Liturgy, published by Blessed Joseph Maria Tommasi. It is an *Ordo Romanus* of the Tenth Century, taken from the library of the Yallicella, and also found in that of the Abbey of St. Gall. Under the rubric *De Festis Sanctorum, qualiter apud Romanos celebrantur,* the following lines are found in this official document. M Until the time of Adrian, the Passions and Acts of the Saints were only read in the Churches dedicated to these saints. This Pope changed the rule, and directed that they should also be read in the Church of St. Peter." [9]

This important passage does not tell us, it is true, at what epoch the custom was introduced of reading the Passions of the saints at the divine office in their titulary Churches; but the custom was quite an ancient one during the pontificate of Adrian, who was Pope at the end of the VIII. century. If there be any difficulty in reconciling this custom with the primitive usages of the Roman Church, which, during the pontificate of St. Gelasius, might perhaps have shrunk from introducing into the Liturgy, lessons not taken from the Holy Scriptures, we may observe, that without being inserted into the divine office, the Passions of the Saints might have been read to the faithful on the festivals of these Saints, in order to increase the solemnity of the day. We have examples of such reading being made out of the time of divine office. It will be sufficient to mention one fact that occurred in the VI. century. It is well known that the sub-deacon Arator read his poem upon the Acts of the Apostles in the Church of St. Jeter in Chains, by order of Pope Vigilius. With still greater propriety, might the Passions of the Martyrs have been read. The use which the Roman Church made of the Acts of St. Cecilia, in her Liturgy, from the V. century, proves that the text was familiar to the Church, as we will presently show, whether it was read to the people in the daily office, or made the subject of a solemn reading, out of the time of divine worship.

[1] See the text of this Chronicle in the work entitled: Origines de l'Eglise Romaine, tom i, pages 212, 248.

[2] See, among others, the second of St. Stephen, the first in *Natali S. S. Perpetuae et Felicitatis,* etc.

[3] Labb. Concil. tome ii. page 1072.

[4] We attribute this council to St. Gelasius, according to the most common belief, without prejudice to the opinion of those who would date it back to St. Damasus, In the latter case, the recommendation of the Acts would be still more striking, as it would date back to the days immediately following the age of persecutions, and consequently prove the existence of a certain number of Acts of the Martyrs, preserved by the faithful, even after the violent edicts of Diocletian.

[5] Item recipiuntur gesta sanctorum Martyrum qui multiplicibus tormentorum cruciatibus, et mirabilibus confessionum triumphis irradiant. Quis ita esse catholicorum dubitet, et majora eos in agonibus fuisse perpessos nec suis viribus, sed gratia Dei et adjutorio universa tolerasse? *Decret.* i. *pars, distinct,* xv, can. iii. *Sancta Romana.*

[6] Sed ideo secundum antiquam consuetudinem singulari cautela in sancta Romana Ecclesia non leguntur, quia et eorum qui conscripsere nomina penitus ignorantur, et ab infidelibus, aut idiotis superflua, aut minus apta, quam rei ordo fuerit, scripta esse putantur, sicut cujusdam Quirici et Julittae, sicut Georgii, aliorumque hujusmodi passiones, quae ab haereticis perhibentur conscriptae, Propter quod, ut dictum est, ne vel levis subsannaudi oriretur occasio, iu sancta Romana Ecclesia non leguntur. *Canon. Sancta Romana.*

[7] Disquisitio de Cursu Gallicano, page 386. In ordinem Romanum Commentarius. page cxxvii. Musaeum italicum. tome II.

[8] De S. Callixto Papa et Martyre, ejusque Basilica S. Mariae trans-Tiberim, page 206.

[9] Passiones sanctorum, vel Gesta ipsorum, usque Adriani tempora, tantummodo ibi legebantur, ubi Ecclesia ipsius Sancti vel Titulus erat. Ipse vero a tempoere suo rennuere jussit, et in Ecclesia Sancti Petri legendas esse constituit. *B. Jos. M. Thomasii opp.* tome iv, page 325.

Chapter Eighteen - Testimony of the Liturgies of the West in Favor of the Acts of St. Cecilia

It is therefore plain that the Canon of St. Gelasius offers no unfavorable allusion to the Acts of St. Cecilia; it now remains for us to prove that far from considering these Acts as of trifling or doubtful authority, the Roman and Western Churches, from the V. Century, esteemed them so highly, that they borrowed from them the substance of the prayers and canticles addressed to God on the solemnity of St. Cecilia's feast. "We will commence with the Roman Church. Her most ancient Sacramentary, known under the name of *Leonian*, because the greater part of its formulas are attributed to Pope Saint Leo the Great, thus mentions Cecilia, in one of its five Prefaces, all dedicated to our holy Martyr." Cecilia, destined by the will of her parents to become the spouse of a mortal, scorned a union which was to last but a short time, and jealous of the crown of chastity, sought an immortal spouse; preferring the honors of everlasting life to the joys of maternity. Her glory is enhanced by her having prevailed upon Valerian to whom she was united in marriage, to join her in the practice of perpetual chastity, and to share with her the crown of martyrdom." [1] Later in the V. century, the Roman Church thus speaks: "The inconstancy of youth could not arrest Cecilia in the path of virtue; the charms of the senses could not make her look back; nor could the fragility of her sex intimidate her. Although a young woman, exposed to all the torments of the executioners, the chaste Virgin Martyr gained a glorious victory, and to crown her triumph, bore with her to the kingdom of heaven, the man who had been given her as a spouse." [2] In the numerous and elegant compositions stamped by the genius of Leo, allusions to the Acts are evident; we will not stop to point them out. The Gelasian Sacramentary, which also belongs to the V. century, contains a preface of the same style and full of the same allusions," [3] and in its collect commemorates the crowns brought by the angel to Valerian and Cecilia. [4] At the end of the VI. century, St. Gregory, in his Sacramentary, diminished the number of the prefaces of the saints which formed the riches of the Missals of St. Leo and St. Gelasius. Those of St. Cecilia were sacrificed with the others, but in return the most ancient manuscripts of St. Gregory's Responsorial prove, that if the Roman Church in the VI. and VII. centuries, abated nothing of her severity in favor of St. Cecilia, respecting the conciseness of the prayers to be thenceforth used at the Holy sacrifice; she superabundantly compensated for this severity in the chants which accompany the Canonical Hours. [5] All the anthems and responses of the office of the twenty-second of November are taken literally from our Acts, and have remained the same after the lapse of twelve centuries, as they were at the time of St. Gregory.

The Book of the Gospels carried by Cecilia upon her heart, [6] the ardent prayers she addressed to God at her approaching marriage with Valerian, [7] her fasts of two and three days, [8] the hair shirt she wore under her garments, [9] the musicians' concert, during which she sang hymns to the Almighty, [10] the confidence she reposed in Valerian, [11] the words of the latter to the poor Christians in the Appian Way, his interview with Urban, [12] the Pontiff's prayer after hearing the miracles wrought by Cecilia, [13] Valerian's return to his bride, and the apparition of the Angel, [14] Cecilia's conversation with Tiburtius, which resulted in his conversion to the faith, Cecilia's apostrophe to the martyr band at day-break in the house of Maximus [15] the protestation of Almachius' officers, after the exhortation addressed to them by the virgin, [16] the victory she herself gained [17] over the Roman prefect's tyranny, [18] one of the replies of her interrogatory; [19] finally, the request she made St. Urban when expiring; [20] such is a summary of the Gregorian office of St. Cecilia, and, consequently, such are the facts considered authentic by the Church of Rome since the end of the sixth century. These different incidents represent in an abridged form, the narrative of the Acts; the same words even are preserved, except where the necessity of adapting them to the harmony of the ecclesiastical chant, required a slight alteration. We are, therefore, perfectly safe in concluding that there is no history considered more venerable by the Church of Rome, than that of St. Cecilia, as it is related in these pages, and set forth in the Liturgy of St. Gregory. Let us now examine the other Western Liturgies.

We shall begin with that of Milan, called Ambrosian, because the greater part of it was compiled by St. Ambrose. The Mass of St. Cecilia, contained in it, is drawn up with great care, and, judging by its style, can scarcely be dated farther back than the fifth century. The following are the principal passages of the Preface: "Christ lavished upon Cecilia the highest honors of heaven. To merit the palm of martyrdom, she withdrew from the world and its nuptial joys. To her is due the honor of the glorious confession of her husband, Valerian, and of his brother, Tiburtius. Thou, Lord, didst crown them with fragrant flowers by the hand of a celestial spirit. The virgin guided these young men to the kingdom of heaven, thus teaching the world the power of chastity. Through Cecilia's merits they became martyrs, and followed, in the company of the angels, the footsteps of the King of Glory." [21]

The Offertory is composed of St. Urban's prayer, in which he thanked our Lord for having so signally blessed St. Cecilia's eloquence.

In the chants of its canonical office, the Ambrosian Responsorial, like that of St. Gregory, borrows from the Acts of St. Cecilia. [22]

If we now examine the Gallican Church, we shall find that its ancient liturgy, which lasted until the time of Pepin and Charlemagne, bears an analogous testimony to the authenticity of our Acts. The most complete Gallican Missal now extant, although containing but twenty-six Masses, (*Proper*) of the Saints, has one in honor of St. Cecilia. This Mass, compiled in a pompous style, is a summary of the Roman Legends. Its Preface is in the style of the Leonian and Gelasian Sacramentaries, and retraces, in an abridged form, the character of the virgin, her different trials, her martyrdom, her crown, and her entrance into the celestial kingdom with Valerian. [23] This Missal, according to the opinion of B. Joseph Maria Tommasi, is the same which was compiled about the year 460, by Musaeus, a priest of Marseilles, the principal author of the Gallican Liturgy.

Finally the Gothic Church of Spain, whose Liturgy was compiled by St. Leander, Archbishop of Seville, a friend and contemporary of St. Gregory, also offers testimony in favor of the Acts of St. Cecilia. The prayers in its Missal constantly allude to the incidents we have mentioned. The hair shirt with which the Virgin mortified her body; [24] the crowns of roses and lilies brought from Heaven by an angel; [25] Valerian's prayer to the Blessed Spirit to obtain his brother's conversion, [26] are all mentioned; and finally an eloquent comparison is made between the fire which burned beneath Cecilia's feet in the *caldarium* of her palace, and the celestial love which consumed her heart. [27] The circumstances of our Acts are given more fully in the Missal of the Gothic Church of Spain than in its Breviary, the prayers of which are extremely short; however, the latter contains a hymn of fourteen verses, in which the life of St. Cecilia is sung with touching veneration. [28] St. Isidore, the brother of St. Leander, composed the greater number of the hymns of this Liturgy. It is possible that this learned doctor of the Church is not the author of the one just mentioned. However this may be, it cannot be dated later than the seventh century, at which period St. Isidore flourished, because St. Julian of Toledo, the last poet who composed hymns for the Gothic Breviary, lived in 675.

By comparing the monuments most worthy of veneration in the Western Liturgy, we find that throughout the two centuries which followed the compilation of St. Cecilia's Acts, the Roman, the Ambrosian, the Gallican, and the Spanish Gothic churches, all solemnly adopted the facts they contain. We must also acknowledge that even among the most authentic Acts of the Martyrs, scarcely any have been so solemnly approved.

[1] Dum humanis devota nuptiis, thalamos temporales contemneret, sponsum sibi, qui perpetuus esset, praesumpto praemio castitatis adhibuit, et aeternitatem vitae maluit, quam ut mundo procrearet originem. In cujus gloriam etiam illud accessit, ut Valerianum, cui fuerat matrimonii jure copulanda, in perpetuum sibi socians Martyr casta consortium, secum duceret ad coronam. *Muratori. Liturgia Romana vetus,* tome i. *Sacrament. Leonianum,* page 456.
[2] Despecto mundi conjugio, ad consortia superna contondens, nec aetate nutabili praepedita est, nec revocata carnis illecebra, nec sexus fragilitate deterrita, sed inter puellares annos, inter saeculi blandimenta, inter supplicia persequentum, multiplicem victoriam Virgo casta et Martyr explevit, et ad potiorem triumphum secum ad regna caelestia, cui fuerat nupta, perduxit. *Muratori. Liturgia Romana vetus,* tome i. *Sacrament. Leonianum,* p. 456.
[3] Gerbert. Liber Sacramentorum. *Liturgia Alemannica,* tome ii. page 197.

[4] Deus, cui beata Caecilia ita castitatis devotione complaenit, ut conjugem suum Valerianum, affinemque ejus Tiburtium tibi fe, cerit consecrari, cum et Angelo deferente micantium odoriferas florum coronas, palmam martyrii perceperunt: tribue, quaesumus, ut ea intercedente pro nobis, beneficia tui muneris percipere mereamur. *Gerbert Ibid,* page 196.

[5] See the manuscript of St. Gregory's Responsorial, published by Dionysius of St. Martha, and by Blessed Joseph Marie Tommasi.

[6] Virgo gloriosa semper Evangelium Christi gerebat in pectore.

[7] Et non diebus neque noctibus vacabat a colloquiis divinis et oratione.

[8] Biduanis ac triduanis jejuniis orans, commendabat Domino quod timebat.

[9] Cilicio Caecilia membra domabat, Deum gemitibus exorabat.

[10] Cantantibus organis, Caecilia Domino decantabat dicens. Fiat cor meum immaculatum, ut non confundar.

[11] Est secretum, Valeriane. quod tibi volo dicere: Angelum Dei habeo amatorem, qui nimio zelo custodit corpus meum.

[12] Caecilia me misit ad vos, ut ostendatis mihi sanctum Urbanum, quia ad ipsum habeo secreta quae perferam.

[13] Domine Jesu Christe, pastor bone, seminator casti consilii, suscipe seminum fructus, quos in Caecilia seminasti. Caecilia famula tua, quasi apis tibi argumentosa deservit.

[14] Valerianus in cubiculo Caeciliam cum Angelo orantem invenit.

[15] Beata Caecilia dixit Tiburtio: Hodie te fateor meum esse cognatum, quia amor Dei te fecit esse contemptorem idoloram.

[16] Dum aurora finem daret, Caecilia dixit: Eia milites Christi, abjicite opera tenebrarum, et induimini arma lucis.

[17] Credimus Christum Filium Dei verum Deum esse, qui sibi talem elegit famulam.

[18] O beata Caecilia quae duos fratres convertisti, Almachium judicem superasti, Urbanum episcopum in vultu angelico demonstrasti.

[19] Nos scientes sanctum nomen ejus, omnino negare non possumus.

[20] Triduanas a Domino poposci inducias, ut domum meam Ecclesiam consecrarem.

[21] Per Christum Sancta Caecilia, coelesti dono repleta, ut martyrii palmam assumeret, ipsum mundum est cum thalamis exsecrata. Testis est Valeriani, et Tiburtii provocata confessio: quos angelica manu odoriferis floribus coronasti. Viros Virgo duxit ad gloriam. Mundus agnovit quantum valeat devotio castitatis; quae ita promeruit, ut Martyres efficerentur, et iter Regis gloriae cum Angelis graderentur. *Missale Ambrosianum. In Natali S. Coeciliae. Virg. et Mart.*

[22] Breviarium Ambrosianum. xxii. *Novembris.*

[23] Mabillon. *Liturgia Gallicana,* page 226, 217.

[24] Illa denique procul dubio poterit apud Deum veniam nostris impetrare offensis, quae suam tegens cilicio carnem, multorum animas convertit ad fidem. *Missale mixtum secundum Regulam B. Isidori, dictum Mozarabes. In festo S. Caeciliae Virginis.*

[25] Splendificos aspectus angelicos destinasti ad terras, per quos illis (Martyribus) concretas liliorum ac rosarum floribus destinasti coronas. *Ibid.*

[26] Qui Tiburtium fratis prece perduxit ad fidem, ipse per vos accendat plurimos ad diligendam aeternae gloriae mansionem. *Ibid.*

[27] Gloriosam Virginem Caeciliam die integro et nocte tota thermis inclusam, nec ullo modo laesam fuisse fatemur. Servari quippe meruit in balnei calore, quae gestabat Christum in pectore. Duae quippe ignium divisae faces ardebant; una in Virginis corde, altera sub Virginis pede; una combustioni parata, altera refrigerio debita; una minabatur supplicium, pollicebatur altera regnum; una morituris corporibus necem, altera vivituro spiritui futuram praeparans libertatem. *Missale mixtum secundum Regulam B. Isidori, dictum Mozarabes. In festo S. Caeciliae Virginis.*

[28] We give a copy of this hymn, a true historical monument of the life of St. Cecilia. The imperfection of the verses does not invalidate the testimony thus rendered by the Church of Spain in the seventh century.

Inclytae festum pudoris
Virginis Caecilice
Gloriosa praecinamus
Voce prompti pectoris;
Quo soluta lege mortis
Tollitur in aethera.

Germine haec Virgo clara,
Sanctitate clarior;
Pectore Christum praestans,
Huncque solum praestans,
Ore sponsum, mente scelus,
Vicit hostem sanguine.

Pectoris sacri recessum
Munit Evangelio;
Squalido corpus beatum
Proterit cilicio:
Noctis horas et diei
Mentis implens cantico.

Haec enim sortita sponsum
Germinis praefulgidi;
Angelum Dei fatetur
Se habere vindicem:
Hunc verendo ut pudori
Det honorem commonet.

Sponsus hic furore caeco
Comminatur virgini;
Sed beata Virgo factis
Dicta prorsus comprobans;
Angelum, munusque ex coelo

Mox adesse praestitit.

Adfuit promissus idem
Vir coruscis vestibus;
Exhibens serti coronas,
Floribus praefulgidis:
In rosis docens cruorem,
Castitatem liliis.

Munere hoc provocatus
Sponsus ad Christi fidem:
Illico fratris salutum
Impraecatus obtinet,
Hincque ambo passionis
Consecrantur sanguine.

Hunc inde virgo Christi
Consequens Caecilia,
Hanc triumphalis honoris
Promeretur gloriam:
Igneis imis retrusa,
Fit caloris nescia.

Plus calens sic igne Christi,
Vicit ignem saeculi,
Et vibrantis ensis ictum
Ter valenter sustulit;
Postque terris membra ponit,
Spiritu coelos petit.

Inde nobis sacra Virgo
Mitte coeli munera;
Liliorum, vel rosarum

Munus inde proroga:
Unde hausisti superna
Veritatis gaudia.

Liliis corusca in nobis
Castitas praefulgeat:
Punicis rosis voluntas
Passionis ferveat;
Criminis mole subacta
Innovemur gratia.

Ecce adventum futuri
Praestolamur judicis;
Sustinemus, et beata
Illa lucis gaudia;
Non rei tunc puniamur,

Non crememur ignibus.

Martyrum, et sacrosanctis
Aggregati coetibus,
Evadamus, quod timemus
Continentis gloriam,
Regis almi ad coronam
Evocati dexteram.

Ut tuam Christe videntes
Servuli praesentiam:
Gratulemur, gaudeamus,
Personemus gloriam;
Curiae coelestis arce
Confovendi in saecula. Amen.

Chapter Nineteen - The Appian Way from the Fourth Century to the Ninth

After having proved the authenticity of the accounts transmitted to us respecting the virtues and combats of St. Cecilia, we must now collect the testimonies of love and veneration which, throughout the course of ages, have been offered to her memory by the faithful in every part of Christendom. We have already mentioned Cecilia's dying wish that her palace should be converted into a church. St. Urban fulfilled this pious desire, and the Basilica of St. Cecilia became one of the most venerated sanctuaries of Christian Rome. It is time to recommence our pilgrimage through the Appian Way, that we may seek some traces of our heroine, whose body reposed there for several centuries. Our first visit to this celebrated Way was in the time of Alexander Severus; we shall glance at the Christian memorials with which it has been enriched since that period. We shall pass over the profane monuments doomed to be destroyed by the ravages of time, or the hands of barbarians, and devote all our attention to the Martyrs' tombs. The Capena gate no longer exists, Aurelian having extended the limits of Rome a mile further upon the Appian Way. The subterraneous cemeteries between the old and the new gate have been abandoned for those of Callistus and Pretextatus, the galleries of which commenced before the second mile. The most illustrious Martyrs have been buried here. We will examine their tombs with the assistance of the very incomplete guidebooks, the first of which dates from the seventh century, the Acts of the Martyrs, and other documents.

After having traversed the memorable place where our Saviour met the Prince of the Apostles, still ascending the acclivity, we shall find to the right the cemetery of Callistus, the descents into which are marked by small churches with three or four arches. These Churches ordinarily bear the name of some Martyr, and each one opens upon a staircase which gives entrance to that part of the Catacombs where its Patron is buried. These edifices, which are very similar to many of the Pagan tombs upon the Appian Way, were erected during intervals of peace, and the Roman Pontiffs have piously watched over their preservation. They are adorned with votive inscriptions in honor of the Martyrs; other inscriptions were placed in the crypts near the tombs of the Saints. Pope St. Damasus composed many of them, expressing the combats of the Martyrs, and his own humble devotion to them.

The first church we meet upon the cemetery of Callistus, is that of the holy Virgin Sotera, [1] who suffered in the persecution of Diocletian. This edifice forms the entrance to the Martyr's tomb, which St. Ambrose certifies belonged to her family. [2]

As we proceed towards the right, the Church of St. Cornelius meets our eyes; a marble staircase which has been recently discovered, with the remnants of the Damasian inscription, conducts to the cubiculum which contains the remains of the glorious Pontiff. The great Bishop of Carthage, St. Cyprian, is also honored in this place, although his body never reposed there. [3]

On the same side, farther on, is the Church called ad Sanctam Caeciliam, also named ad Sanctum Sixturn, because it gives entrance to the crypt, where the Virgin Cecilia and Pope Sixtus II. are buried. In this crypt, destined to receive the bodies of the Pontiffs, St. Urban buried St. Cecilia. It also contains the remains of St. Zephyrinus, who was buried by St. Callistus [4] upon the upper story; Pontianus, the successor of St. Urban, whose body was transported from the island where he had been exiled; Anterus, celebrated for his zeal in preserving to posterity the memory of the Martyrs; Fabian, whose Pontificate was decided by the flight of a dove; Lucius, who so promptly culled the palm of martyrdom and whom we shall see later associated in Cecilia's triumph; Stephen, who defended the tradition of baptism against the Africans, and was assassinated in his episcopal chair; Sixtus II, whose martyrdom preceded by three days that of his Archdeacon, Lawrence, and who shares with Cecilia the honor of giving his name to this region of the Callistus Cemetery; Dionysius, who received from another Dionysius, Patriarch of Alexandria, a confession of his faith; Eutychian, of whom we know little but his martyrdom; Eusebius, who notwithstanding his short Pontificate, left many proofs of sanctity; and finally, Melchiades, who had the happiness of seeing peace dawn upon the Church. [5]

Among this illustrious band, Cecilia sleeps her glorious sleep. Near her, repose Tharsicius, an acolyte of the Roman Church, who had the honor of lying in the same tomb with Zephyrinus; [6] Calocerus and Parthenius, officers of the court of Decius [7] Finally, in a lower gallery, twenty-four other Martyrs whose names are not mentioned upon the monuments of the VII. century, from which we borrow this description, form as it were the Virgin's guard of honor. [8] In later years, so great was the veneration for Cecilia's tomb that the region which bore her name, was enlarged, and the Martyrologies of Bede, Adon, and Usuard, mention nine hundred Martyrs buried ad Sanctam Caeciliam. [9]

As we have before remarked, this part of the cemetery of Callistus also bore the name of Sixtus; but the Church, through which the crypts were entered, was called after Cecilia. [10] The martyrs we have enumerated, were not all buried in the same cubiculum. Popes Fabian, Sixtus II, and Dionysius, were the only ones interred near St. Cecilia. The subterranean corridors branched out in every direction, and, at certain distances, other sepulchral chambers were excavated for the Pontiffs and principal Martyrs.

Cecilia's tomb was towards the south, rather far from the Church above mentioned, and situated on a corridor which joined the galleries under the Church of St. Sebastian. It was a cell, shaped like a square oven, lined with four marble panels. This sepulchre, the form of which is unusual in the Catacombs, was rather high, being built near the arched roof of the corridor; it was closed by a small marble tablet which concealed the cypress coffin containing the remains of St. Cecilia. The absence of the decorations so profusely lavished upon other sepulchres of the Catacombs, joined to the mysterious character of this one, easily account for all traces of it being lost when the faithful of Rome ceased to frequent the Catacombs. Saint Damasus, as we have previously stated, wrote inscriptions in verse for the principal sepulchres of the Martyrs. The greater number of those referring to the tombs we have enumerated, have been destroyed; those only remain which relate to the holy Popes Stephen and Eusebius, and to the acolyte Tharsicius. Fragments of the Damasian inscription, consecrated to Pope St. Cornelius, have been lately found. It is more than probable that St. Damasus dedicated a special inscription to St. Cecilia, as that virgin occupied too distinguished a place in the Appian Way, not to have obtained such an honor; we shall soon relate under what circumstances this precious marble must have disappeared, and how Divine Providence made use of the hands of barbarians to preserve for Christian Borne one of her greatest treasures.

The Pontiff, who had been so zealous in preserving the Memoirs of the Martyrs, erecting in all parts of the Catacombs, magnificent epitaphs, many of which are still in existence, had a special devotion to the band of martyrs buried upon the Appian Way, near Sts. Sixtus and Cecilia. Although he reigned during the time of peace, he might have arrogated to himself a resting-place in the Crypts containing so many heroes, but his humility prevented his aspiring to such an honor. Not far from the church ad Sanctam Caeciliam, but more to the right, and nearer the Ardeatine Way, which is parallel to the Appian, he caused another Basilica to be built, giving access to the sacred cemetery whose repose he had not ventured to disturb; it was called the Church of Damasus. It was there that he buried his mother and sister; and there, also, that, after eighteen years of a brilliant and laborious pontificate, his own remains were interred.

The inscription which Damasus had prepared for his own tomb, was placed in the church. In it, the Pontiff extolled the martyrs grouped around St. Sixtus, and concluded with these words: "I, Damasus, must acknowledge that I had thought of choosing among them, a place for my own body; but I feared to insult the ashes of the Saints" [11]

Pursuing our pious pilgrimage, after praying at Cecilia's tomb, let us continue to explore the sacred monuments presented to us on the right side of the Appian Way. We will pass by the Churches of St. Damasus, of Pope St. Mark, and of the two brothers Marcel and Marcellinus, because they belong to the Ardeatine Way, as well as the vast cemetery of Sts. Nereus and Achilles, and descending the hill, we reach the place properly called the Catacombs. In this place, is venerated the mysterious well, where, for forty years, the bodies of the holy Apostles were concealed; we have already mentioned it. After the age of persecution, a splendid church called after the great Sebastian, was erected upon this spot, and is one of the seven churches in which Christian Rome glories, as Pagan Borne formerly boasted of her seven hills. Several galleries of the Callistus Cemetery extend round this church. The valiant soldier of Christ, St. Sebastian, reposes here; not far from him the military tribune Quirinus, who was buried here by his pious daughter, the virgin, St. Balbina; [12] and Eutychius who suffered a cruel martyrdom, as we learn from the long inscription which is still preserved. Leaving the Church of St. Sebastian, we will retrace our steps towards Rome, exploring as we go, the Christian monuments upon the left of the Appian Way. Down in the valley, is the Pagan temple, memorable for having been the retreat of St. Urban. In the same direction, we can see in the distance, the Church of St. Eugenia, [13] which gives entrance to the cemetery of Apronianus upon the Latin Way, which, like the Ardeatine, runs parallel to the Appian. This illustrious virgin, who suffered martyrdom during the persecution of Galienus, was buried here by her mother, Claudia. We next walk along the cemetery of Pretextatus, and meet the small church built upon the spot where Pope St. Sixtus was beheaded, with his deacons, Felicissimus and Agapitus. [14] St. Cyprian says in one of his letters, that their execution took place in this very cemetery. The ministers of Decius hoped that by choosing, for the holy Pontiff's place of martyrdom, one of the cemeteries excavated by the faithful, they would more effectually terrify the Christians. The martyr's body was transported, as we have said, from the other side of the Way to the cemetery of Callistus, where the body of Cecilia reposed. The two deacons, who were martyred with the Pontiff 1 , were buried near the place where they shed their blood. A church forms the entrance to their tombs. Januarius, [15] Magnus, Vincent, and Stephen, who were also companions of Sixtus, are buried in the same place. On this account, the church is called, *Ad Sanctum Januarium*. The large crypt which contains St. Urban's body, is near the church of which we speak. [16] We have seen how Marmenia, in her pious zeal, prepared this sepulchre for the holy Pope, and this accounts for his not being buried with Cecilia and Zephyrinus.

Two other churches open upon the cemetery of Pretextatus, forming a group with that of Januarius, on the left side of the Appian Way. The smaller one is called after the holy martyr St. Zeno; [17] the other, which is larger, bears the name of Saints Tiburtius, Valerian, and Maximus. [18] The Basilica of Cecilia and Sixtus, on the right of the Appian Way, is directly opposite to the Church of Valerian upon the left. The votive inscription to the three martyrs is exposed near their tombs. It is written in characters of the fourth and fifth centuries, and runs thus:

SANCTIS MARTYRIBVS TIBVRTIO BALERIANO [19] et MAXIMO QVORVM
NATALES [20] EST XVIII. KALEDAS [21] MAIAS.

This marble which gives some idea of the inscriptions placed in the crypts to designate the names of the principal martyrs honored by the faithful, still exists, and in the ninth century was transported to the Church of St. Cecilia. [22] After having venerated the sepulchres of our heroes, we will continue our course upon the Appian. Passing again the little Church, commemorative of the meeting of our Saviour and St. Peter, we arrive at Aurelian's wall, and going through the gate which afterwards received the name of St. Sebastian, we re-enter the Holy City.

[1] See the guide-books Salisburgense, Einsidlense, Malmesburiense, and the Papyrus of Monza. We leave the honor of commenting upon these monuments to M. le Chevalier de Rossi, who has our best wishes for the publication of his Codex *topographicus urbis Romae.*
[2] S. Ambros. de Virginibus, lib. iii. cap. vii. n° 38.
[3] Itiner. Salisburg. Einsidlen. Malmesbur.
[4] Salisburgense.
[5] Itiner. Salisburg. Malmesburiense.
[6] Salisburgense.
[7] *Ibid.*
[8] *Ibid.*
[9] See also the Roman Martyrology of 4th of March, Page 191.
[10] Malmesburiense.
[11] Hic fateor Damasus volui mea condere membra;
    Sed cineres timui sanctos vexare piorum.
    S. Damasi opp., carme xxxiii (Maï. Script. Vatt. nov., Coll. t. v. p. 37).
[12] Itinerar, Salisburg. Malmesbur.
[13] Itinerar. Einsidlense.
[14] Epist. lxxxii.
[15] The Salzburg guide-books confound this Januarius with a son of St. Felicitas, who bore the same name.
[16] Itinerar. Salisburg. Malmesbur.

[17] Itinerar. Salisburg. Malmesbur.

[18] *Ibid.*

[19] Baleriano for Valeriano. B is substituted for V upon many of the Christian and Pagan inscriptions of the first ages.

[20] Natales for Natalis. This replacing E for I, is also very frequent in the ancient monuments. With respect to the word Natalis, birthday, being used for the day when the martyrs, disengaged from their bodies, were born to eternity, it is the usual liturgical style since the first ages of the Church.

[21] Kaledas for Kalendas. These omissions of letters often disfigure the most beautiful inscriptions.

[22] In the first edition we accepted the opinion of all authors who had spoken of this inscription. With them we thought it belonged to the third century. Since then we have examined the marble more attentively, and it seems impossible to date it so far back. The inscription is still quite beautiful, but the inferiority of the letters is such that it must have been engraved after the reign of Constantine, probably during the latter part of the fourth century, and perhaps in the beginning of the fifth. Our learned friend, M. le Chevalier de Rossi, is of the same opinion. Before proceeding further, we must speak of a monument in the cubiculum of the Catacombs of St. Sebastian. It bears this inscription:

SANCTO MARTYRI MAXIMO.

Many have supposed it to be the sepulchral inscription of St. Maximus, but it is not. This marble is simply a detached fragment of the upper part of a Christian sarcophagus. We have examples of these large marble sarcophagi, ornamented with symbolical bas reliefs, with the portrait of the deceased in the centre, and an inscription above, in honor of the martyr under whose protection he wished to repose. The thickness and dimensions of the stone of which we speak, and the traces it still bears of having adhered to a solid mass of the same material, take away all doubt of its origin.

Chapter Twenty - Events Relating To St. Cecilia and Her Church throughout the Seventh Century

The Librarians of the Apostolic See, compiled at an early date in Rome, a chronicle of the Roman Pontiffs, more extensive and full of incidents than that written in the fourth century, and ending with the pontificate of Liberius. This second chronicle has been preserved, and extends to Felix IV., who occupied the Holy See from 526 to 530.

It served as a basis for the famous biography of the Popes, so long attributed to Anastasius, the librarian, who merely continued it. [1] If we examine this precious document, which dates back to the first half of the sixth century, we shall find therein the following passage relating to St. Urban. "He baptized a number of persons, among others Valerian, husband of Cecilia; and many of those whom he instructed, received the crown of martyrdom." [2] Thus the official tradition of the Roman Church, as well as the Liturgy, placed, in the pontificate of St. Urban, the events related in the Acts of St. Cecilia, and confirmed these recitals as far as was compatible with the extreme brevity of a chronicle so concise as that of Felix IV. The Church of the holy martyr, although deprived of the relics of its glorious patroness, continued to be venerated by the faithful.

It was greatly honored in 530, when its Titulary Cardinal, Boniface Sigisvult, or Sigisband, was elevated to the Apostolic See, as successor of Felix IV., under the name of Boniface II. [3] In later years, the Basilica of St. Cecilia frequently enjoyed this honor.

The Roman Pontiffs were in the habit of celebrating the Holy Sacrifice in this church, on the martyr's festival. In the year 540, this solemnity was interrupted by an attack upon the person of the Vicar of Jesus Christ.

The Emperor Justinian, in one of the outbreaks of his theological mania, published his famous edict against the "three chapters." He formed the design of forcing Pope Vigilius to confirm, by apostolic authority, the edict which was causing so much trouble in the Eastern Churches. His design was to seize the Pontiff, and carry him off to Constantinople. Anthemius, an officer of Theodora, wife of Justinian, was charged with the execution of this project. He was ordered by the Emperor, to seize the Pontiff wherever he could meet him, excepting at St. Peter's, which he consented to respect as the inviolable asylum of the head of Christianity.

On the 22d of November, Feast of St. Cecilia, Vigilius, according to custom, went to celebrate the Holy Sacrifice in the church of the martyr. The concourse of people was great, as this day was also the anniversary of Vigilius' episcopal consecration, or of his exaltation to the chair of St. Peter. The Pope, following the example of his predecessors, was engaged in distributing largesses to the people. The emissary from Byzantium succeeded in eluding the vigilance of the faithful; and, by a bold stroke, the Pontiff was seized and carried to the banks of the Tiber, which flows near the church. He was placed on board a vessel, and in spite of the cries and moans of the people, taken away from Rome. His absence lasted during seven of the most stormy years of his troubled pontificate. [4]

Pelagius succeeded him in the Apostolic chair, but was soon followed by John III., who governed the Church, until 572. The *Liber Pontificalis* remarks of this Pope, that: "He venerated the cemeteries of the holy martyrs, and restored many defaced monuments to their original state." [5] This passage of the Papal chronicle leads us back to the Catacombs, which had been cruelly ravaged thirty years before the pontificate of John III. The sleep of the martyrs had been disturbed by the barbarians; the noise of military arms had been heard even beneath the sacred vaults where the conquerors of Pagan Rome reposed in peace. In 586, under the pontificate of St. Silverius, Rome had been besieged during an entire year, by the Goths under Vitiges. Not satisfied with destroying [6] the magnificent aqueducts, which, flowing over the Appian, Latin, and Tiburtine Ways, had, for centuries, supplied Rome with water, these barbarians had also descended into the cemeteries, and, with sacrilegious hands, had demolished the decorations with which the Pontiffs and faithful had embellished the sacred crypts. They had vented their blind and impious rage even upon the inscriptions placed near the martyrs' tombs.

The pontificate of Vigilius was too stormy to permit him to repair such devastations. We have, nevertheless, a proof of the interest he took in this pious work, in the inscription which is still extant, relating to three holy martyrs whose Damasian epitaph had been destroyed by the Goths. These martyrs were Vitalis, Martial, and Alexander, and the following is the inscription found on the monument substituted by Vigilius, for that broken by the barbarians: "When the Goths encamped beneath the walls of Rome, in their senseless triumph, ignorant of the overthrow which awaited them, they began by declaring war against the Saints. In their sacrilegious insolence, they overthrew the tombs consecrated to these martyrs, from the earliest ages. Damasus, divinely inspired, had proclaimed them worthy of veneration, and had composed verses in their honor. But although the sacred marble which bore this inscription has been broken, it is not just that their memory should perish forever. Therefore, Pope Vigilius, whose heart was deeply afflicted at such an outrage, repaired the sepulchres, after the enemy had been driven from Rome." [7]

We have every reason to suppose that the Cemeteries of the Appian, suffered very much at this time from the insults of the barbarians, who had so brutally destroyed the aqueduct of this Way. After the defeat of Vitiges, the Goths again besieged Rome under the command of Totila. They must have naturally wished to search these immense subterranean galleries, either to seek treasures, or in the hope of finding some secret entrance into the city. Their Arian fury was at this time exercised against the Catholic sanctuaries, and the most precious monuments of antiquity were exposed to their violence. It is certain, that in the VIII. century, Cecilia's tomb had no longer any precise inscription, since the Lombards vainly sought the Virgin's body that they might carry it away. We may, therefore, conclude, with sufficient probability, that this marble was destroyed by the Goths in the VI. century, and that it was not renewed because the faithful were so well acquainted with the locality of the martyr's tomb. The pious zeal of Pope Vigilius with regard to the three martyrs, of whom we have just spoken, refers principally to the rebuilding of their sepulchres, to which he added a new inscription. We have no proof that either he, or his successors, undertook the restoration of all those which had been defaced. The faithful of Rome, who at this time, frequently visited the cemeteries, had not forgotten the tombs of the principal martyrs; the work undertaken by John III. must therefore have been principally the consolidation of the galleries and halls, and the restoration of the sepulchres injured by the barbarians.

We learn from the *Liber Pontificalis*, that under this Pontiff, divine service was not only still performed in the sacred crypts, on the days commemorating the triumph of the Martyrs, but that the Holy Sacrifice was offered there regularly every week John III. ordained that the Lateran Church should furnish the bread, wine, and lights, required every Sunday for the holy functions. [8]

This pious Pontiff displayed on another occasion his confidence in the protection of the holy martyrs.

The Romans, annoyed by the presence of Narses in Italy, where he represented the authority of the Emperor Justinian, formed a cabal to oblige this great general to abandon the government of the peninsula. They even went so far as to write to the Emperor that they preferred the tyranny of the Lombards to that of Narses. The latter, wounded by the ingratitude of the Romans, retired to Campania, and in his indignation invited the Lombards to take possession of a city which had so ill requited his services. In reality, this intrigue had been plotted by the schismatics of Italy, who never ceased protesting against the V. General Council whose authority Justin, as a Catholic prince, sustained, John III. trembled for his country, and hastened to Narses. He succeeded in inducing him to return to Rome; but the Pontiff had become odious to the party whose designs he had frustrated. On his return, instead of going to the Lateran Palace, he concealed himself, as Urban had formerly done, under the shadows of the martyrs' tombs. He chose that part of the Cemetery of Pretextatus, which, in honor of the husband and brother of Cecilia, was called the Cemetery of Saints Tiburtius and Valerian. [9] Over the funereal galleries, where the Pontiff came to learn patience from the example of the holy martyrs, rose the Church of which we have spoken, surrounded by several buildings for the accommodation of the priests and different functionaries. John III. resided some time in this obscure retreat. He celebrated the divine Mysteries sometimes in the Church, and sometimes in the subterranean chapels; and the Popes' Chronicle adds that he even consecrated several Bishops while concealed in the cemetery. [10]

At the same time, about the year 570, the holy Archbishop of Ravenna, Agnellus, finished the mosaics of the superb church, erected, under the title of St. Apollinaris, by the great king Theodoric. [11] We may even attribute this splendid embellishment to that munificent prince who died about the year 526. However this may be, this vast groupings of mosaics is of great interest in our history, because, of all the monuments which Christian art dedicated to the memory of St, Cecilia, it is the most ancient which has been preserved to our own days. It represents the following picture:

"A band of twenty-five martyrs advance towards our Saviour, to present him the crown they hold in their hands, whilst twenty-two Saints direct their steps towards the Mother of Christ, who holds her divine Son upon her knees. The name of each virgin is written above her head: St. Cecilia is placed between Lucy and Eulalia. They are all standing dressed in rich and elegant costumes, and holding crowns in their hands. According to the style of the Byzantine mosaics, a tree is placed between each figure, to indicate that
104

those represented, inhabit the garden of heaven." The sixth century closed during the pontificate of St. Gregory the Great, who occupied the Holy See, until the fourth year of the following century. This illustrious Pontiff arranged the Liturgy in its present form, and gave to the office of St. Cecilia the prominent place it occupies. A fearful contagion having desolated Rome in 590, Gregory, in order to avert the anger of God, ordered seven processions, which were to commence from seven different churches, and all to repair to the Basilica of St. Mary Major, the last invariable refuge of the faithful in such calamities. The first procession, which was that of the clerks, advanced from the Church of St. John Lateran; the second, composed of laymen, from that of St. Marcellus; the third, of monks, from the church of Sts. John and Paul; the fourth, that of the religious, from the church of Sts. Cosmas and Damian; the fifth, that of married women, from the church of St. Stephen; the sixth, that of widows, from the church of St. Vitaiis; and, finally, the seventh, composed of the poor, and of children, from the church of Cecilia. [12]

The Pontiff thus placed under the protection of the martyr, the feeble and the suffering, to whom, during her life, she was so devoted. The Lord heard the supplications of his people, and through the intercession of the Queen of Heaven, the exterminating Angel was commanded to sheathe his sword.

The Basilica of St. Cecilia seems to have been rebuilt and rededicated under Gregory's Pontificate. At least, we may draw this conclusion from the famous charter of St. Paschal, of which we shall soon speak. [13]

It is not surprising that towards the close of the sixth century, this edifice needed repairing, and the fact recorded in the charter of St. Paschal, connects the name of St. Gregory in a particular manner with, the Church of the great Martyr. Moreover, this fact is confirmed by the very expressions of St. Paschal, which are to be read in every copy of his charter, and in which he declares that he has nominated St. Gregory as one of the patrons of the monastery which he erected near the Church of St. Cecilia.

A last fact relative to the homage paid by St. Gregory the Great, to St. Cecilia, may be found in the present he sent to Theodolinda, the Queen of the Lombards, of several vials containing oil from the lamps which burned in the cemetery of the martyrs.

It is well known how great was the paternal affection of the Pontiff towards this princess, who remained true to her faith in the midst of an Arian court, and who had the happiness of converting her nation to Catholicity. His intention in sending her these vials of holy oil, was, that she might unite with the faithful of Rome in venerating the martyrs. To facilitate this, he sent her at the same time a topographical index of the different Saints from whose lamps the oil was taken, that so she might picture more vividly to herself the sacred ways of Christian Rome. This valuable list, written upon parchment, is still preserved in the Church of St. John the Baptist at Monza. The names of the Saints are frequently grouped together according to the locality of their tombs in the crypts. This order was also indicated upon each vial by means of small labels, most of which are still preserved, either fastened to the bottles or detached from them. In most cases the oil taken from lamps belonging to several tombs,. was mingled in one vial. That relating to our illustrious Martyr bears the following inscription:

SCA. SAPIENTIA SCA SPES. SCA FIDES. SCA CARITAS. SCA CAECILIA. SCS TARSICIVS. SCS CORNILIVS. ET MVLTA MILLIA SCORVM.

This inscription at once carries us back to the Appian Way. We find in it the names of four celebrated Roman Saints, St. Sophia with her three daughters, Faith, Hope, and Charity, who like their mother obtained the crown of martyrdom. [14] The place of their sepulture was not positively known, but this monument proves to us that it was upon the right side of the Appian Way. On the parchment, these Saints are placed between Saints Sotera and Cecilia, who were incontestibly a short distance from each other in the same region of the Callistus Cemetery; hence we find their names in the same inscription with that of the glorious Martyr in whom we are so deeply interested. After these four names, comes that of Cecilia, followed by that of Tarsicius, who, as we have said, reposed near her in the cemetery of Sixtus; St. Cornelius is the next mentioned; his tomb, recently discovered upon the Appian, forms another proof of our assertion; and the number of martyrs mentioned later, confirms all we find in the guidebooks relative to the Cemetery of Callistus. We have, therefore, a monument of the Gregorian period respecting St. Cecilia. This modest vial has been preserved for centuries, and a portion of the oil it contains was taken, during the pontificate of St. Gregory, from a lamp which burned near the virgin's tomb. The crypt of Cecilia and Sixtus has since been laid waste; the monuments and lamps have disappeared; Cecilia's body has been carried to Rome; the subterranean vaults, formerly the object of such ardent veneration, have been silent and desolate for centuries, whilst the vial still exists, and is a proof of the veneration of the Romans of the sixth century towards this spouse of Christ. But this is not all. Another vial in the treasury of Monza, containing oil from the lamps which burned near the tombs of Cecilia's husband and brother, bears the following inscription:

SCI SEBASTIANI. SCS EVTYCIVS. SCS QVIRINVS.
SCS VALERIANVS. SCS TIBVRTIVS. S. MAXI
MVS. SCS VRBANVS. SCS IANVARIVS.

Here we again find the many groups of martyrs we described as reposing at the extremity of the Callistus Cemetery, upon the right of the Appian: Sebastian, Eutychius, and Quirinus. Next follow three heroes, Valerian, Tiburtius, and Maximus, who were buried upon the left side of the Appian. Sts. Urban and Januarius, whose tombs were situated in the same region, are very naturally added to the preceding. Here again a fragile vial, preserved by the piety of the faithful, serves, at the present day, to prove the faith and confidence reposed by the Christians of Rome and the Queen of the Lombards, in the noble heroes whose memory we have celebrated. These bottles were carried to Theodolinda by a person named John, who signed the parchment upon which they are described, without adding any titles to his signature, but those of sinner, wretched and unworthy. [15] Before concluding this chapter, we will mention a circumstance which refers at least indirectly to our history. St. Eulogius, Patriarch of Alexandria, wrote to St. Gregory, begging that he would send him a copy of the Deeds of the Martyrs, formerly collected by Eusebius. The holy Pope answered that he knew of no Acts of the Martyrs compiled by Eusebius, except those which are still found in his Ecclesiastical History. "I know of no other," adds the Pontiff, [16] either in the Archives of our Church or in the Roman Libraries, unless it be a small number contained in a simple volume.'"

[1] Origines de l'Eglise Romaine, vol. i, page 191-249.
[2] Hic sua traditione multos convertit ad baptisma, etiam Valerianum sponsum S. Caeciliae, et multi martyrio coronati sunt per ejus doctrinam. *Chronique de Felix IV.,* in Urbano.
[3] Ciacconius. Vitae Romanorum Pontificum, Tome i. page 358.
[4] Anastas. *In Vigilio.* Pagi. Breviarum Pontificum Romanorum, Tome i. page 295.
[5] Hic amavit et restauravit Caemeteria sanctorum martyrum. *Anastas.* in Joanne iii.
[6] Proeop. de bello Gothico. Lib. ii. cap. iii.
[7] Dum peritura Getae posuissent castra sub urbe,
    Moverunt Sanctis bella nefanda prius.
Istaque sacrilege verterunt corde sepulchra
    Martyribus quondam rite sacrata piis.
Quos monstrante Deo, Damasus sibi Papa probatos
    Affixo monuit carmine jure coli.
Sed periit titulus confracto marmore sanctus,
    Nec tamen his iterum posse latere fuit.
Diruta Vigilius nam mox haec Papa gemiscens,
    Hostibus expulsis, omne novavit opus.
                    Gruter (Inscript. antiq. tome iii, page mclxxi. 4)
[8] Instituit ut oblationes et amulae, vel luminaria, per eadem Caemeteria omni die Dominico de Lateranis ministrarentur. *Anastas. in Joanne* iii.
[9] Tunc sanctissimus Joannes Papa retinuit se in Coemeterio sanctorum Tiburtii et Valeriani. *Anastas. In Joanne* iii.
[10] Habitavit ibi multo tempore, ut etiam episcopos ibidem consecraret. *Anastas.* in Joanne iii.
[11] "Vid Ciampini. *Vetera Monimenta,* tome ii, page 100." The Mosaic is engraved in full upon several plates.
[12] Litania Clericorum exeat ab Ecclesia beati Joannis Baptistae. Litania virorum, ab Ecclesia beati Martyris Marcelli. Litania monachorum, ab Ecclesia mar-

tyrum Joannis et Pauli. Litania ancillarum Dei, ab Ecclesia beatorum martyrum Cosmae et Damiani. Litania feminarum conjugatarum, ab Ecclesia beati primi martyris Stephani. Litania viduarum, ab Ecclesia beati martyris Vitalis. Litania pauperum et infantium, ab Ecclesia beatae martyris Caeciliae. *Oratio ad plebem, de mortalitate. S. Gregorii opp.,* tome v, page 278. Edit Galliccioli.

[13] "Titulus quem piae devotionis affectu sanctus Papa primus Gregorius doctor eximius dicaverat." Sec the text of this charter, with this important version, in Bosio, *Acta S. Coeciliae,* p. 44, and in Laderchi, p. 204.

[14] Acta SS. Augusti. Tome i. *Die 1° Augusti.*

[15] Marini. Papiri diplomatici. N. cxliii.

[16] "Nulla in Archivio." Moretti observes with reason that, these words of St. Gregory should he understood in a relative, not in an absolute sense: *pauca quaedam.* The holy Pope had just told the Patriarch of Alexandria that the Roman Church possessed a book containing the names of nearly all the Martyrs *pene omnium Martyrum,* meaning the Martyrology; it is very evident that there is no proportion between the number of Acts now extant, and that of the Martyrs whose names we know. Were the Acts of St. Cecilia to be found among the authentic collection of which St. Gregory speaks? There is no doubt of it; otherwise the Roman Church would not have taken from them the hymns consecrated to this Martyr upon her festival.

Chapter Twenty-One - Events Relating to Cecilia and Her Basilica throughout the Seventh and Eighth Centuries. In the Seventh, the Bodies of the Martyrs are Disinterred and Translated to the Churches of Rome

In 610, Pope St. Boniface IV. obtained from the Emperor Phocas, the famous temple, known as the Pantheon, to be converted into a church. We will not enlarge here upon this subject. Joseph de Maistre has treated it so nobly, that it would be presumptuous even to attempt it. [1] In one of its circumstances, however, the Christian inauguration of the Pantheon is of some importance in the annals of our saint, and we cannot pass over it in silence. Until the year when this took place, the Romans had not thought of removing the remains of the martyrs to the numerous churches of the city. The faithful chose their sepulchres by the side of their valiant protectors, hoping to rise with more confidence in their company on the day of the general resurrection. Even after peace had been restored to the Church, the Popes themselves desired to be buried near the martyrs. We have already spoken of St. Damasus' humble wish to repose with the saints of the Appian Way, and of his having erected his own tomb at the entrance of the Ardeatine Crypts. His predecessors, Mark, Julius, and Liberius, expressed the same desire. The first selected his sepulchre in the cemetery of Balbina, on the Ardeatine Way; the second, in the cemetery of Callipodius on the Aurelian; and the third in the

Cemetery of Priscilla on the Salerian. Siricius and Celestinus prepared their tombs on this same way. Anastasius and Innocent in the cemetery called *Ad ursum pileatum;* Zosimus in that of Cyriacus in *agro, Verano;* Boniface in that of St. Felicitas.

Everything seemed to promise undisturbed repose to these venerated bodies, confided to the silent vaults, which even the Pagans had rarely violated during the persecutions.

But Almighty God, in His Providence, had other designs with regard to the crypts of the Holy City. He intended they should be an inexhaustible mine, from which the bones of the Saints. should be translated, to repose under the altar of sacrifice, and thus signify the union of the members with their divine Chief.

We have seen John III. repairing the cemeteries after the incursions of the Goths; these barbarians had scarcely disappeared, when the Lombards began to establish their power in the Italian peninsula. They frequently besieged Rome, and while encamped round the city, often entered the crypts and committed many sacrilegious devastations. From that time, the Popes felt it necessary to make the successive translations which almost depopulated the cemeteries. But such was, according to the beautiful idea of Prudentius, the holy fertility of the Roman soil, [2] that although immense cohorts of martyrs reascended in triumph to the light of day during the seventh, eighth, and ninth centuries, many tombs are still found from time to time, some with the martyr's name engraven upon the sepulchral stone, [3] others bearing no inscription, the names of those who repose within them, being known only to Christ, for whom they shed their blood. [4] The first solemn translation was made by order of St. Boniface, at the dedication of the Pantheon. Twenty-eight chariots, filled with bones of the martyrs, taken from the different crypts, traversed the streets of Rome, and St. Boniface deposited under the new altar the relics mutilated for Christ, but reserved for an endless triumph. [5]

The temple of all the Gods received the name of "Sanctae Mariae ad Martyres," thus blending under this title the great Queen of heaven and earth, and those to whom the Christian Church owes one of the most invincible arguments of her divinity. Cecilia was not among those who were removed by Boniface. Two centuries were destined to elapse before the tomb sealed by St. Urban was to be opened.

We will not enumerate the different translations made by the successors of St. Boniface up to the pontificate of Paschal I., who had the glory of transferring Cecilia's body to the altar of her Basilica. These imposing translations continued until the twelfth century. After this period, subterranean Rome remained in the silence of its sacred gloom for nearly three centuries, not being even disturbed by the ravages made by the troops under the command of the Constable de Bourbon. Men shrunk from these gloomy cities of the dead, and, with the exception of the corridors which opened near the Basilicas or in the light of day, the immense city of Martyrs was rarely visited by the faithful. Towards the close of the sixteenth century, Borne awoke to the consciousness of the marvels buried in her bosom, thanks to the courageous devotedness of Antonio Bosio, who, with pious boldness and profound erudition, entered upon this colossal enterprise of exploration. In the following century, the Apostolic See authorized the search for the bodies of the Martyrs, and determined with great prudence the only unquestionable signs by which they could be discerned. We shall, before long, again visit these mysterious vaults, and return with the precious treasure too long hidden in the bowels of the earth. In the meantime, the Roman faith was being propagated throughout the north of Europe by the indefatigable preaching of the Benedictines. From the day when St. Gregory sent the monk Augustine to plant the standard of the Cross in the Isle of Britain, a number of apostolic preachers, principally monks, continued up to the twelfth century to preach to the Saxons, Germans, Scandinavians, Slavonians, and Livonians. They all came to visit the Eternal City, some before beginning their missions, others in the midst of their combats, eager to imitate the Apostle of the Gentiles, who, after being wrapt to the third heaven, nevertheless thought it his duty, as he himself tells us, to visit St. Peter and compare his gospel with that of the supreme Pontiff. [6] In 696, St. Willibrord, Apostle of Friesland, visited Rome. Pope St. Sergius wished to consecrate as bishop this herald of the divine word. On the feast of St. Cecilia, and in her Basilica, he imposed hands upon Willibrord, to whom he gave the name of Clement, as a new link to bind him to the Roman Church, which had been so gloriously illustrated by this disciple of St. Peter, [7] Thus the episcopal see of Utrecht was founded by St. Willibrord under the auspices of St, Cecilia. About the same time, a marvellous book appeared in the Isle of Britain, consecrated to the glory and merit of Christian Virginity, and worthy to be ranked with those written upon the same subject by Saints Cyprian, Methodius, Ambrose, and Augustin. Its author was the monk St. Adhelm, Bishop of the Western Saxons, who thus celebrated, in the most melodious verse and delightful prose, the glory and happiness of the Spouse of Christ. Such was the elevated opinion, entertained by the pious Bishop of Sherburn, of Cecilia's merits and the honor she enjoyed in heaven, that after having exalted the incomparable prerogative of Mary, the Queen of Virgins, he places Cecilia first in the rank of those who follow her to the heavenly spouse. She is attended by Agatha, Lucy, Eugenia, Agnes, Dorothy, and many others, whose virtues he extols. This holy prelate died in 709. He composed, about the year 680, this graceful work which he styles "de Laude Virginitatis," and borrowed from our Acts all that he says with regard to St. Cecilia. [8] England, that daughter of the Roman Church, had therefore received from her august mother, together with the holy gospels, the touching recital of the virtues and triumphs of Cecilia. We have another proof of this in the martyrology, which Bede, the celebrated doctor and historian of the Anglo Saxon Church, composed about the same time in his monastery of Weremouth. The eulogium which he consecrated to Cecilia, notwithstanding its brevity, contains an analysis of the Acts. It is stated that the Saint converted to the faith of Jesus Christ, her husband Valerian and Tiburtius his brother; that she prepared them for martyrdom; and that she herself, after having withstood the fire, perished by the sworcl, under the Prefect of Rome, Almachius. [9]

About the year 731, St, Gregory III. undertook to repair the Churches of the Pretextatus Cemetery. He rebuilt the arch of that of St, Tiburtius and Valerian, which seemed fast decaying. He also directed his attention to the Basilica of Sts. Urban and Januarius, which he repaired like the former. In the course of time, these venerable edifices, more and more neglected in consequence of the martyrs' bodies having been transferred to the city, crumbled away, some partly, others entirely, and covered the ground with their ruins. The Church of St. Cecilia in Rome continued to receive the homages of the faithful. Under the Pontificate of St. Gregory III., the deacon Moschus was buried therein, and his epitaph, which is still preserved, expresses the love and confidence he had vowed to this holy martyr. It is under the portico of the Basilica towards the right and runs thus:

SEPVLCHRVM QVOD IN HANC AEDEM VENERANDAE CHRISTI MARTYRIS CAECILLAE SITVM EST IN QVO ET QVIESCIT IN PACE MOSCVS HVMILIS DIACONYS S. SEDIS APOSTOLIAE OMNES EXPOSCENS VT PRO ME DOMINVM EXORETIS QVATENVS EJVSDEM SACRATISSIMAE VIRGINIS INTERVENIENTIBYS MERITIS CVNCTORVM CONSEQVI MEREAR INDVLDGENTIAM DELICTORVM [10]

Four other sanctuaries were erected in honor of St. Cecilia, either outside the city or within its walls. Outside the city, on the Appian Way, that called "Ad Sanctam Caeciliam," with which our readers are already acquainted; another upon the Tiburtine Way, which has been entirely destroyed. About the middle of the seventh century, Pope St. Zachary undertook the restoration of the latter, embellished it with paintings, endowed it, and made it a dependency of the Church of St. Peter. [11] In the interior of the city, the Basilica of Saint Cecilia de Domo, of which we have spoken; and another, called Saint Cecilia de Lupo Pacho, and elsewhere de Turre Campi. Later, it was distinguished under the name of Sancta Cecilia a .Monte Giordano, because the quarter in which it was situated, formerly belonged to Giordano Orsini. [12] We shall again refer to these two Churches. In the year 768, for the second time, the titulary Cardinal of the Basilica of St. Cecilia, who had been named to that office by St. Zachary, ascended the Apostolic Chair, under the title of Stephen IV. This election took place in the Church itself. Two years after, in 770, St. Opportuna, the pious abbess of Montreuil, was warned of her approaching death in a vision in which Cecilia appeared to her on the 10th of April, at day break. Opportuna's cell was suddenly illuminated with the most dazzling light and embalmed with delightful perfumes. Two celestial virgins descended towards her, radiant with glory. They were Cecilia and Lucy, resplendent with light and beauty. The holy Abbess, recognizing them through divine inspiration, thus addressed them: "Hail, Oh my sisters, Cecilia and Lucy! What does the glorious virgin Mary, Queen of Heaven, Virgin of Virgins, ask of her humble servant?" The two messengers of the Mother of God replied: "Opportuna, faithful Spouse of Christ, the most pure Virgin Mary awaits thy coming. The moment has arrived when thou shalt be united in Heaven to her Son whom thou hast loved upon earth with all the strength of thy love. Put on thy crown of glory; light thy lamp; the moment approaches when thou shalt be presented to thy heavenly Spouse." Twelve days scarcely elapsed before the virgin breathed her last sigh in the arms of the Queen of Angels. [13]

St. Leo III., who had terminated the eighth century with so much glory, by placing the imperial crown upon the head of Charlemagne, on Christmas day, A. D. 800, was distinguished for his liberal donations to the churches of Rome. To the Basilica of St. Cecilia, he presented an altar-cloth of a material called *Stauracin,* which was a kind of gold brocade, studded with crosses. He also presented one of the silver crowns, which at that time were suspended before the altar, and served as chandeliers. This silver ornament weighed ten pounds and one ounce. [14]

[1] Du Pape. Tome II., pages 284-288.
[2] Vix fama nota est, abditis
    Quam plena Sanctis Roma sit,
    Quam dives urbanuin solum
    Sacris sepulchris floreat.
                            Prudentius, peri stephanon, Hymn. S. Laurentii.
[3] Plurima litterulis signata sepulchra loquuntur
    Martyris aut nomen, aut epigramma aliquod.
                                        Ibid. Hymnus S. Hippolyti.
[4] Quorum solus habet comperta vocabula Christus.   *Ibid.*
[5] Boldetti. Osservazioni sopra i Cimiterj de' santi Martiri. Page 666, We readily accept this tradition, which is based upon an ancient manuscript found by Baronius, *Martyrol. Roman. ad diem* xiii. *Maii.* in the archives of Sanctae Mariae ad Martyres. Facts of this nature are seldom invented, and although the martyrs were removed from the Catacombs principally during the eighth century, it is natural to admit that the ravages made by the Goths, in the sixth, must have so completely destroyed some of the galleries as to render it impossible to repair them. The Pontiff wished to ensure a suitable and safe resting-place for the bones of the saints, and the dedication of an edifice like the Pantheon, furnished him an opportunity of carrying out his design. It is true that the Liber Pontificalis does not give in detail this translation of the martyrs, but merely remarks that Boniface IV., in dedicating the Pantheon, placed therein, some relics, *et reliquias in ea collocavit,* but this indication, which of itself would be insufficient, on account of the vague idea conveyed by the word *reliquias,* is fully explained by the testimony of the manuscript cited by Baronius, whilst it also accords with histor-

ical conjectures.

[6] 1 Gal. 18.

[7] Von. Beda. Histor. Eccles. Anglo, lib. v., cap. xii.

[8] We transcribe the verses of St. Adhelm as being the most ancient poems extant on St. Cecilia after the hymn of the Gothic Breviary.

Porro Caeciliae vivacem condere laudem,
Quae valeat digno metrorum pagina versu?
Quae sponsum proprium convertit dogmate sancto,
Mellea carnalis contemnens ludicra luxus:
Basia dum potius dilexit dulcia Christi,
Candida praepulchris complectens colla lacertis.
Quamvis harmoniis praesultent organa multis,
Musica Pierio resonent, et carmina cantu;
Non tamen inflexit fallax praecordia mentis
Pompa prophanorum, quae nectit retia Sanctis,
Ne forto properet paradisi ad gaudia miles.
Taliter interea compellans vocibus, infit,
Dum secreta petunt, concessa lege thororum:
Angelus en, inquit, superis tranavit ab astris:
Hic me, patronus, coelesti foedere fulcit,
Ut nequeam prorsus quidquam carnalis amare;
Namq'ue meum jugiter conservat corpus in sevum,
Ut nnllus valeat spurco succensus amore
Contrectare mea probroso crimine membra:
Sed mox Angelicis ulciscens vindicat armis,
Qui me pollutis nituntur prendere palmis.
Sic devota Deo convertit foemina sponsum.
Nee non, et levirum solvens errore vetusto,
Donee credentes sumpsissent dona lavacri.
Facti municipes in summis arcibus, ambo
Martyres effecti, carnis tormenta luentes.

Biblioth. Vet. Pat., tome xiii. page 14.

[9] *X. Kal.* Natale S. Caeciliae Virginia, quae et sponsum suum Valerianum et fratrem ejus Tiburtium ad credendum Christo ao martyrium perdocuit: et ipsa deinde martyrizavit, ignem quidem superans, sed ferro occisa, sub Almachio Urbis Praefecto. *Martyrologium Bedae. Acta SS. Martii,* tome ii. page xxxix.

[10] According to the opinion of the learned Gaetano Marini, this deacon, Moschus, is the same with the arch deacon of the same name, mentioned in the celebrated inscription found in the Vatican Crypts. The inscription contains also important fragments of the Acts of a Council, held, against the Iconoclasts, by Gregory III., near the Confession of St. Peter. Vid. Maii. Scrip, vett. Tome v. p. 466.

[11] Anastas. *In Zacharia.*

[12] See the diploma of Urban III., in Fonseca do Basilica S. Laurentii in Dainaso, Page. 252.

[13] Mabillon Acta S. S. Ordinis S. Benedicti. Saec. iii., part ii., page 230.

[14] Anastas. *In Leone III.*

Chapter Twenty-Two - Discovery of Cecilia's Body by Pope St. Paschal

The moment had at length arrived when the discovery of the long-lost sepulchre of St. Cecilia, was to verify the numerous traditions concerning this saint, to which not only Rome, but the entire West, had clung for centuries, with ever increasing enthusiasm. In 817, Paschal ascended the Apostolic chair, and seemed to have been especially chosen to people the churches of Rome with the relics of the martyrs. It became almost a necessity to remove these holy remains from those grottos, the vaults of which were crumbling to decay, and which were no longer visited so eagerly by the pious faithful.

In 761, the holy Pope, Paul I., had opened an immense number of tombs, in the crypts which seemed most liable to be destroyed, and had distributed the martyrs' bones among the churches, [1] monasteries, and Basilicas. The Papal Chronicle particularly designates the Church of St. Silvester's Monastery, on the Campus Martius, which had been founded by the Pope, as having been more favored than the others. In a document relating to this monastery, Paul gives his motive for disturbing these venerated remains. "Throughout the course of ages," he says, "many cemeteries of the Holy Martyrs and Confessors, have been neglected and destroyed. During the impious invasions of the Lombards, they were ravaged from one end to the other. These barbarians even went so far as to search the sepulchres, and carry away many glorious bodies. From this disastrous period, these cemeteries were no longer treated with the same honor, the faithful having become very negligent in visiting them. Must I say they have even allowed their animals to enter freely into these sacred vaults, and some have not hesitated to use them as enclosures for their flocks." [2] Nevertheless, throughout the eighth and ninth centuries, the numerous pilgrims who yearly visited Borne, considered it a duty to descend into the cemeteries of the martyrs, and visit the Basilicas which gave entrance to them. Divine Providence has permitted that many of the guide-books in which they noted down all that their piety rendered them anxious to remember after their return home, should be preserved to the present day. These documents, drawn up without art, frequently even incorrectly, give us, among other things, the topography of the cemeteries upon the different Ways, the details of their accompanying Basilicas, the more or less precise locality of several martyrs' tombs in the same crypt; in a word, they are the only light with which we can illumine the gloom of the Catacombs. All the authors who have formerly spoken of subterranean Rome, have, on account of not using them, made numerous and inevitable errors.

With the assistance of these documents, many obscurities have been cleared up, and positive facts have been substituted for the erroneous assertions which learned men had derived, either from statements drawn up at a period when traditions concerning the Catacombs had perished, or from conjectures totally void of foundation. With the assistance of these valuable guide-books, we cheerfully contribute the little that is in our power to that renovation of the antiquities of Christian Rome which, we doubt not, will be effected at some future day: and we earnestly pray that our illustrious friend, who seems to have been chosen by heaven for this noble mission, may successfully accomplish the task. His genius has conceived it; his vast science can compass it; and his piety convinces him of its importance. The series of guide books of which we speak, commences at the last year of the sixth century, with the list of the holy oils sent to Theodolinda; it is continued by two descriptive documents taken from a manuscript of St. Peter of Salzbourg, the first evidently belonging to the seventh century; these two documents are more detailed than others, and have already corrected many errors. That inserted by William of Malmesbury in his history follows, and is also filled with the most precious topographical documents. It must have been written previous to the year 818, since he describes many Martyrs as reposing in the Catacombs, who were transferred to the Churches of Rome by St. Paschal in that year. Finally, the last is that which Dom Mabillon found in the Library of Einsiedelen, and which, according to its topographical details, can scarcely be dated earlier than the ninth century. It is true there are not many details with respect to the Martyrs, as he confines himself to the description of the Basilicas erected upon the Cemeterial Ways. But we know that after the relics were taken away, these churches were not visited, and being deplorably neglected, gradually crumbled into ruins.

As we have already seen, in the document of St. Paul L, the neglect of the Romans towards these sacred cemeteries, caused them to be totally abandoned. In the beginning of the ninth century, the inconvenience of this state of things was still more sensibly felt, and it became necessary to put an end to it. The cemeteries of the Appian Way had been generally kept in better order, either on account of the restorations made at different epochs, or of the special veneration in which they were held; but the condition into which they had fallen on account of the devastations of the Lombards, joined to other causes which we have mentioned, imperiously called for some decided measures on the part of the Roman Pontiff. In the second year of his Pontificate, Paschal commenced the course of solemn Translations which marked his reign in so special a manner. We may form some idea of the importance of the removals made by Paschal at this time, by reading the contemporaneous inscriptions exposed in the crypts of the Church of St. Praxedes. Two thousand three hundred Martyrs are therein mentioned, as having been buried by the Pontiff, either under the principal Altar, or in other parts of the Basilica, situated upon the right of the entrance, or finally in a chapel dedicated to St. Agnes.

We learn from this precious inscription, that the Pontiff transferred the bodies of the most illustrious martyrs of the Appian Way, to the Church of St. Praxedes. Many of the Pontiffs of the cemetery of Sixtus, were included in this translation. First, Sixtus himself; afterwards, Pontianus, Anterus, Fabian, Lucius, Stephen, and Melchiades. Urban had been brought from the cemetery of Pretextatus and united to his colleagues. The bodies of other Pontiffs, taken from different cemeteries, completed this imposing collection. [3] Then followed a legion of martyrs, some designated by their names, others by their total number in each section. Holy women who had been the ornament of Christian Rome, completed this assemblage of the elect. The most illustrious were Praxedes and Pudentiana, Symphorosa, Felicula, Zoe, Daria, and Emerentiana. [4] Cecilia was not among them.

One day, in the year 821, Paschal [5] was praying in the Basilica of St. Cecilia, when he was struck with the dilapidated state of this august sanctuaiy. The walls, which had been restored by St. Gregory, more than two centuries before, were fast decaying, and there was every reason to fear that, unless prompt and efficacious measures were taken, the ancient church, to which many sublime remembrances were attached, would soon be a heap of ruins. Paschal immediately made a resolution to repair the church throughout, and to rebuild it in a style of magnificence even far surpassing its original splendor. Paschal had been so zealous in recovering the remains of the holy martyrs, that he could not conceive such a project without desiring to find Cecilia's body, that he might translate it solemnly to the house which she had sanctified by her presence, and consecrated with her blood. Before the Pontificate of Paschal, her body had been vainly sought in all the crypts of the Appian Way. Many reasons had rendered these researches fruitless. It is true that Cecilia's tomb could not be far distant from the church that bore her name, and that of Sixtus; but the gallery which concealed this glorious sepulchre was at some distance from the entrance to the Basilica. There was nothing about the tomb calculated to attract attention. A narrow and rather elevated recess, closed by a marble slab without inscription, might easily be overlooked among so many tombs, placed one above the other. Cecilia's tomb, although near the Papal Sepulchres, was totally different, and before opening it, it would have been impossible to understand why St. Urban chose so honorable, and yet so modest a sepulchre for the virgin.

As we have already seen, the Goths, in the sixth century, made great ravages in the Catacombs, destroyed sepulchres, and shattered the inscriptions. This violence and the gradual abandonment of the sacred crypts, accounts for the disappearance of the epitaph which St. Damasus, or his successors, must have dedicated to St. Cecilia, and which in any case could not have been fastened upon the tomb, on account of its peculiar form. However this may be, we find in the guide-books of Salzbourg, that Cecilia's tomb was well known in the seventh century, and that it was not far from the sepulchres of the holy Popes, Fabian, Sixtus, and Dionysius.

On the other hand, the Malmesbury guide-book, which must have been written previous to the year 818, in which St. Paschal removed the bodies of the holy Pontiffs, Sixtus and Dionysius, relates that these Popes still reposed in the Cemetery ad Sanctam Caeciliam, and yet makes no mention of St. Cecilia; all traces of the latter must have been lost between the end of the seventh, and commencement of the ninth century. This therefore must have been the period at which the sacred Cemeteries began to be less frequented. But God willed that this very forgetfulness should preserve the tomb of St. Cecilia, under circumstances when it would otherwise have been despoiled of the sacred treasure it contained.

The Lombards, commanded by Luitprand, and later by Astolphus, besieged Rome several times during the eighth century. They entered the sacred Cemeteries and carried off the relics of many martyrs. They were very anxious to find the body of St. Cecilia, but after a persevering search were unable to discover it. Such zeal in these converted barbarians will scarcely surprise us when we reflect that Luitprand purchased with gold from the Saracens, the body of St Augustin, which he transferred from Sardinia to Pavia.

But God would not permit Rome to be deprived of a treasure which, for a moment, she did not fully appreciate. It finally became the general opinion in the Holy City that Cecilia's body had been carried away by the Lombards. Paschal was not discouraged, and eager to consecrate the restored Basilica, by placing its illustrious patroness under the altar, he commanded that the search should be recommenced. He even visited the crypts himself, but could not find the Virgin's body in any of the tombs he opened. Finally, yielding too readily to the general opinion, he gave up the search in despair, but the time had arrived when Cecilia was to re-appear and enter triumphantly into Rome.

One day, Paschal (he himself relates the circumstance) was assisting at the divine office in the Basilica of St. Peter, near the Confession. The clerks were melodiously chanting Lauds, and the Pontiff listened to the harmonious canticles with pious delight. He was finally overcome by drowsiness, the consequence of his protracted vigils. [6] The sacred chants sounded in his ears like a distant echo; but his eyes, closed to exterior objects, were suddenly struck by a luminous vision. A young virgin of great beauty and adorned like the Spouse of Christ, stood before him.

Looking steadily at the Pontiff, she said in a firm voice: "We owe thee many thanks! Hast thou then, on simple reports and false rumors, abandoned all hope of finding me? Nevertheless at one time thou wert so near me, we could have conversed together." [7]

"Who art thou," asked the Pontiff, deeply agitated, "who speakest to me with so much assurance?"

"If thou wouldst know my name," said the virgin, "I am called Cecilia, servant of Christ." [8] Paschal who knew that apparitions are not always an index of heaven's will, replied: "But how can we believe thee? Men say that the body of this holy martyr was carried away by the Lombards." "They did seek me," said the Virgin, "for a long time and with great perseverance; but the Virgin Mother of God protected me. She would not permit them to carry me

117

away, and I am still in the same place where I first reposed. Thou hast commenced researches; continue them, for it has pleased the Almighty God, in whose honor I suffered, to reveal my tomb to thee. Take away my body, together with those of the other Saints near me, and place us in the Church thou hast recently restored." [9] After these words she disappeared.

Re-animated by this vision, Paschal caused a new search to be made in the Cemetery of Sixtus. The name of this holy Pontiff united to that of Cecilia in designating the same Church of entrance, naturally guided the explorers. Much time had been lost in searching the Cemetery of Pretextatus, and always in vain. At this time the crypts of Callistus were frequently confounded with those of Pretextatus, at the point where these two cemeteries were blended into one, near the Church of St. Sebastian. This is very evident from the text of Anastasius, [10] a contemporary historian, whose description of the discovery of Cecilia's body perfectly accords with Paschal's account. The Pontiff did not now seek on the left of the Appian, a tomb which from the locality of the Bacilica ad Sanctam Casciliam, he felt assured was on the right. He descended the steps and once more explored the sacred labyrinth. He finally reached the subterranean galleries near the Church of Sebastian. At a point where two roads crossed, a hitherto unexplored tomb, placed in the angle of intersection, struck his eyes. This sepulchre had been overlooked on account of its extreme simplicity, but its peculiar shape and the remembrance of Cecilia's words, induced the Pontiff to examine it. He ordered the marble to be removed, and to his excessive joy, discovered in this deep and narrow cell, the tomb he had so vainly sought. Cecilia reposed in her cypress coffin, dressed in the antique robe of silk and gold in which Urban had buried her; and the linen and veils which had been used to staunch her wounds, were rolled together and placed at her feet. Paschal certifies that he touched with his own hands the venerated remains of the daughter of the Cecilii. [11] The bodies of Valerian, Tiburtius, and Maximus, were at a short distance; [12] nothing remained but to restore this illustrious family of martyrs to Rome.

But Urban was destined to share with his noble daughter, the triumph prepared for her. St. Paschal had already transferred the body of this holy Pontiff to the church of St. Praxedes; after recovering Cecilia's body, he formed the project of placing the remains of the holy Pope under the same Altar with those of Cecilia and her companions. He made every preparation to celebrate the Translation of these venerated Martyrs with all the pomp and solemnity so great a ceremony required.

[1] Anastas. *In Paulo*.
[2] See a long passage of this letter of Pope Paul 1st, in Boldetti, p. 96.
[3] They were Popes Alexander, Felix, Julius, Siricius, Anastasius, and Celestin.
[4] See the inscription given for the first time in full, by His Eminence Cardinal Mai *Scriptorum veterum nora collectio*, tome v. pages 38, 40. The bodies of the

martyrs to whom this inscription is dedicated, with the exception of a very few which have been transferred elsewhere, still repose behind the marble slabs which at some future day, may be removed to take out these sacred bones, when the galleries of the Catacombs are at length exhausted.

[5] Anastas. *In Paschali.*

[6] Unde tamen, Domini annuente clementia, quadam die dum ante Confessionem Beati Petri Apostoli, psallentium matutinali lucescente Dominica residentes observaremus harmoniam, sopore in aliquo corporis fragilitatem aggravante. *Paschalis Papae diploma.*

[7] Astitit nobis pnella pulcherrima virginali aspectu, vel habitu decorata, taliaque nobis, intuens, ait: Multas tibi gratias referimus: certamen quod in me diu apposueras, frustatoriis relationibus pervulgatis, sine causa reliquisti? Qui tanto penes me fuisti, quod ore proprio loqui communiter valebamus. *Paschalis Papae diploma.*

[8] Et dum a nobis diligenter interrogata fuisset: Tu quis es? Vel quod est nomen tuum, qui talia me praesumendo conaris? Si e nomine quaeris, Caecilia, inquit, famula Christi vocor. *Ibid.*

[9] Cui subjungens dixit: Quomodo hoe credere possumus, quia olim fama relata est, quod ejusdem sacratissimsc Martyris corpus a Longobardis inde fuisset ablatum? Quae ita respondent dixit: Veritas est, quod multum me desideranter quaesierunt, sed gratia Dominae meae semperque Virginia Dei Genitricis affuit, quod qualiter quotidie praesto sum, nullatenus me longius abire pormisit; sed sicut coepisti perage, et sicut operaris indesinenter operare, quia omnipotens Deus tibi me placuit revelare, et corpus meum cum aliis corporibus Sanctis, quae sunt juxta me, reconditis, in Titulo quem nuper reparari mandasti, recondere stude infra muros urbis. Et haec dicens abcessit. *Ibid.*

[10] Anastase. *In Paschali.*

[11] Tunc etenim pro hujus revelationis manifestatione, omni postposita difficultate, incunctanter et absque ambiguitato ipsius venerabilis Virginis corpus inquirendum decrevimus; qui etiam annuente Deo, ejusque solito juvamine properantes, in Coemeterio sancti Sixti situm foris portam Appiam, sicut in sacratissima illius Passione manifeste narratur, inter collegas episcopos, in aureis indumentis, cum venerabili sponso reperimus, ubi etiam linteamina, cum quibus sacratissimus sanguis ejus abstersus est de plagis, quas spiculator trina percussione crudeliter ingesserat, ad pedes beatissimae Virginis in unum revoluta, plenaque cruore invenimus; quae omnia nostris manibus pertractantes, cum venerabili corpore honeste infra muros hujus Romanae Urbis induximus. *Paschalis Papae Diploma.*

[12] We should not understand literally that Paschal found Cecilia with her husband. It is evident that the two bodies were not in the same tomb, but the sepulchres were close together: so Cecilia related to St. Paschal when she appeared to him. Mereover, if Paschal had found Cecilia and Valerian buried together, he would not have separated them in the trans-Tiberian Basilica.

119

Chapter Twenty-Three - Translation of the Bodies of Saints Cecilia, Valerian, Tiburtius, Maximus, Urban, and Lucius. St. Paschal's Munificence towards the Basilica of St. Cecilia

Cecilia was about to return to the Holy City which had been honored by her presence so many centuries before. The house where she had won so many souls to Christ, which she had sanctified with her blood, and transmitted to Pope Urban, to be converted into a temple of the Lord, she would now find restored by another Pontiff, and faithfully preserving the destination she had given it at her death.

Several months had elapsed since the day when Paschal had resolved to restore this sanctuary. On the 8th of the Ides of May (8 May) [1] 822, the Pontifi solemnly dedicated St. Cecilia's Church, and doubtless upon the same day he placed her holy relics under the Confession.

He placed a white marble sarcophagus for the virgin, who richly merited the first honors of so magnificent a triumph. Paschal, following Urban's example, respected the attitude of the Virgin. He left her in the cypress coffin just as he had found her; but he lined the inside of it with a rich fringed silk damask, called *quadrapulum;* over her body he threw a light silken veil, also fringed, and made of a material called *stauracin.* [2] When he had concluded these arrangements, he closed the tomb with a marble slab which was destined not to be removed for eight centuries.

The three bodies of Valerian, Tiburtius, and Maximus, were placed in a second sarcophagus; Valerian between the two other martyrs, and each one wrapped in a separate winding-sheet. Before closing the second sepulchre, Paschal took the head of Tiburtius which had been severed by the sword, and placed this precious relic in a silver casket, weighing eight pounds, wishing that the faithful should have continually before their eyes, so eloquent a testimony of the martyr's courage. [3]

Paschal prepared a third sarcophagus for the body of Urban, whom he wished to place with his spiritual children. That the holy Pope might not repose alone, he removed the body of Lucius, a successor of St. Urban, and also a martyr, from the church of St. Praxedes, and interred the Pontiffs together. Urban and Lucius were also wrapped each in a separate winding-sheet. Paschal having closed this third sepulchre, caused a circular wall to be built round the place where the martyrs reposed. A marble slab, bearing a mosaic cross and an inscription, was placed inside the sepulchre, near the tombs, to certify to posterity, the value of the treasure which Paschal had interred there.

The following verses were engraved on the marble:

HANC FIDEI ZELO PASCHALIS PRIMVS AB IMO ECCLESIAM RENOVANS, DVM CORPORA SACRA REQVIRIT, ELEVAT INVENTVM VENERANDAE MARTYRIS ALMAE CAECILIAE CORPVS, HOC ILLVD MARMORE CONDENS. LUCIVS, VRBANVS, HVIC PONTIFICES SOCIANTVR; VOSQVE DEI TESTES, TIBVRTI, VALERIANE, MAXIME, CVM DICTIS CONSORTIA DIGNA TENETIS. HOS COLIT EGREGIOS DEVOTE ROMA PATRONOS. [4]

The principal altar of the church was erected over the tombs; according to custom, an opening protected by a movable grating, and called *fenestella,* was cut in the solid stone; and within was a perpendicular conduit, by means of which, pieces of linen, called *brandea,* were lowered down to the tomb. After having been sanctified by this sacred contact, these linen cloths were distributed as relics. Paschal covered the altar, and the interior of the abovementioned aperture with silver plates, and placed on the altar a magnificent ciborium of the same metal, weighing five hundred pounds. He adorned the Confession with a statue of St. Cecilia, also of silver, weighing ninety-five pounds. Three other statues, probably those of Valerian, Tiburtius, and Maximus, were grouped around that of the virgin. They were made of the same material, but were gilded, and the three together weighed forty-eight pounds. One hundred pounds of silver were employed in the decorations of two columns of Byzantine workmanship, which supported an arcade, the whole interior of which was covered with silver plates. [5]

The Papal Chronicle also gives an inventory of the sacred vessels and furniture presented by Paschal to the Basilica. We mention these details to prove this Pontiff's veneration for the holy martyrs, also to give some idea of the wealth of the Roman churches in the ninth century. Among the offerings were twenty-six silver chalices for the different altars, weighing together one hundred and nine pounds; two silver lamps, each weighing two pounds; a basin of pure gold, weighing three pounds; a silver censor weighing one pound; a purple altar-cloth, the centre of gold brocade, upon which was embroidered an angel distributing crowns to Valerian, Cecilia, and Tiburtius, the whole trimmed with gold fringe of marvellous workmanship; costly veils and tapestry, some destined for the Confession, others for different altars of the Basilica, and for the Presbytery, without counting the large and rich curtain, hanging at the entrance of the church. [6]

A description of these fabrics, all of the richest material, would detain us too long; we will, however, mention another altar-cloth which Paschal presented a short time before his death. It was of gold brocade, and enriched with a magnificent piece of embroidery, representing the resurrection of our Lord. [7]

This Basilica, which the Pontiff had decorated with such magnificence, was built according to the style observed in all the Roman churches. A court surrounded by a portico, with a fountain in the centre, was in front of the building.

The bath room in which Cecilia breathed her last sigh, was upon the right, at the entrance of the Basilica. Above the columns of the grand nave, Paschal caused to be painted a series of the Roman Pontiffs, from St. Peter to himself, similar to those in the churches of St. Peter and of St. Paul. [8]

Between the apsis and the grand nave, a triumphal arch was erected covered with a brilliant mosaic. In the centre, the mother of God was represented seated upon a throne, and holding the Divine Infant on her knees. She is accompanied by two Angels, one standing on her right, the other on her left. On either side, five Virgins are advancing towards the throne of the Son and His mother, each presenting a crown. These virgins are separated one from the other by palm trees. Lower down, the twenty-four elders of the Apocalypse, twelve on either side, are represented raising their crowns to Christ, to whose glory this triumphal arch was consecrated. [9] The mosaic of the apsis was not executed until after the translation of the Martyrs, as Paschal desired by its means to perpetuate the remembrance of this event so glorious for the Basilica.

It has been preserved until the present day, and although the rich enamel is somewhat faded, the mosaic is none the less venerable. In the centre, our Saviour is represented standing, and clothed in a mantle sparkling with gold. With His right hand, he is giving a blessing according to the Greek manner, while, in his left, he holds a roll of the Gospels. The Byzantine artist represented St. Peter on the left of our Saviour, because among the Greeks, that was considered the post of honor. The prince of the Apostles wears a silver cloak, and holds two keys, the symbols of his power. Valerian and Cecilia stand next to him; the former also wears a silver cloak, and holds a crown in his hand; the Virgin has her hair fastened with a band, and her neck adorned with a necklace formed of three rows of pearls. Her dress and mantle are of gold, and she holds a crown composed of two rows of pearls. The picture terminates on the left with a palm tree laden with fruit. St. Paul stands on the right of our Saviour, enveloped in a golden mantle, and holding a book of the Gospels richly bound. St. Agatha stands next, crowned with a diadem, and clothed in a golden robe, the beauty of which is enhanced by a rich trimming of pearls. She rests her right hand upon the shoulder of Paschal who wears the antique Chasuble and Pallium, and holds in his hands a little edifice representing St. Cecilia's Church, in the dedication of which he added the name of Agatha to that of the Roman Virgin. The picture on this side also, is terminated by a palm tree laden with fruit; a phoenix stands upon one of the upper-branches of the tree, as if to recall the symbolical bird which Cecilia caused to be engraved upon the tomb of Maximus.

On the lower part of the mosaic, the Lamb of God is represented with five rivers flowing under his feet, ancient symbols of the vivifying fountains which flow from the Redeemer's wounds. On either side, six lambs, representing the Twelve Apostles, advance towards the Divine Lamb. [10]

The monogram of Paschal is placed at the top of the apsis, and on the lower part of this immense picture, the inscription in verse, in which he dedicated this sumptuous monument of the Byzantine art to St. Cecilia. It runs thus:

HAEC DOMVS AMPLA MICAT VARVS FABRICATA METALLIS OLIM QVAE FVERAT CONFRACTA SVB TEMPORE PRISCO. CONDITIT IN MELIVS PAS-CHALIS PRAESVL OPIMVS. HANC AVLAM DOMINI FIRMANS FVNDAMINE CLARO. AVREA GEMMATIS RESONANT HAEC DYNDIMA TEMPLI. LAETVS AMORE DEI HIC CONIVNXIT CORPORA SANCTA CAECILIAE ET SOCIIS RVTILAT HIC FLORE VENTVS, QVAE PRIDEM IN CRYPTIS PAVSABANT MEM-BRA BEATA. ROMA RESVLTAT OVANS SEMPER ORNATA PER AEVVM. [11]

Such were the testimonials of Paschal's devotion to St. Cecilia, and such were the ornaments with which he enriched her Basilica. In his distribution of relics to the different churches, he could not forget that of St. Cecilia. Nine hundred bodies of Martyrs were placed in her Basilica, as if to form an escort for the glorious Spouse of Christ, and also to increase the dignity of her august sanctuary. [12]

Paschal was not satisfied with merely restoring the dwelling of St. Cecilia; he also wished to ensure a tribute of homage which day and night should ascend to heaven from this holy place. He therefore by his largesses installed a choir of monks near the church to sing the Divine Office. He caused a monastery to be built in a place called *Colles Jacentes*, and endowed it with the revenues of a hospital which his predecessor, St. Leo III., had founded near St Peter's, upon a tract of ground formerly used for aquatic games. This hospital had not prospered, and had consequently been abandoned.

After having paid so much honor to the Virgin Cecilia, Paschal happily end-ed his Pontificate which is signalized among all others by acts of piety to-wards the holy martyrs. The Pontiff had acquitted the debt of gratitude which the church owed to those who had cemented it with their blood. If the triumph he reserved for Cecilia, exceeded that of all the other martyrs whose relics he translated, it was because Paschal, like Urban, felt that there are many mansions in the house of the Heavenly Father; [13] and that the daughter of the Cecilii had heroically ascended to one of those reserved for the most magnanimous souls.

Paschal died in the year 824. In the following century, Flodoard [14] a canon of the Church of Rheims, and one of the first historians of France, wrote a poem commemorating the deeds of the Roman Pontiffs. He eulogized the virtues of Paschal; but dwelt particularly upon Cecilia's apparition to that Pontiff, and described the glorious tomb where she reposed in her rich apparel, surrounded by the bloodstained evidences of her martyrdom. Thus even the churches, in foreign countries, were deeply interested in the events which had taken place in Rome, and the glory of Cecilia seemed to be appreciated throughout Christendom. Whilst Alexander Severus was remembered only in the pages of history, the renown of the noble young Roman maiden, who had suffered in his reign a cruel death, increased with every succeeding age. We will quote the eloquent lines of St. John Chrysostom, who, wishing to impress the people with an idea of the ever increasing glory of the martyrs, contrasts it with that of the Caesars, among whom he particularly names Alexander Severus.

"The Roman Senate," says this eloquent Bishop, "decreed the apotheosis of Alexander Severus, and made him the thirteenth of their principal gods; [15] for this assembly had the power of creating and declaring gods. If these Pagans are asked: 'How can Alexander be a god? Is he not dead? Did he not die a miserable death?' They reply: 'During his life, Alexander accomplished many and noble actions. He subjugated cities and nations; he was victorious in wars and combats; he erected innumerable trophies.' I see nothing either new or surprising that a man who was at once a king and a great general, having under him large armies, should gain victories; but I am filled with astonishment when I find that a man, who suffered on the cross and was laid in the tomb, daily performs so many miracles both on land and sea; this proves a secret and divine power. After the death of Alexander, his empire was divided and annihilated, and yet he did not restore it. What could that dead man do? Christ, on the contrary, founded an empire, but it was not until after his death that he accomplished his work. But why do I speak of Christ, when he has granted to his very disciples so much glory beyond the tomb? Tell me, where sleeps Alexander's dust? On what day did he die? What I *do* know is, that the tombs of the servants of God are erected with magnificence; they are the ornaments of the royal city; every one knows the day that is consecrated to them; it is celebrated throughout the world. The Gentiles cannot point out Alexander's tomb; they know not where it is. The very barbarians know those of the Martyrs. The sepulchres of those who served the Crucified, surpass the palaces of emperors, not only by their extent and beauty, but still more by the concourse of people who visit them. Even kings prostrate themselves before their tombs, and renouncing their pomp, beseech the servants of God to intercede for them. The fisherman and the tent maker are both dead, and he who now wears the diadem humbly implores their protection." [16]

[1] See the ordo of the church of St. Cecilia 8 May, and the titles published by Laderchi vol. ii. page 10.

[2] Fecit etiam in arcella ad corpus jam dictae Virginis vestem de quadrapulo cum periclysi. Item et aliam vestem de stauraci cum ericlysi de olovero. *Anaias. In Paschali.*

[3] Anastasius, or his copyist, erred in attributing to Cecilia the head of which we speak. When the virgin's tomb was opened the second time, the head was found with the body; and the tradition of the Basilica, which attributed the head to Tiburtius, was confirmed by opening the tomb of the latter.

[4] When Paschal restored this church, he sought for and discovered the body of the martyr, Cecilia, which he placed under this marble. The Pontiffs Lucius and Urban are with her, and you, also, Tiburtius, Valerian, and Maximus, occupy an honorable place. Here repose those whom Rome reveres as her powerful protectors.

[5] Anastas. *In Paschali.*

[6] *Ibid.*

[7] *Ibid.*

[8] Marangoni. Cose gentilesche ad uso delle chiese. Page 311.

[9] The design of this mosaic, which has been destroyed, may be found in Ciampini, Vetera Monimenta, tome ii. page 157.

[10] This mosaic may also be seen in Ciampini. Vetera Monimenta page 160.

[11] This vast temple, was falling to ruins when Paschal, in his munificence, restored it. He placed this temple of God upon the richest foundation; the sanctuary, brilliant with gold, sparkles with precious stones. Paschal reunited in this Church the bodies of Cecilia and her companions. This family, composed of young patricians whose remains were so long concealed in the crypts, now reposes here.

[12] Sixtus V. Bref *Salvator noster.* Laderchi, tome ii. page 410. This tradition is open to criticism. It seems at first sight to have originated from a text of the Roman Martyrology of the 4th of March, where nine hundred Martyrs are mentioned as being buried *ad Sanctam Caeciliam*, viz., in the cemetery of Cecilia and Sixtus. But as Laderchi remarks, Paschal may have transferred these martyrs to the church after the Translation of Cecilia's body. This would explain every thing.

[13] John xiv., 2.

[14] We will give the passage of Flodoard's poem referring to the events we have related

Caeciliae cernens incumbere casibus aedem
In meliora levat restructis culmina septis.
Defessum precibus, quem Caecilia visere Virgo
Affarique probat dignum: taraen increpat, ut quid
Liquerit incertum quaerendi membra laborem,
Quae sublata putat popularis credulus aurae?
Ut se res habeat referens, nomenque roganti
Adnotat, hortaturque piis persistere coeptis;
Gaudeat invento dum munere: nam placet, inquit;
Aeterno Domino, cujus splendoris amore
Me passam constat, noviter quo me ipse repertam
A te constructi templi munimine condas.
Hic dictis celeri repetit coelestia saltu.
Papa revelato laetus tam lucis aperte
Indicio, indagans thesauri celsa talenta
Reperit, eximiis pretiosa monilia gemmis.
Aurea virgineum celabant tegmina pignus:
Carbasa Martyrii rutilabant sanguine clari;
Quae pater almificus manibus pia munera tractans

Colligit, inducens Urbi instrumenta salutis:
Atque locat thalamo candentia membra decoro.

D. Mabillon. Acta SS. Ord. S. Ben. saec. iii. part. ii. p. 587

[15] This remark of St. John Chrysostom is not strictly correct. There is no certain proof that the Senate by special decree placed Alexander among their gods; but Lampridius expressly says, that during Alexander's lire a temple was elected to his honor.

[16] In Epist. ii, ad Corinth. Homil. xxvi, No. 4, 5.

Chapter Twenty-Four - Confirmation of the Acts of St. Cecilia by the Circumstances Attending the Discovery of Her Body. Digression upon the Relics of St. Cecilia

Before resuming our history, let us dwell for a moment upon the facts contained in the account of the finding of St. Cecilia's body; facts which serve to verify our Acts. We have taken them principally from Paschal's official document and the contemporary chronicle of Anastasius, both unknown to the compiler of the Acts, since he lived three centuries before, and his recital had been admitted into the Liturgies from the sixth and seventh centuries. They were also circulated throughout the Churches of the West, at least a century before Paschal's pontificate, as we have already seen in the Chronicle of Felix IV., the verses of St. Adhelm, and Bede's Martyrology. We found in Paschal's document, and in the narrative of Anastasius, not only the names of Cecilia and Valerian, but also those of Tiburtius and Maximus, and it was also stated that these four martyrs were first buried upon the Appian Way. Although Paschal's recital is so laconic, he mentions that Cecilia was dressed in a robe of gold and silk. The Acts had already given us this information which is indeed of secondary importance. Yet its confirmation serves to prove the veracity of the compiler. Paschal does not say that he discovered near the body the ampullas filled with blood, which are still found in the martyrs' tombs; but he mentions pieces of linen which had been saturated in blood, lying at Cecilia's feet. Here is an additional proof of the fidelity of our historian who was the first to mention this fact. The circumstance of the linen cloths is characteristic of the martyrdom of our Saint. They prove the staunching of a wound inflicted by a sword; they are not to be confounded with the sponges used to collect the martyr's blood, which was afterwards pressed into vases destined to preserve it. The linen cloths in Cecilia's tomb were rolled up with great care and placed at her feet as a trophy. By their mute but eloquent testimony, they recalled the tragic scene of the *Caldarium*. Later we shall see Cecilia's tomb again reopened, and then new discoveries will give additional proof of the minute accuracy of our Acts.

The circumstances of the discovery of Cecilia's body, in 822, also serve to enlighten the critic upon the value of the virgin's relics, which several churches boasted of possessing, before the pontificate of Paschal. St. Venantius Fortunatus, in the seventh century, speaks of those which St. Vitalis, Bishop of Ravenna, had placed in the Church of St. Andrew. [1] It is very evident that these relics could not have been those of our holy martyr, since her tomb was not opened until the year 822. Many relics are spoken of, after this period, as being those of St. Cecilia. Ehaban Maur commemorates in a poem, the bones of St. Cecilia, which he declares that he placed in his church at Fulda, with those of Sts. Valerian and Tiburtius; [2] in another place, he mentions nine altars, which he says he enriched with her relics. [3]

A statement of the relics preserved in the Basilica of St. Cecilia, at Rome, and which appears to have been compiled about the beginning of the twelfth century, mentions four altars of this same church, as containing relics of the glorious patroness; in two of the altars, the relics were bones. [4] The treasury of the celebrated Church of St. Martin of Tours, which was pillaged by the Calvinists, in 1562, contained a head of St. Cecilia, enclosed in a reliquary partly of gold, partly silver gilt, and enriched with precious stones. [5] A second head was kept in the church of St. Nicholas des Champs, in Paris; [6] a third in the treasury of the Abbey of St. Lucien de Beamais. [7] It would be easy to extend this enumeration, with the assistance of different inventories of relics found among the Bollandists and elsewhere; but we cannot pass over in silence, the arm of St. Cecilia, and the relics of Sts. Tiburtius, Valerian, and Urban, which Paul II. presented in 1346, to John Jofroy, Bishop of Alby, who placed them in his cathedral. [8] All these relics, which we by no means intend to stigmatize as pious frauds, could not possibly belong to the Roman virgin, whose history we are relating. When Cecilia's tomb was opened in 1599, the body was found entire, just as St. Paschal had placed it, under the altar of the trans-Tiberian Basilica. Du Saussay, in his Martyrologium Gallicanum, frankly acknowledges this, and he thinks that the head preserved in the church of St. Nicholas in Paris, must have belonged to Cecilia, Abbess of Remiremont. [9]

It is difficult at first, to explain the mistake made at Rome, and even in St. Cecilia's church, where, from the twelfth century, they supposed that some of the saint's bones were under several of the altars. But it is easily accounted for, if we remember that, besides the virgin married to Valerian, there were at least three other holy martyrs, named Cecilia, two of whom suffered in Rome. The first mentioned in the Martyrology, attributed to St. Jerome, is marked on the 2d of June; the second, on the 16th of September. [10] The third Saint Cecilia, suffered martyrdom in Africa, during the persecution of Diocletian, .with Sts. Saturninus, Dativus, and Felix, who are mentioned in the Roman Martyrology, on the 11th of February. [11]

In the interval which elapsed between the first discovery of Cecilia's body, in 822, and the second, which took place eight centuries later, there was no certainty as to the condition in which St. Paschal had left the body in closing the tomb. It was universally the custom to remove some portions of the holy relics before sealing the new sepulchre; [12] this may have given rise to the supposition that the sacred bones attributed to Cecilia, belonged to the jnost celebrated martyr of that name. This was firmly believed; the reopening of the tomb could alone solve this great problem and supply the records omitted in Paschal's document. The two heads preserved in the Churches of St. Martin of Tours, and St. Lucian of Beauvais, may be attributed to either of the two Roman martyrs of whom we spoke, or to the one who died in Africa.

Again, it would be necessary to know whether there were two entire heads or simply different parts of the same head. Churches frequently glory in possessing the body of a saint, when they have only a valuable portion of his bones; it is the same for the head, arms, or other principal members, and this mode of expression, which is perfectly familiar to all persons acquainted with this branch of religious archaeology, was already in use in the fourth and fifth centuries. [13] It, is, therefore possible, that the two relics preserved in the Churches of St. Martin of Tours and Saint Lucian of Beauvais, were but two portions of the same relic, under the name of the Head of St. Cecilia. If we come now to the relics of Fulda, which Rhaban Maur, a contemporary of Paschal, expressly declares to be those of the great Roman Martyr Cecilia, and of Saints Tiburtius and Valerian, we have the same reasons to allege.

In 1599, the body of St. Cecilia was found entire; hence the error in this case, as in the former one, probably resulted from similarity of name. The bones, of which Ehaban speaks, must have been those of another Cecilia, and must also have been very considerable, since he was able to distribute them among nine altars of his abbey.

We find less difficulty in believing that this Church possessed some of the bones of Valerian and Tiburtius. It is certain that Saint Paschal, in 822, separated the head of Saint Tiburtius from his body, and placed it in the Basilica. The bodies of the two martyrs were not found, in 1599, in the same state of preservation as that of St. Cecilia. It is very probable that St. Paschal had distributed some of their bones and that Rhaban had received a portion.

However, we will not be positive, because when the tomb was last opened, the bodies of the two brothers seemed complete, with the exception of Tiburtius' head, and we are rather inclined to believe that the relics of Fulda belonged to two other martyrs of the same name. A Saint Tiburtius is mentioned in the archives of the Roman Church, on the 11th of August, — he is still commemorated in the office of that day. A St. Valerian suffered also at Rome, with several other Martyrs, about the year 167; and finally the Western Martyrologies have preserved the remembrance of several other Sts. Valerian and Tiburtius, whose relics may have been removed, according to the usual custom, from one place to another, and this may have caused confusion.

We will add a few words respecting the relics of St. Cecilia which were preserved in the Church of St. Andrew at Kavenna, in the sixth century. At this period, and even long after, not only the linen which had touched a Saint's tomb, but also that used to cover his altar were considered relics; indeed even the oil of the lamps which burned before his body. The relics of which St. Venantius Fortunatus speaks, must have been of this nature, since for two centuries after this bishop's death, Cecilia still reposed in a sealed tomb of the Callistus Cemetery.

We trust the reader will pardon this little digression. We considered it absolutely necessary in a book, intended to contain every fact relative to our holy martyr. They will perhaps thank us for throwing some light upon the relics honored under her name. The solution was very easy in as much as it related to our history; but the matter required to be delicately handled, since it concerns the honor of churches. Too frequently, thoughtless or prejudiced men have attributed to fraud, what was the result of an innocent error proceeding from a similarity of names. We frankly acknowledge that it has given us great pleasure to proclaim on this occasion a new privilege extended to Cecilia even in her tomb. Buried by the hands of a martyr Pope, guarded in her sepulchre by the vigilance of the Mother of God, revealed to a supreme Pontiff in a heavenly apparition, her saintly body was found in a perfect state of preservation, surrounded by the eloquent tokens of her martyrdom. Paschal left it as he found it, that future generations might share the happiness he had enjoyed of contemplating the Spouse of Christ, trail quill v reposing in her glorious sleep. New wonders await us; but let us leave Cecilia, for some centuries yet, calmly resting, not beneath the crumbling vaults of the Callistus Cemetery, but amidst the splendor of her own palace.

[1] Venantii *Fortunati Carmima.* part i. lib. i. carra. ii.
[2] *Rhabani Mauri.* Opp. tome iv. page 231.
[3] *Rhabani Mauri.* Tome vi., pages 215-221.
[4] Laderchi. tome ii., pages 11-14
[5] Gervaise, Vie de St. Martin., page 426.
[6] Du Saussay, Martyrelogium Gallicanum, tome ii., page 1231.
[7] Baillet, Vies des Saints, 22 Novembre.
[8] Gallia Christiana, tome i., page 33.
[9] Du Saussay. *Ibid.*
[10] Florentini. Martyrolog. St. Hieronynii. anj jours indiques.
[11] See also Dom Ruinart. *Acta Sincera Martyrum.* page 409.
[12] Although in olden times relics were not often divided, still the numerous miracles wrought after the finding of St. Stephen's body, did not prevent the precious bones of this martyr being dispersed throughout Africa, as St. Augustin attests. At the period in which St. Paschal lived, this practice had become still more common, and if the holy Pontiff left Cecilia's body entire, as was proved later, it must be attributed to a special dispensation of Providence.
[13] St. Basil, in his homily upon the forty Martyrs (opp. tome ii. p. 155) remarks that although the relics of these saints were divided among a large number of cities, yet each city was justified in considering that it possessed the entire body.

Theodoret is still more explicit: "Although the entire bodies of the martyrs are not in the casket, although these frequently contain but a small portion of their bones, still we commonly call these relics the bodies of the Martyrs." Epist. cxxx. ad Timotheum. Opp. Tom. iv. p. 1218. Halae. 1771.

Chapter Twenty-Five - Events Relating to Cecilia and Her Basilica throughout the Course of the Ninth & Tenth Centuries. Homage Rendered to Cecilia in the Greek Liturgy

The ninth century, celebrated for the Translation of innumerable martyrs from the obscurity of the Catacombs to the Churches of Rome, was also remarkable for the Martyrologies compiled in various countries. Those attributed to St. Jerome and Venerable Bede, were too incomplete to satisfy the piety of the faithful, and the glory of the church imperatively demanded new and fuller details of the heroism of her saints.

About 847, Rhaban Maur published a work intended as a supplement to the Martyrology of Bede. Soon after, (859), St. Ado, Archbishop of Vienna, followed Rhaban in the same career, and in 876, Usuard, a monk of St. Germain des Près, published a Martyrology, at the request of Charles the Bald. This being more correct than those of his predecessors, he has the honor of having prepared the venerable text which the Apostolic See, after having submitted it to the learned Baronius, presented to the universal Church under the name of the Roman Martyrology. Such was the Catholic enthusiasm in this matter, in the ninth century, that even in the year 850, Wandelbert, a monk of Prum, opened, by a martyrology in verse, the magnificent series of poems for every day of the Ecclesiastical year, which comes down to the seventeenth century.

All these Martyrologists speak of St. Cecilia with considerable detail; but no one develops the subject so clearly as St. Ado, who seems to have wished to give an abridgement of her Acts. The approbation of so many men, versed in the study of sacred monuments, gives additional authority to this document, handed down with so much respect from the fifth century. The authors of the martyrologies of the ninth century, may have made some errors here and there; but it would be a serious literary injustice not to recognize as a confirmatory argument, their unanimous opinion, concerning the value of an historical document; particularly when this document had been considered authentic in preceding ages. Men, influenced by undue partiality, may affect to despise the testimony of Ado and Usuard, but we can produce in favor of these learned men, considered simply as critics, the testimony of Dom Ruinart and of Bossuet, neither of whom can be accused of too blind admiration for the legendaries of the middle age. [1]

The successors of Paschal inherited his interest in the Basilica which he had restored with so much splendor, and adorned with such precious treasures.

In 827, Gregory IV. presented to the Altar of St. Cecilia, a fabric of velvet embroidered with eagles and griffins, and fringed with purple and gold. [2]

In the ninth century, devotion to St. Cecilia began to spread throughout the Churches of the East, where her name had not hitherto been inscribed on the list of Saints; later, the West accepted in return into her Calends the illustrious virgins Catherine, Barbara, and Margaret. The discovery of Cecilia's body not only filled the Latin Church with joy, but spread her fame in countries where she was comparatively unknown. A Greek version of her Acts appeared in Constantinople towards the end of the same century. Its translator was the famous holy writer Simon Metaphrastes, Chancellor of the Emperor Leo VI., the philosopher, who reigned from 886 to 911. "We do not undertake the task of defending this pious and celebrated personage from the accusations made against him, but we do certify that Metaphrastes translated with scrupulous fidelity the Roman manuscript of the Acts of St. Cecilia. It is easy to compare his translation with the original, and we have done so with much pleasure, as it has enabled us to justify this laborious writer whose services have been hitherto repaid with ingratitude.

The Greek Menology, which corresponds to the Latin Martyrology, was definitively compiled towards the close of the tenth century. All the amateurs of antique liturgies are well acquainted with the celebrated manuscript of this book, compiled by order of the Emperor Basil Porphyrogenetes, who ascended the Byzantine throne in 976. This Menology, which was published at Urbino 1727, with curious vignettes of the first six months, from September to February, contains a notice of St. Cecilia on the 24th of November, in the style of the "Western Martyrologies. To avoid repetition we will not transcribe the passage. We merely wished to mention this first notice of the martyr in the Greek liturgy. The Church of Constantinople, then still united to the Apostolic See, was not satisfied with this purely historical homage rendered to St. Cecilia. At this time, was completed that part of the Greek Liturgy which corresponds to our Proper Masses of the Saints; they were compiled by the most pious and skilful among the Greek writers of sacred verses. The following are some of the stanzas dedicated to the Roman virgin:

"Cecilia, worthy of all praise! thou hast preserved thy body from all stain, and thy heart from sensual love! Thou hast presented thyself to thy Creator aa an immaculate Spouse, whose happiness was consummated by martyrdom; He received thee as a spotless virgin, and owned thee as His Spouse!

"The Lord, in his wisdom, vouchsafed to crown thy brow with the fragrance of roses, O holy virgin! Thou wert the link which united two brothers in the same happiness, and thy prayers assisted them.

"Abandoning the impure worship of idols, they proved themselves worthy of the mercy of Him who was born of a Virgin, and who permitted His blood to be poured out for us like a precious perfume.

"In thy desire for the treasures of heaven, thou didst despise the riches of earth; disdaining the love of mortals, thou didst chose a place among the choir of virgins, and thy wisdom guided thee to the heavenly Spouse.

"Thou didst valiantly combat and trample underfoot the malice of the demon, O, thou honor of the Athletes of Christ!

"Glorious Cecilia, august martyr! thou art the holy temple of Christ, His noble dwelling, His pure abode. Deign to intercede for us who celebrate thy praises.

"Ravished with the beauty of Christ, strengthened by His love, sighing after His joys, thou didst die to the world, and wert found worthy of eternal life.

"A spiritual love made thee disdain the affections of earth; thy discourse, replenished with wisdom, inflamed the heart of thy Spouse with the love of holy virginity; thou art now united with Him in the choirs of angels. O, martyr, worthy of heaven's reward!

"An angel of light was ever by thy side, surrounding thee with divine splendor; His arm guarded thy purity, and kept thee ever chaste and pleasing to Christ.

"Thou, O, Valerian, didst desire baptism; an envoy from heaven appeared; he enlightened thy mind, declaring to thee the sacred oracles; he enrolled thy name among the heavenly choir, whilst thou wert yet combating on earth."

"Thou, O, Tiburtius! quitting the path of error, didst gain the knowledge of heavenly things; despising this perishable life, thou didst eagerly hasten to immortality; believing in the adorable Trinity with thy whole soul, thou hast combated as a valiant warrior! O, Cecilia! the desire of possessing God, and His holy love, burned in thy inmost soul, and consumed thy entire being; thou wert an angel in a mortal frame. With intrepid courage thou didst bare thy neck to the sword; thy blood consecrated the ground which received it, and thy soul sanctified the air in its flight to heaven.

"The three children changed the flames of the fiery furnace into dew, and thou, Cecilia, by the virtue of the baptismal waters, sang, like them, in the midst of seething vapors: 'Be thou blessed, O God of my fathers!' Thou art the enclosed garden, the sealed fountain, the veiled loveliness, the glorious Spouse adorned with a brilliant diadem, the blooming paradise of the Heavenly King, O, Cecilia, replenished with God!"

[1] Dom Ruinart, in his History of the Persecution of the Vandals, wishing to prove the antiquity and authenticity of the Acts of the holy Martyrs, Liboratus and his companions, cites in full the notice given by the Martyrologists of the ninth century, and thus expresses his confidence in them: "Haec fusius referre visum est, prout in illis authoribus habentur, ut clarum sit jam nono saeculo persuasum fuisse *viris Historiae sacra studiosis,* Victorem nostrum hujus sanctorum monachorum Passionis authorem fuisse." (*Historia persecutionis Vandalicae,* page 97, n° 3.)

Bossuet in *la Defense de la Declaration,* citing, in support of his Thesis, (the responsibility of which we are far from assuming) a passage from the Acts of St. Eusebius, a priest of Rome, thus declares his favorable opinion of these Acts; Hactenus Acta, ubi innata simplicitate ipsa se prodit antiquitatis, et quibus ejus generis Actorum aliquis inest gustus, hoc sapient. *Tum Usuardus monachus, et Ado Viennensis haec Acta viderunt;* ex quorum qurppe verbis brevem illam quam suis Martyrologiis inserunt, sancti Eusebii contexunt historiam." *Defensio cleri Gallicani,* part ii, lib. xv, cap. xxxiv.
[2] Anastas in Gregor. IV.

Chapter Twenty-Six - Events Relating to Cecilia and Her Basilica throughout the Eleventh, Twelfth, Thirteenth, and Fourteenth Centuries. Veneration Paid to the Roman Virgin in France

The eleventh, one of the greatest of Christian centuries, owes its principal glory to Saint Gregory VII. This Pontiff could not fail to venerate the generous virgin, who had won the admiration of Urban, in the heroic days of faith. Gregory, the martyr of Christian liberty, whose energetic and tender soul showed its power in the struggle against the Empire, at the same time that it poured forth its sweetness in his letters to the pious Countess Matilda, was devoted to Cecilia's glory, and humbly solicited her patronage. He renewed the altar of the trans-Tiberian Basilica, embellished it with a silver statue of the saint, and solemnly dedicated it in 1075, the third year of his Pontificate. The inscription which recalls this event, was placed in the crypt, where it was seen in the thirteenth century, when the altar was renewed. It is thus conceived:

DEDICATVM EST HOC ALTARE DIE III. MENSIS IVNII PER DNVM GRE-
GORIVM PP. VII. ANNO DNI MLXXV.

When this giant of the Lord had finished his course, and traced out a path for his successors, he expired at Salerno, pronouncing these forcible words, which will re-echo throughout ages: "I have loved justice and hated iniquity; therefore do I die an exile." His death occurred on the twenty-fifth of May, feast of St. Urban; hence the names of these two great Pontiffs were united in the Christian calendar, as they had been in their reverence for Cecilia. This holy martyr assisted the Roman Church in the eleventh century, with even more power than in the days of Almachius. [1]

At this period, the different altars of the Basilica were rebuilt and consecrated anew, and the Cardinal Bishops were so eager to obtain the favor of the Spouse of Christ, that they would not permit any other prelates to dedicate them. We find from an ancient deed, preserved in the archives of the

Basilica, that the altar of our Saviour, situated to the left of that of the Confession, was dedicated on the 22d of May, 1060, by Humbert, Bishop of St. Rufine, the same who was so zealous for the interests of the Apostolic See, when sent as legate to Constantinople, at the time when Byzantium was preparing to consummate her schism. This same bishop was also sent on a mission to France, where, by his zeal, he crushed the heresy of Berengarius.

John, Bishop of Porto, who exerted so much influence in the election of Gregory VII., to whom he remained inviolably faithful, consecrated on the 25th of May, 1071, the altar of the Blessed Virgin; and, on the 3d, of January, 1072, that of St. John, *ad fontem*.

As we before stated, the bath room in which Cecilia suffered martyrdom, had been transformed into a chapel; Ubald, Bishop of Sabine, dedicated its altar on the 17th of September, 1073. [2] Finally, the altar of St. Mammes, situated to the left of the grand altar, was consecrated on the 24th of February, 1098, under the pontificate of Urban II. by Maurice, Bishop of Porto. [3]

Thus, in the latter part of the eleventh century, the Basilica of St. Cecilia seemed to share in the universal renovation, which was felt throughout the whole Church of Jesus Christ.

Before his death, Gregory VII. had designated as his successor, Didier, the Abbot of Mont Cassin, Titulary Cardinal of St. Cecilia's church. After a determined refusal of nine months, the humble monk finally yielded, and, under the name of Victor III. assumed the government of the Church. He directed it with great success for eighteen months, when he was called to receive the reward of the elect. The trans-Tiberian Basilica counted in him the third Pontiff she had given to the universal church.

The twelfth century offers us some graceful stanzas in honor of St. Cecilia, found in a long sequence upon Christian virginity, attributed to the venerable Aelred, a Cistercian monk of the Abbey of Rieval, in England. [4] She is also mentioned with praise in a discourse of the learned and pious Honorius of Autun. We find in the three following centuries, innumerable sermons in honor of this glorious martyr, written by the most talented men of the middle age. William of Paris, Albert the Great, St. Thomas of Aquin, St. Bonaventure, St. Vincent Ferrier, are among the panegyrists of St. Cecilia. We regret that the style of these authors is too dry to admit of our citing any passages from their sermons, which are rather scholastic than oratorical. They are, however, precious links in the uninterrupted chain of homage paid to the memory of the generous martyr throughout the course of ages.

Many other historians of this period were equally eager to celebrate Cecilia's merits; Vincent de Beauvais in his *"Historical Mirror,"* Jacques DeVoragine in his *Golden Legend,* Peter De Natalibus in his *Lives of the Saints,* and finally Saint Antoninus, in his Chronicle, are distinguished among others for the accuracy with which they have adhered to the substance of the primitive Acts. The Church at this time shone with the virtues and prodigies of the Saints who illustrated the last three centuries of the Middle Age. Cecilia's name was dear to all the friends of God, and this glorious Spouse of Christ frequently rewarded their love by appearing to them. St. Dominic saw the Mother of God enter the dormitory of his disciples, accompanied by Cecilia. [5] The Queen of Angels appeared to the Blessed Reginald, to reveal to him his vocation to the order of Friar Preachers and on that occasion also was attended by Cecilia. [6] Some of the brightest spirits of heaven were sent to console St. Peter of Verona with pious colloquies, and the future martyr was likewise favored with a vision of St. Cecilia resplendent with glory, and accompanied by Agnes and Catherine. [7]

The Blessed Oringa, a Florentine virgin, avoided without effort all the dangers which threatened her chastity, and the infernal spirits being interrogated by a libertine, who was tired of soliciting her in vain, replied, that the servant of God was under the guardianship of the same Angel who had protected the virginity of Cecilia. St. Frances, the Roman prophetess of the fifteenth century, before founding her celebrated monastery of Turrem Speculorum, had chosen for her favorite resort the Church of St. Cecilia, which was not far from the palace Ponziani where she dwelt. She loved to partake of the holy mysteries near the Virgin's tomb; where often, rapt in ecstacy, she heard and saw the mysteries of heaven. There also she buried her two children, whom the Lord called to Himself in their infancy — Evangelist, in his 9th year, and Agnes not yet five. [8] France also joined in the homages which were universally rendered to Cecilia. Bernard of Chatenet, Bishop of Alby, on the 15th of August, 1282, laid the corner stone of his magnificent Cathedral, one of the most astonishing specimens of the ogive architecture in France, and the most imposing of all the monuments erected in Cecilia's honor. The work was carried on by the Bishops, Berald de Fargues, Jean de Sayo, Guillaume de la Voulte, and, finally, Louis d'Amboise who dedicated it on the 23d of April, 1480; it was not, however, entirely completed until 1512, wlien Charles de Eobertet was bishop of Alby. Built of brick which has become blackened by time, terminated at the western extremity by an immense tower which rests on four galleries and rises four hundred feet above the waters of the Tarn, the Church of St. Cecilia d'Alby, with its severe aspect, and walls one hundred and fifteen feet in height, looks more like a formidable fortress, than a temple consecrated to the Virgin whose name it bears. But the interior of this noble building is such as befits the sanctuary of the Queen of Harmony. Its vast nave, destitute of columns, rearing its vaulted roof ninety-two feet above the pavement, and surrounded by twenty-nine chapels, presents an animated appearance, not only on account of the graceful and yet imposing effect of its domes and arches, but also from the admirable blending of statuary and painting. This Church is deservedly considered the most complete in all its parts, of any, this side of the Alps.

In an architectural point of view, we cannot sufficiently admire the marvellous art with which the progressive developments of the ogival style are blended. All is correct; no violent transition offends the eye, or disturbs the

135

graceful effect of the united whole. The choir corresponds with the rest of the edifice. Louis d'Amboise placed opposite to one of the side doors, the effigy of Constantine, and opposite to the other, that of Charlemagne. The interior is adorned with a prodigious number of graceful and elegant statues, placed in fanciful stone niches. That nothing may be wanting to this sublime Cathedral, the whole edifice is covered with paintings. Scenes from the Old and New Testament and from the Lives of the Saints, the History of the Church, the Last Judgment and the torments of hell, cover the pilasters, the walls, and the small chapels. The rich azure of the vaulted ceiling is also resplendent with brilliant and graceful designs, a harmonious profusion of fanciful arabesques, ornaments of the acanthus, escutcheons, and medallions, sparkling with gold, which is as fresh as the ultramarine ground work that relieves the whole. Such, in a few words, is a description of the superb sanctuary which the piety of France has dedicated to Cecilia, but the veneration of the French people towards the heroic virgin, was manifested even in Rome. Guillame de Bois-Eatier, Archbishop of Bourges, in his zeal for Cecilia's glory, descended into the crypts of the Appian Way, and finding that the tomb which, for six centuries, had preserved her body, was unornamented, he caused the empty sepulchre of the great martyr to be embellished at his own expense. [9] The monument which he erected has been destroyed; but the inscription which may still be seen, bears the following words:

HIC QVONDAM RECONDITVM
FVIT CORPVS BEATAE CAECILIAE
VIRGINIS ET MARTYRIS.
HOC OPVS FECIT FIERI REVERENDISSIMVS
PATER DOMINVS GVILLELMVS ARCIEPS
BITVRICENSIS ANNO DOMINI MCCCC NONO. [10]

More than once, French Cardinals presided as Titularies, in the marble pulpit which was erected in the centre of the apsis of the Church, so proud of containing the relics of its noble patroness. The most illustrious of all was unquestionably Simon de Brie, who was created Cardinal by Urban IV., in 1262, and placed upon the Apostolic Chair under the name of Martin IV., in 1281. He was the fourth Pope appointed from the Church of Saint Cecilia. This Pontiff, who governed Christendom with honor during the short space of four years, presented two donations to the Basilica as a proof of his devotion. The first was a silver statue, adorned with precious stones; [11] the second, a much more valuable gift, was the promotion of John Cholet, Bishop of Beauvais, to the Cardinalate with the Title of Presbyter of St. Cecilia's church. This prelate was very successful in important legations to France and Arragon; he also founded in Paris the college which for a long time bore his name. [12]

In 1283, he rebuilt with magnificence the Altar of the Confession, which had been consecrated by Gregory VII. two centuries previously. With the exception of some embellishments made in the seventeenth century, of which we shall speak later, the altar is the same used at the present day. The inscription engraved upon it by the architect of John Cholet in the thirteenth century, runs thus:

HOC OPVS FECIT ARNVLFVS ANNO MCCLXXXIII.

Vasari thinks that the Arnulphe above mentioned is the celebrated ornamental painter Arnolfo di Lapo. The altar is ornamented with a rich mosaic upon a slab of that beautiful violet-colored marble called *paonazzetto*. Arnolfo's work is completed by a *ciborium* formed of four columns of black marble, spotted with white, called by the Italians *preconesio.*

Under Clement V., in 1312, the Church of St. Cecilia was again confided to a French Cardinal, Guillaume Godin, of the order of Friar Preachers, who at a later period was appointed Bishop of Sabine. [13] Clement VI., in 1342, entrusted it to Guy of Boulogne, Archbishop of Lyons, who resigned that See in the same year, and became Bishop of Porto. [14] In the following century, in 1426, Martin V. bestowed the title of St. Cecilia upon the last French bishop, whose name was placed among the Beatified. This was Louis d'Alleman, Archbishop of Aries, famous for hostility to the Holy See in the conventicle of Basle, but more happily celebrated for the generous confession of his fault, at the feet of Nicholas V. [15] who restored to him the title of which Eugene IV. Had deprived him. Louis d'Alleman was succeeded in the Church of Saint Cecilia by another French prelate, who had followed him in the path of error, and who had also imitated the sincerity of his repentance, Louis de la Palu, whose public career commenced with the council of Constance. He had been created cardinal by Nicholas V., in 1449. In the sixteenth century there were many French cardinals who held the Church of St. Cecilia. The first was Gabriel de Grandmont, Bishop of Tarbes, who was promoted to the purple by Clement VII. He died in 1534, after having occupied the Sees of Poitiers, Bordeaux, and Toulouse. The next, under Paul III., was John of Bellay, Bishop of Paris, who governed at the same time the Churches of Limoges, Mans, and afterwards Bordeaux; he was but a short time titulary of the Church of St. Cecilia. In 1560, he died, Bishop of Ostia [16] Robert de Lénoncourt, Bishop of Chalonssur-Marne, created cardinal by Paul III., obtained in his turn the title of St. Cecilia. [17] This prelate, who, according to a still prevailing abuse, possessed at the same time several bishoprics, is the same who erected in the Church attached to the Abbey of Rheims, the magnificent tomb of the Apostle of the French. Finally, the last French cardinal, who held the title of St. Cecilia, was Charles de Guise of the house of Lorraine, Archbishop of Rheims, who received the cardinal's hat in 1547. Like the two preceding, he was promoted to this dignity by Paul III. [18] The influence of this prelate in the general affairs of the Church, more especially at the Council of Trent, is well known.

We cannot conclude this chapter without mentioning an illustrious cardinal who held the title of St. Cecilia in the fourteenth century. He does not indeed belong to France, like those we have just mentioned, being an Englishman and a Benedictine; but his literary fame sheds a glory over his country and his order. Adam Eston, a professed friar of the Abbey of Norwich, was the most accomplished hebraist of his time, and the catalogue of his writings would alone be sufficient to place him at the head of the learned men of his age. Urban VI. rewarded such exalted merit with the honors of the purple, Eston's career was, nevertheless, a stormy one, and from the time of his elevation to the cardinalate, he knew no repose until the day when, having yielded his soul to God, his mortal remains were deposited in the Basilica of St. Cecilia. The following epitaph was placed upon his tomb:

ARTIBVS ISTE PATER FAMOSVS IN OMNIBVS ADAM
THEOLOGVS SUMMVS CARDI-QUE-NALIS ERAT.
ANGLIA CVI PATRIAM TITVLVM DEDIT ISTA BEATAE
AEDES CECILIA MORSQVE BEATA POLVM [19]

[1] This blending of the names of Sts. Urban and Gregory VII. on the 25th of May, was remarked in the eleventh century by the contemporary biographer of the latter Pontiff, and we cannot resist the pleasure of citing his eloquent remarks upon the heroic death of Gregory:

Itaque septiformi gratia plenus Septimi Gregorii spiritus, qui mundum et principes ejus arguebat de peccato, et de injustitia et de judicio, in fortitudine caelestis cibi nuper accepti, caelestem viam arripiens, meritoque divini zeli, velut igneo curru instar Eliae subvectus, *Urbani praedecessoris sui cujus ea die festivitas extitit,* omniumque beatorum laetitiam in caelesti gloria cum Christo gaudentium excellenter ampliavit. *Paulus Bernrieden S. Gregorii VII. vita, Cap.* xii. *Acta SS. Maii. Tome* vi. page 102.

[2] Altare Sanctae Ceciliae, quod est in Balneo ejus.

[3] See in Laderchi, Vol. ii, page 10-15, the deed which relates to the dedication of these altars.

[4]

Istos flores virtutis geminae,	Quos attulit Sanctae Caeciliae,
Transplantavit in mente virgine	De secreto divinae patriae
Filius hominis.	Coelestis nuncius.
Quos diversos facit nativitas,	Ne flagraret carnis concubitu,
Non disjungit nlla diversitas	Conflagrata divino spiritu
In caput Virginis.	Caro puellulae.
Rosa floris coruscat libere,	nec timeret ensem sanguineum
Flos lilii non minus prospere	Vel catastae stridorem ferreum
Candet interius.	Corpus juvenculae.

Mancipata divino cultui,	Spiritali rore refrigerans
Consecravit Sancto Spiritui	Aestus carnis, mundique temperans
Suum conjugium.	Omne ludibrium.
	Biblioth, vett Patrum, tome xxiii, page 168.

[5] Acta SS. Augusti, vol. i.

[6] Theodorio *de Appoldia.* lib. ii. cap. xiii.

[7] Acta SS. Aprilis, tome iii.

[8] Acta SS. Martii tome ii. We regret that it is impossible to insert among the communications which the servants of God have had with St. Cecilia, several admirable incidents of the life of the Venerable Mother Agnes of Jesus, prioress of the Dominican convent at Langeac. This great Saint professed a special devotion to our martyr, and was frequently honored by her visits. The interviews which took place between the glorified and the militant Virgin, may be found in full in La vie de la Mere Agnes de Jesus par l'Abbe de Lantages pages 230, 608, 611. We shall find in these interviews all the strength and tenderness so admirably depicted in the Acts of the Roman Virgin.

[9] Labbe. *Biblioth.* MSS. t tome ii. page 130.

[10] Here formerly reposed the body of the Blessed Cecilia, Virgin and Martyr. This monument was erected by order of William, Archbishop of Bourges, the year of our Lord 1409.

[11] Ciaccouius. *Vitae et res gestae Pontificum Romanorum et S. R. E. Cardinalium,* tome ii, page 238.

[12] *Ibid.* page 239.

[13] Ciacconius, tome ii., page 384.

[14] *Ibid.,* page 403. Gallia Christiana, tome iv., p. 105.

[15] *Ibid.,* page 841.

[16] Ciaccoilrus, tome iii., page 568.

[17] *Ibid.,* page 646.

[18] *Ibid.,* page 724.

[19] Ciacconius. *Ibid.,* tome ii., page 649. Ziegelbauer, *Hist, rei litterar.* O. S. B., tome iii., p. 185 et seq.

Chapter Twenty-Seven - Events Relating to Cecilia and Her Basilica throughout the Fifteenth and Sixteenth Centuries. Homage Paid by Literature and the Arts to the Roman Virgin

In the year 1484, the Bacilica of St. Cecilia gave a fifth Pope to the Church, John Baptist Cibo, under the name of Innocent VIII. [1] A short time after his exaltation, he invested Lawrence Cibo, his nephew, with the purple, giving him at first the title of St. Susanna, which he afterwards changed for that of St. Cecilia. This cardinal was very munificent in his donations to the Basilica.

He restored the inner porch, renewed the chapel of the bathroom, where his coat of arms may still be seen; but he respected the altar and pavement of this venerable sanctuary, and these preserve their mediaeval character.

Numerous modifications successively made in this chapel, had entirely destroyed its primitive character. Pompey Ugonius, who wrote in 1588, declares that in his time this sacred place was called the Thalamus or Oratorium of St. Cecilia, and that there were old men who remembered having venerated in their youth the bathroom, in which the holy virgin suffered martyrdom; but he adds, that all traces of this room had disappeared, either because it had not been considered a monument of much, importance, or from some other reason.

In the eleventh century, tradition expressly declared that Cecilia's bathroom was in this place, and that Cardinal Ubaldus, Bishop of Sabine, had dedicated an altar there in 1073. Before long all uncertainty will cease, and we shall see this holy place, such as it appeared on the day of Cecilia's martyrdom, thus restoring to her dwelling its most important apartment to which are linked the most sacred remembrances.

The monks of the monastery, which St. Paschal built near the Basilica of St. Cecilia, did not persevere in the practice of the Benedictine Rules, and the building, like many others, was finally changed into a collegiate church. Thenceforth Divine service was not celebrated with the same zeal at Cecilia's tomb. In 1417, Martin V. gave the Church and monastery to the congregation of the Saviour, founded by St. Bridget; [2] but these religious did not long retain possession of it, and before the end of the fifteenth century the Benedictines were once more established at Sancta Cecilia. [3]

The Lombard congregation of the Humiliati, a branch of the Benedictines, were installed in the monastery after the departure of the Brigittines; but from the beginning of the sixteenth century, the congregation became so reduced that their number was not sufficiently large to take charge of the monasteries placed under their care. Clement VII. concluded to make it a commendatory benifice, and, in 1532, conferred it upon Cardinal Franciotto Orsini. [4] This venerable sanctuary had been so sadly neglected during these disastrous years, that it was barely possible to celebrate the Divine office in it on the feast of St. Cecilia, and on the day of the station which was solemnized each year in this Basilica on the Wednesday of the second week of Lent. It seemed God's will to send these dark clouds as a prelude to the incomparable splendor which was destined in 1527 to illuminate this Basilica and restore the glory which had suffered a momentary eclipse.

At the time when the commendary seemed about to destroy Paschal's pious foundation, the Lord inspired one of his servants with a design which saved it. Maura Magalotta, the pious abbess of the Benedictines of the Campus Martius, urged Clement VII. to allow her the privilege of going to dwell with those of her sisters who wished to accompany her in the monastery of St. Cecilia, and that she might not interfere with the congregation of the Humiliati, to whom the house was supposed to belong, she offered to adopt their Constitutions.

The Pope was both edified and pleased with the proposition of the abbess; but he could not grant her request without the consent of the Titulary Cardinal. This Franciotto Orsini generously gave, and in honor of St. Cecilia resigned the rich benifice which had been bestowed upon him four year's previously. Clement VII. had at this time retired to the Castle of St. Angelo, where he was besieged by the Constable de Bourbon. From this fortress he dated the Bull which ensured the permanent celebration of the Divine office in the Basilica, according to St. Paschal's intentions. The Bull was dated the seventh of the Calends of July, in *Arce Sancti Angeli;* it authorized the removal of Mother Maura Magalotta to the monastery of St. Cecilia, creating her abbess of the congregation of the Humiliati, under the rule of St. Benedict. [5]

It is well known that this order was suppressed by St. Pius V. in 1575, in punishment of an attempt made by one of its members at Milan to assassinate St. Charles Borromeo; but the Pontiff, far from extending this chastisement to the monastery of St. Cecilia, which was flourishing with so much edification, took it under his special protection, and enriched it with new privileges. Later, the female congregation of the Humiliati having become extinct, the Benedictines of the Campus Martius were called upon to take charge of the monastery. In memory of their sisters, who had been established here by Clement VII., the nuns of St. Cecilia wear the white habit formerly worn by the Humiliati.

Maura Magalotta devoted herself with zeal to the reparation of her dear Basilica, which was somewhat dilapidated, and made important improvements in the monastery, the enclosure of which she enlarged. An inscription placed over the principal door of this holy house records the services of the worthy abbess, [6] who died on the 17th of May, 1566, aged seventy-two years. She was buried in the Basilica, before the altar of the Confession, by Mother Scholastica Serleoni, who succeeded her. [7]

In 1584, under Gregory XIII., two altars were re-dedicated in St. Cecilia's Church. One of the two had borne the title of St. Mammes, and had been consecrated in 1098, as we before stated, by Maurice, Bishop of Porto, under Urban II. It was now destined to be the altar of the blessed sacrament, and was dedicated on the 7th of August, by Thomas Goldwell, Bishop of St. Asaph. [8] The relics which had served for the first consecration, in 1098, were again placed in the altar. Among these relics, were found some bones attributed to St. Cecilia; we have already spoken of them, but the moment was now approaching, when it was to be fully proved that they could not have belonged to our martyr.

In the preceding year, Gregory XIII. had given the purple to Nicholas Sfondrato, Bishop of Cremona. This Prelate, who was of an illustrious Milanese family, and of distinguished piety, received the Title of St. Cecilia, and seven years after was elected to the chair of St. Peter. He took the name of

Gregory XIV. and was the seventh Pope from the Basilica of St. Cecilia. After ten months of a brilliant Pontificate, he died, but fortunately not before he had elevated to the Cardinalate, his nephew, Paul Emile Sfondrato, whose name is held in veneration by all who are interested in the glory of our illustrious virgin.

But before relating the great event which heaven seemed to have held in reserve, only to throw more vivid light upon the Acts of St. Cecilia, and to re-animate the enthusiasm of the faithful towards this Spouse of Christ, we will devote some pages to recording the homage paid her by literature and the arts. We have already listened to the harmonious cadence of the Sacramentaries, the musical hymns of the Mozarabic rite of Christian Greece, the epithalamium of the Saxon Bishop, the uncultivated verses of Flodoard, the flowing sequence of the twelfth century; all these have formed a poetical concert to Cecilia's glory. The pious Thomas A. Kempis now offers his tribute of veneration to the Roman virgin, in a most devotional hymn, and a charming acrostic. [9]

He is soon followed by the celebrated Latin poet, Baptista Spagnuolo, called the Mantuan, who consecrated to Cecilia his seventh Parthenia, dedicated to Isabella, Duchess of Mantua. This poem of nine hundred verses, filled with profane reminiscences, like all the compositions of the Mantuan, is written in the pagan style of the period in which its author lived; it nevertheless contains many graceful and easy verses.

We will not extend this list of the compositions which form the poetical crown of Cecilia, but we cannot pass over in silence the Epithalamium of Angelo Sangrini, Abbot of Monte Casino, in which the author extols the holy martyr, whom Italy particularly venerated in the sixteenth century. This century, which gave to the Church the Annals of Baronius, and the Controversies of Bellarmine, had also the glory of collecting the Acts of the Saints, thus preluding the immortal compilation of the Jesuits of Anvers. The different collections of this nature, which appeared at this epoch, all make honorable mention of Cecilia. From Bonino Mombrizzio, who opened this new path to sacred erudition in the early part of the fifteenth century, by his *Sanctuarum,* dedicated to Simonetta, secretary of the Duchess of Milan, down to the Carthusian friar, Lawrence Surius, who, in 1568, published his Original Lives of the Saints, (comprising in the interval, the *Agiologium* of George Wicklius, in 1541, and the collection of Louis Lipoman, Bishop of Verona and Bergama) the Acts of St. Cecilia were faithfully reproduced. Surius was inclined to follow Metaphrastes, who, as we have said, borrowed them from the Latin; and the translation from the Greek, compared with the Roman manuscript, shows the great respect with which the religious writer of Constantinople treated the touching relation of Cecilia's virtues and martyrdom. The arts were even more eager to glorify the daughter of the Cecilii. Architecture paid its tribute in an elegant Roman Basilica, with its marbles, mosaics, and sumptuous decorations, and in the magnificent Cathedral of Alby, with the majesty, grace, and boldness of its proportions. The statuary of the Middle Age paid its homage by placing the noble and placid image of St. Cecilia, under the porticoes of our Cathedrals, where she stands like a queen among the Spouses of Christ. We shall hereafter speak of the masterpiece with which Stephen Maderno enriched the Roman Basilica. It represents the virgin sleeping in her mysterious tomb. [10]

But Catholic *painters,* have, as it were, surpassed themselves, in endeavoring to express the charm and grandeur recalled by Cecilia's name. We will not undertake here an enumeration which would far exceed the limits of this monograph. We leave to others, the pleasure of describing the large stained windows on which is traced the history of our martyr, the graceful illustrations of liturgical manuscripts, the inspired works of the mystical school of the fifteenth century, and all the marvellous testimonies of love given her by so many artists. We shall content ourselves with mentioning the mosaic of Ravenna in the sixth century, already described, as well as that which St. Paschal caused to be executed in the apsis of the Basilica when the Virgin's body was translated thither; these two mosaics seem to be the most ancient representations of St. Cecilia which have reached us. The ninth century offers us a miniature, in the Menology of the Emperor Basil, representing the martyrdom of the Saint. We next mention a fresco of the twelfth century, painted in a crypt of the Basilica of St. Lawrence outside the walls. The painting is copied with great care in the magnificent collection of the frescos of the Catacombs, executed by M. Perret, and published by the French Government. There are many other interesting paintings, relating to the illustrious Virgin, in the ancient pagan temple near which St. Urban lived, and which has been converted into a Church. These paintings have been reproduced by Agin court in his *Histoire de l'Art par les monuments,* and are referred to the thirteenth century; they represent several incidents from the Acts of St. Cecilia. We trust that at some future day these frescoes will be published in a more suitable manner, as they are doubly interesting, both on account of their tasteful execution and of the Church which they ornament. At this same epoch, Cimabue painted a portrait of Cecilia. She is represented seated, veiled, and wrapt in a deep blue mantle, holding in one hand a palm branch, whilst the other rests upon a book of the Gospels. Eight small pictures of incidents taken from the Acts, surround the main figure, forming as it were a frame. By this representation, we see that in the thirteenth century, no special attribute was assigned to Cecilia. This painting, now in the gallery at Florence, was designed for a Church of St. Cecilia, which formerly stood in that city, but which has been destroyed. We refer to the thirteenth, and not to the ninth century, the graceful paintings in compartments which formerly adorned St. Cecilia's Church, only one of which has been saved. The others are only known by the copies which were taken before they had totally perished, and which are preserved in the Barberini Library, and also by the very imperfect engraving published by Bosio [11] in his edition of the Acts of Saint

Cecilia. The fresco which remains, represents the burial of the Virgin by St. Urban, and her apparition to Paschal; this latter scene is admirably executed. The mitre and pluviale [12] of the Pontiff do not permit us to date this picture before the thirteenth century; it may even be placed in the fourteenth. In the fifteenth century, we cannot omit Pinturicchio. who painted five subjects taken from the life of our illustrious Virgin, with that indefinable charm which characterizes all his productions. They may be seen at the gallery of Berlin. We must also speak of a charming fresco of the same century, now placed in the sacristy of the little Church, which, according to its ancient title, we have called St. Cecilia *de domo.*

It represents the Angel crowning Cecilia and Valerian; Tiburtius and Urban are also introduced. Although considerably defaced, the picture breathes an air of piety and recollection, and recalls the calm repose which is the charm of Angelico da Fiesole's productions. We do not intend to enumerate all the monuments of St. Cecilia, but we consider it a duty net to omit mentioning the admirable frescoes pain by Francisco Francia and his pupils, in a chapel of St James' Church, at Bologna. These pictures are composed often compartments: the subjects are borrowed from the Acts of the Saint, and are deservedly ranked among the noblest works of Catholic art, in its most brilliant period.

They have been inexcusably neglected and allowed to deteriorate, yet they still preserve much of their original beauty. The fresco which represents Cecilia's martyrdom, [13] is the only one which can be positively attributed to Francia; it is far superior to the others. These ten frescoes were engraven and published in 1825; but the engravings are so very imperfect, that it is to be hoped others will be made. Unfortunately, the entire series of paintings upon the Life of Saint Cecilia, executed by Taddeo Bartolo, in St. Dominic's Church at Perugia, has entirely perished. These different compositions show how highly the artists of this period appreciated our Acts. A precious document of the fifteenth century, recently published by M. Guignard, bookseller of Dijon, reveals to us that profound study, which enabled these artists to delineate with so much soul and truth, all the most delicate and dramatic incidents in the lives of the Saints.

This document contains the notes given to the artists who were charged with executing the cartoons of a tapestry destined for the collegiate Church of St. Urban de Troyes. The plan comprised six large pieces of tapestry, divided into twenty two subjects, ten of which were to represent events taken from the Acts of Saint Cecilia. The exactitude and attention with which the scenes chosen were first analyzed, and afterwards arranged in accordance with the simplicity of the times: the sentiment to be expressed, the attitudes of the figures introduced, the costumes; the details of surroundings; all prove a careful study of the Acts, and it is much to be regretted that this beautiful composition has perished, or, as Mr. Guignard is inclined to think, was never executed. We mention it, however, as one of the most touching homages offered by art to the memory of St. Cecilia. [14]

The great artists of the sixteenth century, did not forget Saint Cecilia. Their style was indeed little suited to the supernatural, yet we find that many among them delighted in painting Saint Cecilia. We might cite Garofalo, Procaccini, Paul Veronese, Salimbeni, Tempesta, Guido Reni, Carlo Dolci, etc.; but these painters sink into the shade by the side of the immortal Raphael. Who does not know that the Saint Cecilia of the Museum of Bologna, is classed among the great works of this prince of modern artists. Still we must acknowledge that many of the figures are wanting in that heavenly expression which characterizes all his early paintings. For the honor of Cecilia, we prefer therefore, mentioning first, the beautiful picture in the royal gallery at Naples, although she only figures in it as an accessory. Raphael painted it in 1505, for the religious of Saint Anthony of Perugia, The principal subject represents our Saviour taken down from the Cross and placed on his mother's knees, Saints Peter and Paul stand on one side, Saints Cecilia and Catherine on the other. The wonderful talent of the artist is very evident in these four figures, and thus we have a Cecilia truly worthy of the divine Raphael. [15] The painting at Bologna is chiefly valuable as a work of art: St. John the Evangelist and Saint Paul stand on the right of the martyr, St. Augustin and St. Mary Magdalen on her left. All these figures are incontestably beautiful, but there is no mystical expression about them. Magdalen in particular does not at all correspond with our idea of a holy penitent. There is a heavenly expression about Cecilia, but her embonpoint badly accords with our notions of a saint. Emblems of profane music are scattered at her feet; her lyre rests upon her knees; her eyes are raised to heaven and she seems listening to angelic concerts. This much admired painting was destined for the chapel of St. John *in Monte,* at Bologna. Vasari has asserted that Francesco Francia, after looking at it, died of jealousy. Happily for the honor of Catholic art, this is a mere fable. Raphael commenced his picture of St. Cecilia towards the end of the year 1513, and finished it in 1514, and Francesco Francia did not die until 1533. Finally, that we may omit nothing relating to the famous St. Cecilia of Bologna, we will remind our readers that it was this painting which awakened in Corregio the consciousness of his own talent, and made him exclaim, "And I too am a painter."

Among the noble works of *Domenichino,* we find no less than six pictures, wherein Cecilia occupies the principal place. Besides these, we must also mention the frescoes he painted at Rome in St. Cecilia's chapel in the Church of St. Louis des Français. They embrace the entire life of the saint. The angel conversing with Valerian and Cecilia; the Virgin distributing her fortune to the poor after Valerian's martyrdom; Almachius seated on his tribunal, and the calm and imposing attitude of Cecilia, refusing to offer incense to the idols; finally and pre-eminently, the immortal scene of Urban's interview with the expiring virgin; the bathroom inundated with generous blood which the faithful eagerly collect, the poor assisting at the last moments of their faithful benefactress, the Pontiff's ineffable emotion at the sight of so sublime a sacrifice; the martyr's legacy to the Father of the faithful. The blending of all these incidents portrays the Acts of Saint Cecilia far more vividly than the most eloquent words could do. We will conclude with a mention of Lionello Spada, who died in the seventeenth century, twenty years before Domenichino. In his admirable painting, preserved .at St. Michael *del Bosco,* at Bologna, he has represented Saint Cecilia in the midst of the heated vapor of her caldarium. He is, we believe, the first artist who ever attempted this subject, and it must be confessed that he has both conceived and executed it in an admirable mariner. Artists of the French school have, in these latter days, represented our Saint in a manner unworthy her dignity.

Every one is well acquainted with the picture painted by Mignard, for Louis XIV., in which he represented the virgin appareled like a coquette. A renowned artist of our own day, has degraded Saint Cecilia to the level of a lady in her boudoir. May Catholic art soon resume her empire in our dear France, and may her artists ere long present us with a Cecilia worthy of the name! Music claims the Roman Virgin as its special patroness; she is the Queen of Christian Harmony. Her name is blended with all the triumphs of music in the sixteenth century. Musical Societies were placed under her protection, and her Festival was celebrated by melodies composed in her honor. How often has a mass in honor of St. Cecilia, or a hymn in her praise, been the first composition of some talented musician! How many artists of superior or secondary merit, have considered their compositions worthless until they had dedicated a hymn to the Virgin whose protection they craved! Even at the present day, the feast of St. Cecilia is celebrated wherever music creates the slightest interest.

In the annual concerts, which bring to the foot of the altar so many men, who, during the rest of the year, are wholly absorbed in worldly occupations, masterpieces may be rare, the execution defective, the motives for the assembly indifferent, if not worse; but it is delightful to find the most seductive of arts acknowledging each year that the superior sentiment of harmony emanates from purity of mind and heart, personified in Cecilia. It is then that more than one soul, animated with heavenly thoughts, aspires after more harmonious and durable concerts than those of this world of sorrows, where the chords of the lyre, having been broken by sin, can only be joined for a moment; and can never resound with a full and perfect accord, except when employed to honor God, in concert with the angels. An English poet has most happily expressed this thought in a canticle which he composed for the Feast of St. Cecilia.

Our joys below it can improve,
And antedate the bliss above.
This the divine Cecilia found,

And to her Maker's praise confin'd the sound.
When the full organ joins the tuneful choir,
    Th' immortal pow'rs incline their ear;
Borne on the swelling notes our souls aspire,
While solemn airs improve the sacred fire:
    And Angels lean from heav'n to hear.
Of Orpheus now no more let poets tell,
    To bright Cecilia greater pow'r is giv'n;
His numbers rais'd a shade from hell,
    Her's lift the soul to heav'n.

Pope: Ode for music, on S. Cecilia's day.

[1] Among the gifts presented by the Cardinal J. B. Cibo to this Basilica, was an immense bell which he placed in the chapel, although it already contained three of smaller dimensions, dating back to the year 1311: MSS. Vatican, de Galletti. 8025 Santa Cecilia, tome i.

[2] Ciacconius, tome ii., page 825.

[3] This is proved by a sepulchral inscription, found in the Basilica, which dates back to the year 1475, and certifies that from that time the Church and monastery were in the hands of the Humiliati.

[4] Laderchi, tome ii., page 284.

[5] Laderchi, tome ii., page 313.

[6] Maura Magalotta Abbatissa, a Clemente VII., et Franciotto cardinali Orsino praeposito huc accita, sedem banc divae Caeciliae sacram, quam monachi Humiliatorum S. Benedicti obtinebant in praesentis monasterii, ejusdem ordinis monialium formani redegit, eamque pene collabentem restituit, adjectis insuper hortis, quorum etiam ut honestior usus esset, claustrali eos muro cinxit, anno a partu Virginis mdxxxi.

[7] D. O. M. Maura Magalotta, per triennium Abbatissa monasterii Campi Martii, deinde a Clemente VII., Pont. Max. Abbatissa perpetua monasterii Sanctae Caecilise creata, quae instituit, instauravit et dotavit. Obiit anno Dni mdlxvi. xvi. Kal. Junii, vitae suae an. lxxii. Scolastica Serleoni Rom. Abbatissa, et suffecta posuit.

[8] Laderchi, tome ii. pages 340 and 406.

[9]

En virginis Caeciliae
Fulget vita clarissima,
Quam sponsus pudicitiae
Elegit ab infantia.

Quae Christi Evangelium
Abscondebat in pectore;
Ut Jesum nitens filium
Gasto servaret corpora.

Hinc amor et devotio,
Fervebat cum eloquio.
Hinc diebus ac noctibus
Sacris intendit fructibus.

Nam duos fratres nobiles
Christi effecit milites,
Quos per ejus vestigium
Hortatur ad Martyrium.

Haec cernens tunc Episcopus
Urbanus vir Angelicus,
Resolvitur in lacrymis
De fructu tantae Virginis

Domine Jesu suscipe
De manibus Caeciliae
Fructus casti consilii,
Sicut odorem balsami.

O Beata Caecilia,
Devota Christi famula
Per tua sacra merita,
Nos Deo reconcilia.

Deo Patri sit gloria,
Ejusque soli Filio,
Cum Spiritu Paraclito,
Et nunc, et sine termino. Amen.

Consolatrix infirmorum, compassione.
Electrix supernorum, contemplatione.
Confortatrix Christianorum, praedica-
tione.
Imitatrix Beatorum, sacra passione.
Liberatrix perditorum, devota ora-
tione.
Inventrix liliorum, casta conversa-
tione.
Associatrix Angelorum, coelesti reve-
latione.

[10] We cannot mention here as a Catholic statue, the Muse which David sculptured under the name of St. Cecilia, and which may be seen in the choir of the Cathedral of Angers. The statue is graceful, but cannot be classed among the works inspired by Christian faith in honor of Cecilia.

[11] D'Agincourt gives the designs of these pictures, hut in such a miniature form, that it is impossible to form a correct judgment of them.

[12] Cope.

[13] Rio De l'Art Chrêtien, page 250. Montalembert. Du Vandalisme et du Catholicisme dans l'art, p. 147.

Rio. *Ibid,* page 172.

In the Memoirs of the Academic Society of the Aube.

[14] We will refer here to a peculiarity of the fourth piece of tapestry, which needs to be explained, as it is found in the most beautiful frescoes of Francia, at Bologna. The artists of the Middle Age, not understanding the vapor baths which were taken by the ancients in the caldarium, were unable to comprehend the torment to which Almachius condemned Cecilia, otherwise than by supposing that she was placed in a cauldron of boiling water. They were somewhat embarrassed in their efforts to explain the passage of the Acts which refers to the prodigy by which Cecilia's body was preserved from moisture If she had been immersed in boiling water, this passage would have been, to say the least, very singular. In the fifteenth century, the archaeologists were unable to explain to the artists a style of baths which were not then used. Moreover, the latter would have found great difficulty in representing in a painting the saint praying in the caldarium, whilst by representing her half plunged in a caldron, or, as Francia does, in a bath, with a lictor brandishing his sword above her head, they were able to describe both kinds of martyrdom, as they understood them. A little later, Julius Romanus and Guido understood the ancient customs, and represented Cecilia kneeling in her caldarium, and extending her neck to the executioner.

[15] Vasari. Tome iii. p. 166.

Chapter Twenty-Eight - Cardinal Paul Emilius Sfondrato. His Devotion to St. Cecilia. His Discovery of Her Body.

Paul Emilius was born at Milan, 1561. His father, Paul Sfondrato was a brother of Gregory XIV; his mother, whose name was Sigismund, "belonged to the family of Este. In his youth, Paul showed the happiest dispositions, and when old enough to choose a state of life, at once gave preference to the Church. He came to Rome at an early age, and spent some time in the house of the Oratorian Fathers, at St. Maria, in Vallicella, where he had the happiness of becoming acquainted with St. Philip Neri. The ardent piety of young Sfondrato was stimulated by the society of this illustrious servant of God, and in his interviews with the holy old man, he imbibed that charity towards the poor, that zeal for the adornment of the sanctuary, and that fervent devotion towards the martyrs, which were his principal characteristics throughout life. Gregory XIV., who was made Pope on the 5th of December, 1590, created his nephew, Paul Emilius, Cardinal, on the 19th of the same month, a promotion which was universally applauded. The young Prelate, then twenty-nine years of age, was absent from Rome when he received the news of his elevation. He hastened to his uncle, who had always appreciated his virtue, and who now admitted him at once into his councils. Rome was at this time intensely interested in the affairs of France. A Calvinist prince had claimed the crown; he had been vigorously opposed by the League, but the decisive battle of Ivry which had taken place immediately after the death of Sixtus V., had rendered further resistance vain. Urban VII., had reigned but thirteen days. Gregory XIV., supported by his nephew, Paul Emilius, responded to the cannons of the victorious Henry by fresh anathemas. But after a short Pontificate, he was called to his reward. He was succeeded by Innocent IX., who reigned but two months. The cause then passed into the vigorous hands of Clement VIII.

The death of Gregory XIV. restored to his nephew the leisure he so much coveted, and with increasing ardor, he devoted himself to works of piety and mercy. His uncle had magnificently provided him with rich benefices, but he did not make use of them to surround himself with the luxuries which his elevated position rendered perfectly justifiable. His palace, void of hangings or tapestry, proved that he preferred to clothe the poor of Jesus Christ. The Pontifical Court admired this prince of the Church, who never suffered any but earthen vessels to be placed on his table, that he might be enabled to feed a greater number of poor. Such was Sfondrato, when at the very pinnacle of honor; such he remained during his whole life. [1] Two objects engrossed his generous soul: 1st. To glorify Christ in His triumphant members. 2d. To soothe Christ in Ilia suffering members. Sfondrato studied this lesson in the school of St. Cecilia. Gregory XIV., in elevating him to the purple, placed in his hand as a pious inheritance the Church he had himself held, that of our illustrious martyr, who, during her life had been so full of compassion for the poor; so zealous in burying the champions of the faith. It was reserved for Sfondrato to walk in Paschal's footsteps; Christ destined him to place a much more brilliant crown upon the brow of his Spouse than she had received in the ninth century from the hands of a Pontiff. Sfondrato took possession of the title of St. Cecilia on the 25th of January, 1591. The ceremony, was pompous and solemn, notwithstanding the raging of a violent storm, accompanied by thunder and torrents of rain, which being unusual at that season, might well have thrown a gloom over the brilliancy of the festival. The new cardinal paid his respects to the abbess and her community in the parlor; he spoke of his veneration for their Church, and added, with charming simplicity, that if he had felt any desire for the purple, it was only that he might become titulary of St. Cecilia. The result will prove the cardinal's sincerity. [2] About this time Sigismondo d'Este, mother of Paul Emilius, came to visit Borne, accompanied by the cardinal's sister and sister-in-law, and several ladies of the family. They visited the Church of St. Cecilia, and treated the religions with the greatest affability. Not satisfied with conversing with the abbess and sisters in the parlor, they begged to kiss their hands. It was therefore necessary to admit them into the interior of the monastery, which was immediately done. During this interchange of mutual charity, Sfondrato's mother remained upon her knees, through respect for the Spouses of Christ. Thus did all this family testify their affection for our illustrious Saint, by the respect which they showed to the consecrated virgins who guarded her sanctuary. Sfondrato felt that the Basilica which had been restored to the abbess by Maura Magalotta, sixty years previous, required some repairs; and, moreover, he did not consider it sufficiently handsome. He undertook a general restoration, and without destroying the antique and venerable character of the edifice, he threw over it that air of splendor so well suited to the Churches of Rome. Sfondrato's first thought was to enrich the Basilica with the numerous and important relics which he had collected, frequently through the mediation of his uncle. They were contained in a number of silver and silver gilt caskets; and that he might preserve them more worthily, he conceived the idea of placing them under the altar of the Confession. But the accessible space between the altar and the mysterious region of the tombs, was not sufficiently large to contain this precious deposit. The cardinal decided to enlarge the place, and, eagerly desiring to find Cecilia's body, he resolved to pierce through the thick stone wall upon which the altar rested. He thought with reason that the tomb could not be far from the entrance; and, moreover, he knew that the opening in front of the altar must correspond with Cecilia's sepulchre, since formerly the faithful by means of this opening lowered pieces of linen to touch the tomb. In the expectation of a discovery which was to prove the consolation and glory of his life, Sfondrato ordered the workmen to labor only in his presence, commanding them to suspend their operations when he was forced to leave the Basilica. [3]

Finally on Wednesday, the 20th of October, 1599, the Cardinal commanded that the pavement should be taken away from before the altar. They then cleared away the ground from around the stones, and loosened the foundations of the wall which covered the subterranean enclosure. After making with much effort an opening in the thick wall, the space under the altar was clearly seen. Two sarcophagi of white marble, placed side by side, three feet below the ground, at once struck Sfondrato's eye. These, two tombs were directly under the altar. Transported with holy joy, the Cardinal determined, before opening the tomb, to send for some reliable witnesses. He immediately despatched messengers for the Bishop of Isernia, Vicegerent of the Cardinal Vicar, James Buzzi, Canon of the congregation of Lateran, and Fathers Peter Alagona and Peter Morra, of the Society of Jesus. They soon arrived, accompanied by several members of the Cardinal's household. After again examining the place, they hastened to open the first tomb, that which was nearest the subterranean entrance. The workmen having removed the marble slab which covered it, a cypress coffin was seen inside, four feet, three inches in length, thirteen inches in width, and seventeen high. There was no appearance of a lock, and the upper lid was not even fastened with nails. It was very thin, and opened and closed by means of a groove. For some time, Sfondrato and his assistants were uncertain how to open this sacred coffin, which they were sure contained the body of St. Cecilia. Finally, the Cardinal himself discovered the proper means, and, with trembling hands, respectfully removed the frail obstacle which concealed the virgin's body from his eyes.

It was a solemn moment. After eight centuries of obscurity and silence, Cecilia appeared once more to the faithful of Christ, in the ineffable majesty of her martyrdom. The interior of the coffin was covered with the same damask, although somewhat faded, with which Paschal had lined it. [4] Time had respected the thin veil which the Pontiff bad thrown over her body, and through this transparent texture, the gold with which her dress was embroidered, sparkled with brilliancy. [5]

Who can describe the joy of these Catholic hearts to whom heaven had granted the favor of being the first to salute upon her triumphal couch, the martyr of the third century, who, in these tempestuous days, was revealed to the Roman Church, as if to encourage her in her conflict with error, and to give to her children, a sure pledge of the reward that awaited those who should fight courageously until the end. Those heroes of Catholicity, who had so lately shed their blood in England, [6] in Holland, [7] and even on the seas, [8] were also sleeping in the tomb, and Cecilia, rising from the grave, not only wished them peace, but proclaimed by her example, the truth of that oracle of the Psalmist: "The Lord keepeth the bones of His servants, not one of them shall be lost." [9]

All were eager to gaze nearer on the mortal remains of the Spouse of Christ. Sfondrato, with profound veneration, raised the veil, and exposed to view, the treasure confided to the tomb by Urban and Paschal. The martyr

151

was clothed in her antique robe, embroidered with gold, upon which the glorious marks of her virginal blood were still apparent; [10] at her feet was the linen stained with the purple of her martyrdom. [11] She was lying upon her right side, and seemed to be in a profound sleep. [12] The neck still bore the marks of the wounds made by the lictor's sword; [13] the head, by a mysterious and touching curvature, was turned towards the bottom of the coffin. [14]

The body was found perfectly entire, whilst the graceful and modest figure of the saint, preserved so miraculously after so many centuries, vividly recalled the martyr breathing her last sigh upon the pavement of her *Caldarium*. The spectators were transported in spirit to the day when Urban had reclosed the coffin, without disturbing the attitude which the virgin had chosen to yield up her soul to her immortal Spouse. [15] They also admired Paschal's prudence in leaving the body just as he had discovered it, and thus preserving so grand a spectacle for posterity. [16]

They next proceeded to open the second sarcophagus; it was contiguous to that of Cecilia, but buried deeper under the altar, towards the apsis. In it were found three bodies, lying side by side, each wrapped in a shroud. The first was placed with the feet towards the right side of the altar; the head had been taken away. The second with the feet towards the left side of the altar; the head was with the body, although severed from it. The third, with the head attached to the body, was in the same position as the first. [17]

It was easy to recognize Valerian, Tiburtius, and Maximus, in this imposing triumvirate of Martyrs. In the first place, Paschal's inscription enumerated the three bodies which he had interred near Cecilia. The absence of the head, in the one occupying the first place, left no doubt that the body belonged to Tiburtius, whose head, as we have stated, was preserved in a casket in the Basilica. [18] The second was undoubtedly the body of Cecilia's husband, and there was such a striking resemblance between the bones of the two martyrs, that it was evident the brothers had suffered death at almost the same age. [19] There was no doubt that the third body was that of Maximus. This notary of Almachius had not been beheaded, but had been beaten to death with loaded whips. His skull bore evident traces of this punishment. It was fractured in several places, and strange to say, the martyr's brown hair, clotted with blood, was entirely preserved, as if our Lord had willed to accomplish literally in him, the promise he has made to his Athletes. "No one of your hairs shall be lost." [20] The skeleton of Maximus proved that he was much taller than the brothers, and his head adhered so firmly to his body, that when Sfondrato, at a later period, wished to remove it, he had great difficulty in doing so. [21]

The sepulchre of Popes Urban and Lucius, was not discovered on that day. Sfondrato knew from Paschal's document, that he was near the two others, but he was eager to return to Cecilia's tomb, to whom the glory of this second Invention, as well as that of the first, principally belonged.

He ordered the cypress coffin to be removed from the marble sarcophagus, and carried with lighted candles to a place adjoining the church and monastery, generally used for hearing the confessions of the nuns. A wooden chest had been hastily prepared, covered with silk and closed by a lock. Sfondrato deposited therein the cypress coffin, containing the precious treasure which he valued so highly; he then locked the outside chest, and sealed it with his seal. A platform was erected upon which the body of Cecilia was placed, on an even line with the grated window looking into the church, at the extremity of the lateral nave, on the left as you enter the church. The news of so important a discovery spread quickly through Rome and excited the greatest enthusiasm.

[1] Amelot de la Houssaye, editor of the letters of Cardinal d'Ossat, ambassador from Henry IV. to Clement VIII., mentions in the notes of this book, different testimonies of the profound esteem in which Sfondrato was held at the Roman court. According to the expression of Delfini, the ambassador from Venice to the Holy See, this cardinal walked in the footsteps of Cardinal Borromeo. (Lettres de d'Ossat, tome v., p. 304). Cardinal Bentivoglio, in his memoirs, gives a still more precious and detailed account of the virtues of Sfondrato in his private life, and also attests the great veneration he enjoyed. (*Ibid.,* tome i., page 89). D'Ossat, who well understood human nature, speaks with admiration in his correspondence of the firmness of Sfondrato when, in an assembly of cardinals, he alone, of all the Sacred College, refused to give his vote for the promotion of Sylvester Aldobrandini to the cardinalate. This nephew of Clement VIII. was but fourteen years of age, and Sfondrato fearlessly quoted to the Pontiff that canon of the Council of Trent, (Sess. xxiv.) which requires the same age, learning, and qualities for cardinals as for bishops. (Lettres de d'Ossat, tome v., page 317).

[2] Archives of St. Cecilia. Croniche del venerabile monastero di S. Cecilia.

[3] All these details, and those which follow, may be found in Bosio's interesting; relation of the finding of Cecilia's body and those of her companions.

[4] Aperta capsa circumornata undique apparuit intus textili quodam sericae quam vulgo appellant saiae similitudinem referente, coloris ex viridi et rufo permixti, cujus tamen nitorem temporis longiuquitate obiuscatum agnosceres. Hoc illud est textile, de quo sic Bibliothecarius in Paschali, dum dona quae is Pontifex huic Ecclesiae contulit, recenset: *Fecit in arcella, ad corpus jam dictae Virginis vestem de quadrupulo cum periclisin.* Bosio. *Relatio inventionis et repositionis S. Caeciliae et Sociorum.*

[5] Intra hanc capsam beatae Caeciliae Virginis corpus extabat serico, atque fusco coopertum velo, subterque velum vestes aurese virginei sanguinis notas respersae, fugaci tenuique fulgore translucebant. *Bosio. Relatio inventionis et repositionis S. Caecitiae et Sociorum.*

[6] Under Henry VIII. and Elizabeth.

[7] The martyrs of Gorcum.

[8] F. Ignatius Azvedo and his thirty-nine companions.

[9] Psalm xxxiii., 21.

[10] Vestes aureae virginei sanguinis notis respersae, *Relatio Relatio, Ibid.*

[11] Insuper ad pedes sacrati corporis linteaminum glomus jacebat convoluto-rum, illa nimirum quae ipse Paschalis in litteris Inventionis suae commemorat. *Bosio. Relatio* etc.

[12] Jacebat id corpus in dexterum incumbens latus, paululum contractis cruri-bus, brachiisque ante projectis. Bosio, *Ibid.*

[13] Corpus S. Caeciliae adhuc intactum, serica viste auro texta, vulnerum cica-tricibus apparentibus, Clemens Papa VIII., in argentea urna sub ara maxima col-locari curavit. *Fonseca De Basilica S. Laurentii in Damaso,* page 285.

[14] Cervice autem valde relfexa, facieque ad humum procumbente, dormientis instar. *Bosio. Ibid.*

[15] Eam ut credi potest formam retinens, in qua post trinam percussionem, cui triduum supervixit, animam Deo reddens conciderat, fueratque pariter in Cae-meterio ab Urbano Pontifice collocatum. *Bosio. Ibid.*

[16] The cypress coffin must have been the identical one in which St. Urban bur-ied Cecilia. It is very certain that it would have been impossible, in the ninth cen-tury, to transfer the martyr's body to so narrow a coffin, without disturbing her attitude or even disjoining her limbs. Anastasius, in relating the marks of honor paid by Paschal to Cecilia, only mentions the material with which he lined her coffin, proving evidently that the latter was not new, and therefore only needed ornamenting. The small size of the cypress coffin is easily explained by the ne-cessity of placing it in one of those narrow cells, where the bodies of the martyrs were frequently deposited without coffins. The very fact of a coffin in a marble sarcophagus, would be a sufficient proof that it existed before Paschal's discov-ery of the body. The bodies of Valerian, Tiburtius, and Maximus, were also in a sarcophagus, but they were laid upon their backs, simply wrapped in shrouds. So were those of Sts. Urban and Lucius. The learned Protestant writers, Platner, Bunsen, etc, in their great work upon Rome, (Beschreibung der Stadt Rom. vol. iii., part iii. page 641.) find no difficulty in dating the Saint's attitude to the first sepulture; we think we have fully demonstrated that the cypress coffin was equally old.

[17] Bosio. *Relatio,* etc.

[18] Corpus sancti Tiburtii ab illo sancti Valeriani eo argumento recognitum est, quoniam sancti Tiburtii corpus capite carebat, cum foris in Ecclesia proprio in tabernaculo conservaretur ut creditur ab ipso Paschali Papa sublatum. *Bosio. Relatio,* etc.

[19] Corpus deinde sancti Valeriani distinctum est a Sancti Maximi, ex eo quod inventum est illius caput a trunco corporis divulsum. quod ei gladio recisum fue-rat. magnitudine quoque, et formae proportione capiti Sancti Tiburtii ita simile, ut duorum pari fere aetate fratrum esse viderentur. *Bosio. Relatio,* etc.

[20] Luke xxi. 18.

[21] Contra vero Sancti Haximi, qui non capite plexus, sed ad necem plumbatia caesus fuerat, repertum est caput ita cum corpore conjunctum, ut cum ipse Car-dinalis tollere illud vellet, ut extra simul cum aliis Sancti Valeriani, et Tiburtii publico in altari coleretur, magno id conatu et labore perfecerit. Ostendebat etiam idem caput percussionum, quas ex plumbatis acceperat notas, et fractionis signa, licet formam integram retineret, in quo subflava quoque caesaries quasi

viventis, er omne capillamentum repersa sanguine incorrupta cernebantur. *Bosio. Relatio,* p. 311.

Chapter Twenty-Nine - Sfondrato Acquaints Clement VIII., With the Discovery of Cecilia's Body. Joy of the Pontiff. Baronius Comes to Identify the Holy Relics

Sfondrato did not wish to proceed further, or to consummate the Invention of the martyrs, without inviting the Sovereign Pontiff to identify this sacred deposit. Following the example of John, who, running faster than Peter, and arriving first at the Sepulchre, nevertheless abstained from entering, so Sfondrato, through deference for the Chief of the Apostolic College, after giving suitable orders, started for Frascati where Clement VIII. had gone to enjoy the country air. Baronius was with the Pontiff. He will give his own narration of the great event.

"Clement was confined to his bed with a violent attack of gout, and admitted no one to an audience; but as soon as he heard the motive of Sfondrato's arrival, he immediately requested to see the Cardinal, and hear from his own lips, the account of this wonderful discovery. The Pontiff listened to the recital with extreme joy, and was deeply grieved that he was unable, on account of his illness, to go immediately and pay his respects to the great martyr. [1] Now it happened that this disappointment turned to my advantage, for, notwithstanding my unworthiness, the Pontiff commissioned me to identify and venerate the body of St. Cecilia. Without loss of time, Sfondrato immediately set out for Rome; I accompanied him, and the same evening, we reached the Church of St. Cecilia.

"I saw the cypress coffin which had been enclosed in the marble sarcophagus. It contained Cecilia's body, and was closed with a very thin and somewhat injured cover. I gazed with admiration at the simple wooden coffin so perfectly preserved after having been buried in the earth for eight hundred and seventy eight years, where neither light nor air could penetrate, and constantly exposed to decay from the humidity of the marble in which it was enclosed. It was so solid that it could be touched and even handled without being in the least injured. The cover was likewise so perfect that for several days the coffin was continually opened and closed to satisfy the devotion of those who wished to see and venerate the holy Martyr."

"Having fully examined and admired the shrine, we wished to see the sacred body which it inclosed. Then were verified the words of David: 'As we have heard, so have we seen, in the city of the Lord of hosts in the city of our God.'" [2]

We found Cecilia's body in precisely the same condition in which it was when Pope Paschal discovered and buried it. At her feet, the blood-stained linen; the dress of silk and gold, which the Pontiff described, perfectly recognizable, although somewhat impaired by time. [3]

"We remarked other light silken textures upon the body, their depression aided us in perfectly distinguishing the beautiful cumbent figure so modestly and gracefully distended. We were struck with admiration to see that the body was not stretched out in the coffin, as the bodies of the dead generally are. The chaste virgin was lying upon her right side as if gently sleeping on a couch, her knees modestly joined, "her whole appearance inspiring such, respect, that notwithstanding our pious curiosity, no one ventured to touch her. Every one was deeply moved with veneration, as if her heavenly Spouse, watching over her sleep, had uttered these words: 'I adjure, you that you wake not my beloved till she please.' [4]

"We saw, we recognized, we venerated. [5] The next morning we offered the Holy Sacrifice of the Mass upon the altar of the Confession, in memory and in honor of this glorious Virgin Martyr and the other Saints buried near her. We then returned to Frascati, and reported all we had seen to the sovereign Pontiff. Clement listened with satisfaction, and immediately commenced to make arrangements for the translation of this august body to her Confession, a ceremony which he declared he alone would perform to the exclusion of any other prelate, no matter how eminent his dignity. The Feast of St. Cecilia was the day appointed for the translation." [6]

We will discontinue the recital of this great annalist, and beg our readers to consider with us one of the most touching characteristics of the Catholic Church, so divinely manifested in the scenes we have already related, and those which are yet untold. A statesman of our day has remarked, that "Catholicity is the greatest school for respect upon earth;" we will add that religion, as it is taught and practised in the Catholic Church, is the inexhaustible source of the most elevated and noble emotions which man can experience. From it flow the many acts of devotedness, the many generous sacrifices, and the noble enthusiasm characteristic of the Catholic Church. Would you know whence she derives her marvellous power? Doubtless from the doctrine and example of our Saviour, who, since His ascension to heaven, has been pleased to reproduce in his Saints the admirable virtues He himself practised. Hence that love, that continual remembrance in the Church, of the heroes she has produced. Hence the ever old and always new development of charity which is unceasingly going on within her. The Saints live with God in a blessed eternity; and the Church in this valley of tears continually feels their protection. Therefore she unceasingly loves them, rejoices in honoring them, and in proposing them to our imitation. If we cling to our departed friends with that love which the Scripture says is stronger than death, [7] how great must be the confidence of the Church in the intercession of the Saints, who are now far more tenderly interested in each one of her children, and far more powerful to aid them than when they were themselves sojourning in this vale of tears. Behold Clement VIII., the austere old man, who during two entire years had refused to the triumphant Henry of Navarre the absolution which through the medium of his ambassadors, he implored upon his knees. Behold this Pontiff, who inherited all the energy of his predecessors, and unshrinkingly bore the weight of the tiara at the very time when so many provinces of Europe were separating from the Church; behold his great soul filled with joy on hearing that the remains of a Christian lady of the third century had been discovered! As soon as his strength permitted, he repaired in person to venerate the precious relic. He watered it with tears of joy and emotion; he esteemed among the greatest events of his pontificate the translation of Cecilia's coffin to a splendid casket, to purchase which he almost exhausted the papal treasury.

Such a spectacle is incomprehensible to those not initiated in Catholicity, but can any thing more strikingly show the veneration of the Church toward those who have carried the practice of virtue even to heroism? After the lapse of six centuries, Paschal rivals St. Urban, in his respectful tenderness towards the virgin, and eight centuries later, the daughter of the Cecilii finds the same pious affection in the heart of Clement. Add to this, that the sepulture given to the virgin by Paschal was much more solemn than that she received from Urban's hands; and that the enthusiasm manifested at the last translation of her body, far exceeded that shown in the ninth century, when her Basilica was restored by Paschal.

Now, however, the Reformation was triumphing; memorials which had been cherished for centuries, were trampled underfoot; the bones of the saints were thrown into the highways, because they recalled too vividly the example of those sublime virtues which were so uncongenial to a century emancipated from the superstitions of popery. Nevertheless, Rome, the capital of the Christian world, cursed by so many nations, and called the Prostitute of Babylon, was agitated with as deep a joy on hearing that the body of a young Roman matron, martyred under Alexander Severus, had been discovered, as if she had been told that a treasure, sufficient to enrich each of her inhabitants, had been suddenly revealed. And why was this? Because this young Roman virgin, who had been buried for so many centuries, was the model of a purity worthy of Angels, of an inviolable devotedness to the God to whom she had consecrated herself, of an ardent zeal for the salvation of souls, of tender charity for the poor, of invincible firmness in confessing the faith which elevates human nature, of courage in twice braving death, and, finally, of that inexpressible charm resulting from the sublime virtue of Christian virginity.

Such were in the third, the ninth, and the sixteenth centuries, and such will be to the end of time, Cecilia's claims to the love of Christians. Past generations loved her, because, by her example, she traced out for them the path which leads to a better world; and now, at the close of an heretical century, she suddenly reappears, as if to re-enkindle the spark of heavenly fire, almost extinct upon earth. How could Catholicity resist such an appeal? Is it astonishing that the Father of the Faithful, the Supreme Head of that Church, so sadly decimated by heresy, should welcome with joy, and salute with gladness one of its most noble and privileged daughters? Is it astonishing that the pious and learned Baronius should have laid aside his immortal pen, to hasten to Cecilia's tomb, whence the glorious martyr was silently proclaiming to the world that the Church of Clement VIII. is the Church of Urban, because it is the Church of Jesus Christ? Is it surprising that the wealthy and generous Sfondrato henceforth devoted his zeal and his riches to adorning Cecilia's temple, when we consider that the object of this holy profusion was to encourage Catholics to practise those virtues which form the eternal crown of the virgin martyr? This pomp, these gifts, and honors, the transports of the entire city, from the venerable old man who wore the tiara, down to the most humble of his subjects, could not indeed restore to the Church, the half of Germany, which had fallen a victim to heresy, nor England, Sweden, Denmark, and the Swiss Cantons now alienated from the Church, which had been their common Mother for centuries. But they attested that even in this fearful crisis, holiness, purity of life, and the heroism of devotedness, were as much respected in Rome, as they had ever been. The time will come when the misguided nations that have seceded from the Faith, fatigued with doubts and incredulity, will turn towards the only country where the Ideal of virtue can never be lost, since it is placed upon the altar.

[1] Ex eo tamen doluit et ingemuit, quod eo detineretur ex mala valetudine impedimento, et non valeret ad invisendam et salutandam tantam Martyrem properare. *Baronius. Annal. ad annum* 821.
[2] Ps. xlvii. 9.
[3] Etenim ut a Paschali Papa inventum et reconditum fuisse legimus venerandum Caeciliae corpus, ita iuvenimus, nempe ad pedes ejus quae fuerant, madida sanguine vela, et senea fila auro obducta quae visebantur, jam vetustate soluae vestis illius auro textae enjus idem Paschalis meminit, indices erant. Baronius, *Annal. ad annum* 821.
[4] Alia vero supra Martyris corpus serica, levia tamen velamina posita, ipsaque depressa situm ipsum et habitudinem corporis ostendebant. Visebaturque (quod admiratione dignum erat) non ut assolet in sepulchro resupinum positum corpus, sed ut in lecto jacens bones tissima virgo supra dextrum cubare latus, contractis nonnibil ad modestiam genibus, ut dormientis imagineni reddere potius quam defunctae, ipso ita ad insinuandam in omnibus virginalem verecundiam composito situ corporis: adeo ut (quod aeque mirandum) nemo quamvis curiosus inspector ausus omnino fuerit virgineum illud detegere corpus reverentia quandam inenarrabilii repercussus, perinde ac si caelestis Sponsus assisteret vigilans custos dormientis sponsae, monens et minans: Ne suscitetis neque evigilare faciatis dilectam donec ipsa velit. *Annal. ad annum* 821.
[5] Vidimus, cognovimus et adoravimus. *Ibid.*
[6] Baronius. *Annal ad annum* 821.
[7] Cant. viii. 6.

Chapter Thirty - Sfondrato's Preparations for the Translation of Cecilia's Body. Veneration of Clement VIII. For the Roman Virgin.

On his return to Frascati, Sfondrato caused a new search to be made in the hopes of finding the tomb of the holy Popes, Urban and Lucius. It was soon discovered; Paschal had placed it under the sarcophagus which contained Cecilia's cypress coffin. The two Pontiffs were laid side by side, the former with his head turned towards the right of the altar, whilst the latter was turned towards the left. Each body was wrapped in a shroud. Sfondrato venerated with profound respect, the sacred remains of these martyr Popes, one of whom had been Cecilia's director, and her guest in the very house upon the ground of which now rose the Basilica. These precious relics were reserved to enhance the splendor of the festival, which Clement had appointed for the 22d of November. But before this solemn day, Sfondrato determined to take measures to ensure to posterity a part of the joy which he had experienced in contemplating the Spouse of Christ in her mysterious sleep. He therefore commissioned a skilful sculptor, Stefano Maderno, [1] to immortalize with his graceful chisel, Cecilia's attitude in her tomb. The design was made with scrupulous exactness, and the brilliant young artist, only twenty-four years of age, inspired by such a subject, enriched Christian statuary with this master-piece of grace and modesty which is one of the principal glories of the trans-Tiberian Basilica. He even represented the position of the martyr's hands, which so touchingly express her faith. Three fingers of the right hand were extended to denote the three Persons of the Holy Trinity; and the forefinger of the left, held out to represent the unity of the Godhead. Thus did even this symbolical sign prove, after so many centuries, the belief for which Cecilia had shed her blood. Notwithstanding his great desire to take from this marvellous tomb, some portion of its precious relics, Sfondrato's devotion was too delicate to permit him even to think of touching the body which had been preserved entire by Divine Providence during so many centuries. [2] He wished to reserve it for the day when Cecilia, at the sound of the angel's trumpet, would return to resume her glorious body, which virginity seemed already to have stamped with immortality. The virgin appeared anxious to reward Sfondrato's pious reserve. In order to retain at least a memorial of the touching spectacle which had greeted his eyes upon opening the tomb, the Cardinal determined to take away some of the blood-stained linen at Cecilia's feet. He distributed portions of this sacred linen to many of the Cardinals residing in Rome, intending to reserve the last piece for himself. Now it "happened that a splinter of a bone from Cecilia's head had adhered to the piece which fell to his lot. [3] Hence, when looking at this linen, which had been used in staunching the virgin's wounds, the whole scene of the caldarium was present to his mind. Cecilia's head, fractured by the three strokes of

159

the lictor's sword; and the trembling hand of some friend, who, though staunching these large wounds with the utmost gentleness, could not prevent pieces of bone from coming away with the blood. Sfondrato preserved, as a precious jewel, this touching souvenir of the martyr, who had bequeathed it to him at the very moment when her sepulchre was again to be closed. He also wished as a last consolation, to retain a fragment of Cecilia's clothing. Without touching her silk tunic, he cut off a small piece of her dress. It was probably at this time that he discovered the secret of Cecilia's penance; for he declares that he felt upon her breast, through her clothes, the knots of the hair shirt, which like strong armor, had protected the virgin in her combats, and which now shared her honors. [4]

We have said that the head of St. Tiburtius had been placed by Paschal in a casket, at the time of the first Invention, in 821. Sfondrato, before closing the tomb of the three martyrs, took away the heads of Valerian and Maximus, that they might be exposed in the Virgin's Basilica, with that of Tiburtius, to the veneration of the faithful. Cecilia's coffin, as we have said, was placed in a hall, situated at the upper extremity of the left nave of the church, and could be seen through a grated window which opened into the Basilica. The platform and coffin were covered with rich silk drapery, embroidered with gold. Handsome candelabras, numerous lamps, gold and silver flowers, added to the magnificence of the decorations. No perfumes were burned near the body, because, as the reliable author from whom we gather these details, tells us, a delightful odor of roses and lilies, proceeding from the coffin, embalmed the sanctuary in which it was placed.

Rome was in a tumult of joy at the news of so many miracles. Two months had not yet elapsed since the execution of the celebrated Beatrice Cenci, and the emotions excited on that terrible day had not entirely subsided. More pleasing impressions were about to succeed those which had so violently agitated the city on the 11th of September, when the Pontiff', in his justice, ordered the execution of this beautiful and noble Roman lady. Never was a more striking contrast offered to the sympathies of this ardent people. Beatrice, expiating under the repeated blows of the executioner's axe, the parricide of which she had been guilty, and imploring pardon of Heaven in the presence of an immense crowd, which, infatuated with her beauty, clamorously demanded her release; Cecilia, innocent and pure, also struck several times by the lictor's sword, calmly expiring, surrounded by her faithful friends, and leaving behind her a memory of imperishable sweetness.

This double scene must have presented itself a thousand times to the imagination of the Roman people, and if the death of Beatrice taught them how a repentant sinner can die, Cecilia's death proved how sweetly a soul, enamored with the love of Christ, hastens to meet him, rejoicing in the cruel torments of martyrdom. During the days which elapsed before the Translation, the concourse of people was very great. It became even necessary to call upon the Pontifical Swiss guard to maintain order in the midst of this outpouring of the Roman people upon the trans-Tiberian region. More than once, Sfondrato, who seemed to have taken up his abode in Cecilia's house, was almost crushed by the crowd.

The young patricians and Roman princesses hastened to pay their homage to one who had overcome all worldly seductions; but nothing could equal the joy of the nuns of St. Cecilia's monastery, the guardians of this precious treasure. They scarcely knew how to testify their gratitude at having been permitted to gaze upon her body; but by prayers, chants, and tears, endeavored to assure Cecilia of the happiness caused by her presence in their midst. Nearly all the Cardinals came to venerate the Spouse of Christ, and Clement VIII., having at length recovered his health, hastened from Frascati, to prostrate himself at her feet. Baronius has thus related the interviews between Urban's successor and the great martyr of the third century.

Clement, accompanied by the Cardinals, repaired to the Church of St. Cecilia to visit and venerate the sacred remains of this Virgin Martyr. The cover of the coffin having been removed, the Pontiff saw and venerated this body, worthy of the respect of angels. He offered it a homage, far more valuable than gold or precious stones; — prayers poured forth from an overflowing heart, and tears of the tenderest emotion. [5] He then celebrated the Sacrifice of Mass in honor of the Martyr, and declared his intention of solemnizing her approaching feast with all possible devotion. But Clement should be particularly admired for his extreme modesty; he would not consent to raise the silken veil which enveloped the Virgin. The blood which discolored the tomb, recalled too vividly that chaste blush which is the guardian of virginal modesty. He was quite satisfied with seeing the Virgin's body through the veil which covered it, and with reading the characters engraven near the sepulchre and preserved through so many centuries, by a dispensation of Providence; in a word, with finding everything conformable to Paschal's document. [6] Clement afterwards venerated his holy predecessors, Urban and Lucius, and the martyrs Valerian, Tiburtius, and Maximus, whose tombs were opened for a moment in his presence.

The Pontiff would not be outdone in generosity by a Cardinal, and he therefore determined to offer Cecilia on the day of her Translation, a present worthy of her and of the Apostolic See. As soon as he had heard at Frascati, from Sfondrato and Baronius, the report of the discovery, he felt that it was his duty to prove in some way, his veneration towards the Virgin. At first, he resolved upon ordering a gold casket to contain the Martyr's body; but the two Cardinals dissuaded him, representing to him that so rich an object, beneath an altar, might excite cupidity. Clement, therefore, decided upon a silver casket, in the form of a tomb, sufficiently large to hold the cypress coffin.

The silversmith, charged with the commission, was ordered to finish and present his work to the Pope before the day appointed for the Translation. He used two hundred and fifty-one pounds of silver, and his price for his work and materials, was four thousand three hundred and eighty gold crowns. The casket was lined with purple silk; the exterior studded with stars which gave it the appearance of a new heaven, according to the poetical expression of Baronius, who compares the artist to Beseleel, the divinely inspired fabricator of the Ark of Alliance and the Golden Candlestick. [7]

The design was quite simple, [8] four golden cherubim were placed upon the corners of the upper part of the casket. The arms of Clement VIII. with the tiara and keys, all richly gilt, were in relievo on the sides. This immense coffin was hermetically closed. The lid bore this inscription.

CORPVS S. CAECILIAE VIRGINIS ET MARTYRIS
A CLEMENTE VIII. PONT. MAX. INCLVSM.
ANNO M. D. IC. PONTIF VIII. [9]

Whilst admiring this magnificent silver casket, our thoughts naturally revert to the elegant, large, but empty sarcophagus of Cecilia Metella, left without honor under the portico of a palace. This wealthy lady had tasted of all the pleasures offered by the world to its favorites, the monument erected to her memory by Crassus, her husband, had for centuries ornamented the Appian Way; but the name of Cecilia Metella will never make the heart throb; no one has ever expressed the slightest anxiety respecting the fate of the bones which once reposed in this sepulchre, now a mere object of curiosity, whereas, the Christian Cecilia was sought for with care in the vaults of the Catacombs, and saluted with enthusiasm each time that her mortal remains were brought to the light of day. The contrast between the two Cecilias is still more strikingly shown by the symbols upon their sepulchres. The sarcophagus of Cecilia Metella is exposed to the inclemencies of the weather, its decorations awaken no sentiment of piety in the soul. Two horses' heads spring from the centre of the undulating channels which adorn the tomb; the upper part is decorated with a severe and graceful frieze, surmounted by foliage, under the shade of which some animals are sporting; nothing to suggest the hope of immortality, or even a pious thought; it is mere paganism in all its elegant coldness.

What a contrast to the tomb of the Christian Cecilia! If Urban, in his paternal tenderness, could only offer the Virgin and her narrow coffin, an honorable cell excavated in the soft stone of the Callistus Cemetery, Paschal prepared for her a marble sarcophagus; and although he buried her in a crypt under the altar of the Basilica, he enriched the latter with elegant monuments, and took care that posterity should know that beneath the sumptuous altar, Cecilia was resting in peace. Eight centuries later, Clement VIII. deemed a marble tomb unworthy of the cypress coffin; prudence forbade his encasing it in gold; he therefore ordered a silver casket to be prepared for the Christian daughter of the Cecilii. No vain ornaments enrich this casket; its decorations all speak to the beholder of the life beyond the grave. Angels, whose presence reminds us of Cecilia's angelic purity; brilliant gold stars, emblematic of heaven; the tiara and keys, proving the humble and tender respect of the Head of the Church to the virgin and martyr; such are the emblems which adorn Cecilia's tomb and render it far preferable, in the eyes of Christians, to the beautiful sarcophagus of Cecilia Metella. With the artist and archaeologist, we admire the latter, as one of the most remarkable among the monuments, erected by the ancient Romans; but the silver casket, containing the body of St. Cecilia, speaks to our heart, and teaches us lessons which Christians alone can understand and fully appreciate.

The sarcophagus, formerly prepared by St. Paschal, was too small to contain both the coffin and casket; Sfondrato therefore ordered a new white marble sepulchre to be substituted for the old one. The two sarcophagi, containing, one the bodies of Saints Tiburtius, Valerian, and Maximus, the other, the holy Popes Urban and Lucius, were left in the same place in the Confession, the relics not being disturbed, with the exception of the two heads of which we have spoken, and a few bones which Sfondrato took away from each of these venerable bodies. He sent the wooden box, in which the cypress coffin had been enclosed from the day of its Invention to that of the Translation, to the monastery of St. Paul at Milan; where two of his sisters and several other members of his family, had consecrated themselves to God.

[1] He was born in 1576. He sculptured many of the magnificent bass reliefs in the Pauline Chapel at St. Mary Major, among others, that which represents Pope Liberius, tracing upon snow, the foundation of the Esquiline Basilica.

[2] Sfondrato vehementer optanti, precantique saepius aliquid sibi reliquiarum ejus concedi, cum ex sacro corpore nemo, ac ne summus quidera Pontifex ob maximam reverentiam tollere ausus esset, ultro de eodem illi particulam benigna Virgo obtulisse ac donasse visa est. *Bosio. Relatio invent, et reposit. B. Caeciliae.*

[3] Nam cum ex linteaminibus tinctis sanguine, quae ad pedes jacebant (sacra etenim ossa nec ipse quoque tangere audebat) non nihil idem Cardinalis recidere vellet, quorum plerisque aliis purpuratis Patribus particulae divisae fuerunt, ad eam quam sibi recidebat partem sorte adhaerescens virginei cranii fragmentum accessit; de quo conjici potest, quod cervici proximum esset ad triplicem ietum carnificis pene recisum fuisse; ita ut facile cum ejusdem vulnera linteaminibus illis, quemadmodum in historia traditur, a fidelibus abstergerentur, ipsa abstersione in eis attrahi, atque auferri contigerit. *Bosio. Relatio, etc.*

[4] Sed et quemadmodum ipse Cardinalis se animadvertisse testatar, sub aureis vestibua rigidum cilicii tegmen propius sacris ossibus haerescens latebat, do que ita Acta passionis ejusdem commemorant: *Caecilia vero subtus ad camera cilicio induta desuper auro textis vestibus tegebatur.* Bosio. *Relatio invent, et reposit. B. Caeciliae.*

[5] Ubi cum adesset, (Clemens), educto aperculo cupressinae illius capsae, venerandum quoque Augelis sanctissimae ipsius corpus iis quae diximus (ut positum fuerat a Paschali Pontifice) opertum velis vidit, et veneratus est, atque ei tunc quam sciret omni auro, gemmisque esse gratiorem oblationem, preces obtulit, una cum lacrymis oblationis cordis indicibus. *Baronius,* ad an. 821, n° xxv.

The Pontiff's emotion on contemplating Cecilia's body, h an additional example of that sensibility of which he gave many touching proofs throughout his life. These tears of a stern old man, whose soul was nevertheless full of tenderness, recall his heart-breaking distress when forced to condemn the Cenci to death. He absented himself from Rome on the day when Beatrice, her mother-in-law, and her brother, were to be executed. Three discharges of cannon announced to him that these guilty heads were about to fall under the sword of justice. The condemned knew that at this moment the Pontiff would extend his hand to give them the Apostolic Indulgence for the hour of death. No sooner was this paternal act accomplished, than Clement VIII., fell senseless into the arms of his prelates.

[6] Sed ejus plurimum in eo commendata modestia fait quod invitatus licet, noluit reductis velis, nudum Virginia corpus quantumlibet exsiccatum inspicere, cui esse videretur loco ruboris custodis verecundiae virginalis, sanguis aspersus; satis ad fidem esse sciens, membra singula cognovisse per supposita vela, atque vidisse a praedecessore inscripta sepulchro atque descripta diplomats signacula illaesa reperta, atque divinitus conservata. *Bosio. Relatio invent, et reposit, B. Caeciliae.*

[7] In qua elaboranda, instar Beselehelis inspirati divinitus enituit industria excellentis opificis, qui veluti alterum caelam corpori, cujus esset incoelo anima, fabricans, thecam illam stellis auri fulgore micantibus exornavit. *Baronius,* ad. an. 821, n° xxv.

[8] See the design in Bosio. page 168.

[9] The body of St. Cecilia. Virgin and Martyr, entombed here by Clement VIII. in the year 1599, the 8th of his Pontificate.

Chapter Thirty-One - Translation of Cecilia's Body by Clement VIII.

The 22d of November at last arrived, and was greeted by the Romans with the greatest enthusiasm, their joy being sensibly increased by the rumor of the numerous miracles [1] which Cecilia had wrought since the recent discovery of her body. In order to avoid accidents, a papal edict was published, forbidding the driving of carriages through the trans-Tiberian region, on the morning of the Translation. The Basilica was adorned with magnificence worthy of such a festival. The body of Cecilia, in her cypress coffin, covered with a drapery of cloth of gold, rested upon the altar, which had been enlarged for the occasion. The light of a thousand torches was reflected in the beautiful marble columns of the *ciborium,* and in the enamel of Paschal's mosaics. Clement VIII. escorted by the Sacred College and an immense crowd arrived at the gates of Cecilia's palace. He immediately repaired to the sacristy, where he blessed the casket; this was then carried to the crypt, and laid open upon the white marble sarcophagus, which was resting upon the tomb of Popes Urban and Lucius. Valerian, Tiburtius, and Maximus awaited Cecilia, who was soon to resume her place near them. The procession advanced towards the altar, where the Holy .sacrifice of the Mass was to be offered. Forty-two Cardinals, richly robed and mitred, followed the Prelates. In this august body, were Alexander de Medicis, who was destined to govern the Church after Clement, under the name of Leo XL; Camille Borghese, who succeeded Leo, as Paul V.; Caesar Baronius, the historian of the Church; Robert Bellarmin, the conqueror of heresy, who was one day to be placed on our altars. France was represented by d'Ossat; Literature, by Silvio Antoniani; Faith, Piety, and Charity to the poor, by the dignitaries of the Church, among whom Paul Emilius Sfondrato was the centre of attraction.

Clement, robed in his cope, and crowned with the tiara, followed the Cardinals, walking under a splendid canopy, supported by the ambassadors of the Republic of Venice, and of the Duke of Savoy, and by Roman princes.

The French ambassador held up the cope, when the Pontiff descended from the *sedia gestatoria,* and directed his steps to the altar. The Holy Sacrifice was celebrated with all the ceremonies used at St. Peter's, when the Pontiff* officiates. The assistant deacons were Cardinal Francis Sforza, and Cardinal Alexander de Montalto, a nephew of Sixtus V., whilst Cardinal Peter Aldobrandini, Clement's nephew, filled the functions of deacon of the altar. The Pope added the Collect of Sts. Tiburtius, Valerian, and Maximus, to that of Cecilia.

After the communion, according to the ancient custom, they proceeded to the Translation of Cecilia's body. Sfondrato descended first into the Presbyterium, to be in readiness to receive the Virgin and the Pontiff', at their entrance into the crypt. After the Pope had incensed the body three times, four Cardinal Deacons, Odoard Farnese. Antonio Facchinetti, Peter Aldobrandini, and Bartholomew Cesi, raised the cypress coffin from the altar, and, preceded by deacons bearing the cross and seven gold candlesticks, descended into the subterranean vault of the Confession. During the ceremony, Clement laid his hand on Cecilia's coffin, as if to take direct part in the Translation. The members of the Sacred College surrounded the Pontiff, and the choir chanted the following anthem:

"O, beata Caecilia, quae Almachium superasti, Tiburtium et Valerianum ad martyr ii coronam vocasti!" [2]

The distance between the altar and the tomb was very short. Clement, assisted by the deacons, deposited the virgin's coffin in the silver casket, and then, receiving from Sfondrato a plate of the same metal, upon which was engraved an account of this last Translation, he placed it in the inside of the casket. Finally, after again incensing the precious relics three times, the Pontiff prostrated himself, and with abundant tears and fervent prayers, bade adieu to Cecilia in the name of the Church; he then closed the casket, and sealed, with his own seal, the marble slab which was placed over the sarcophagus; and then, preceded and followed by his imposing retinue he returned to the altar, where he recited the concluding prayers of the Holy Sacrifice, and gave his apostolic benediction to the people, who crowded the church, the porch, and the adjacent squares and streets. The concourse of the faithful continued until night; the day had been lovely; the air balmy as that of spring. Such weather, extraordinary for the month of November, was the more remarkable, as the preceding days had been cold and rainy. [3]

The following is the inscription, engraved upon the silver plate presented by Sfondrato to be enclosed in the silver casket.

"Hic requiescit corpus S. Caeciliae. Virginis et Martyris, quod a Paschali primo Pontifice Maximo ipsa revelante repertum, et in hanc Ecclesiam translatum, et sub hoc altari una cum corporibus SS. Martyrum Lucii et Urbani Pontificum, nec non Valeriani, Tiburtii et Maximi reconditum,

Iterum post annos fere DCCC. Clemente VIII., Pont. Max. cum iisdem Sanctis Martyribus lucem adspexit, die xx. Octobris, anno Dominicae Incarnationis M. D. IC. Cujus S. Virginis corpus praedictus D. N. Papa Clemens veteri lignea capsa, in qua jacebat, argenteae inclusa, intactum immutatumque, hoe eodem loco in quo fuerat collocatum, post peracta Missarum solemnia, maxima cum devotione et lachrymis, toto spectante populo, reposuit, XXII. Novembris, ipso festo Virginis die M. D. IC.

Ad cujus latus in alia seorsum capsa praedicti tres Martyres, Valerianus, Tiburtius et Maximus requiescunt; nec non sub ipso Virginis corpore in alia similiter area praedicti duo Martyres, ac Pontifices Lucius et Urbanus, prout a Paschali Pontifice omnes in iis conditi sunt.

Ego Paulus Tituli S. Caeciliae S. E. B. Presbyter Cardinalis Sfondratus, cui licet miserrimo peccatori praedicta corpora, quae diuturnitate temporis fere in tenebris jacebant, et invenire, et videre, et venerari a Deo Optimo Max. datum est memoriam hanc hisce litteris, consignavi. Anno Dominicae Incarnationis M. D. IC. die XXII. Novembris, sedente Clemente VIII. summo Pontifice, ejusdem Pontificatus anno VIII." [4]

This short account, engraved upon a silver plate, buried in St. Cecilia's tomb, was not sufficient for posterity. The learned explorer of subterranean Rome, Antonio Bosio, determined to commemorate the last Translation of the Virgin's body, by publishing a new edition of the Acts of St. Cecilia. After having carefully collated the manuscripts of the Basilica with those of the Vatican Library, of St. Peter's Chapter, and of the Colonna Palace, he published in the next year a new edition of the Acts, accompanied with a number of notes. Ecclesiastical archaeology has doubtless made much progress since the time of Bosio, but this great man certainly merits to share with Baronius, the glory of having been one of the first to open the path of Christian erudition, and of having been rarely surpassed therein.

Bosio added to the Acts of St. Cecilia, the famous document of Paschal, which he enriched with many important notes. He concluded his work with a description of the last discovery of Cecilia and her companions, and the ceremonies observed at the second Translation. Bosio declares that he either witnessed himself, or heard from Sfondrato's lips, all the facts which he relates. [5] This work appeared in Rome, in 1600, with a dedication to the Cardinal, who himself wrote an attestation, by which he certified Bosio's exactitude in the collation of the manuscripts, and his strict adherence to truth in his account of the discovery of the holy bodies. [6]

[1] Bosio. Relatio inventionis. *S. Caeciliae*, page 103.

[2] Happy Cecilia! Thou didst triumph over Almachius; Thou didst call Tiburtius and Valerian to the crown of martyrdom.

[3] At populi frequentia deinceps ad noctem usque affluere non destitit, coelo ipso obsecundante, quod, cum foedis imbribus per dies proximos exundasset, eo die ita placidum ac serenum affulsit, ut hybernus rigor in vernam temperiem versus esse videretur. *Bosio. Relatio inventionis corporis B. Caeciliae*, page 167.

[4] Here reposes the body of Saint Cecilia, Virgin and Martyr, discovered by Pope Paschal I. who transferred it to this Church, and buried it under this altar, with the bodies of the Holy Martyrs, Lucius and Urban, Popes; Valerian, Tiburtius, and Maximus. Nearly eight centuries after, under the pontificate of Clement VIII., the body of this holy Virgin was again discovered on the 20th of October, A.D. 1599, together with those of the same holy martyrs. On the 22d of November, the same Pope, Clement the VIII., after solemnly celebrating the Holy Sacrifice of the Mass, restored, in presence of the people, and with great devotion and many tears, the Virgin's body to the place it formerly occupied. He enclosed the coffin in a silver casket, and did not permit the body to be disturbed. In an adjoining tomb, the three martyrs Valerian, Tiburtius, and Maximus repose. Beneath the Virgin's body, and in another tomb, are the two martyrs, Popes Lucius and Urban, in the very spot, where they were buried by Pope Paschal. I, Paul Sfondrato, Cardinal Priest of the Holy Roman Church, Titulary of Saint Cecilia, to whom although such a miserable sinner, Almighty God deigned to grant the favor of discovering, beholding, and venerating this holy body, which time seemed to have buried in darkness, — I have drawn up this inscription in remembrance of this event. The year of Our Lord, 1599, the 22d of November, under Pope Clement the VIII.— in the eighth year of his pontificate.

[5] Haec sunt, quas in postrema corporis B. Caeciliae Virginis, Sociorumque Martyrum detectione, ac solemni repositione acta sunt, prout cum oculis nostris nos ipsi conspeximus, tum ex ipsius Cardinalis Sfondrati, qui his omnibus diligenter astitit, ac praefuit, fideli relatione cognovimus. *Bosio. Relatio Invent, et Reposit. corporis S. Caeciliae*, page 170.

[6] Nos Paulus Tituli S. Caeciliae S. R. E. Presbyter Cardinalis Sfondratus, has Sanctissimae Virginis Caeciliae, ejusque Sociorum vitas ex quamplurimis, iisque vetutissimis codicibus integras ab Antonio Bosio excerptas fuisse, necnon quae do inventione Corporum eorumdem Sanctorum ab ipso referuntur, omnia fideliter, sincere, atque ad veritatem conscripta esse testamur.

Chapter Thirty-Two - Confirmation of the Acts of St. Cecilia by the Circumstances Attending the Second Discovery of Her Body

The few details left us by Paschal concerning the first discovery of Cecilia's body, all tend to prove the truth of her Acts; these are now confirmed beyond all doubt by the circumstances attending the second discovery of the martyr's precious remains. First, we shall remark that the position of Cecilia's body is very different from that of any other martyr found in Rome or elsewhere. But when we recall the manner and circumstances of her death, as related in her Acts, the reason of this difference is obvious. As she lies there in her sarcophagus, we easily recognize the Roman virgin, expiring on the floor of her own palace, shrinking with virginal modesty from the gaze of those who came in crowds to witness her triumphal death. Secondly, Sfondrato bears witness to the hair shirt mentioned in the Acts, as the armor with which the heroic virgin shielded herself from the seductions of an effeminate world. "We say nothing of the gold-embroidered robe and the bloody linen, for these are expressly mentioned in Paschal's document. Thirdly, the stature of the Saint, as determined in 1599, is a fresh proof of the correctness of her Acts. Bosio declares that her body, as it lay in the cypress coffin, measured only four feet. Of course allowance must be made for the contraction of the limbs produced by pain and by time, also for the position of the body, the knees being slightly drawn up; but with all these allowances, Cecilia's stature must have been below the middle height. This accounts for her having been forced to mount on a marble stand, when addressing the soldiers of Almachius, that she might be heard by all; it also accounts for the first exclamation of Almachius when she was brought before his tribunal: "Who art thou, child?" (*puella*). But it is not only in what concerns St. Cecilia that the discovery of 1599 attests the minute fidelity of the Acts. These relate that Valerian and Tiburtius were beheaded. Now one of the sarcophagi contained the bodies of two martyrs who had evidently suffered death by the headman's axe. The Acts state that Almachius was puzzled with regard to the respective ages of the brothers, and thirteen centuries later, their skeletons were so strikingly alike that it would have been impossible to distinguish one from the other, if each body had not been wrapt in a separate shroud. The Acts relate that Maximus was not beheaded, but beaten to death with loaded whips; now, in 1599, the head of this martyr was found adhering to the body, his skull fractured, and his hair clotted with blood, thus proving by what kind of torment he gained his heavenly crown. There is still another circumstance of the greatest importance in this demonstration of the Acts of Saint Cecilia by archaeological details. Our readers have not forgotten the oratory, opening upon one of the lateral naves of the Basilica, on the right, as you enter the Church, and designated under the name of St. Cecilia's Bath. This sanctuary, which from time immemorial, had been considered as an appendage of the Church, and honored with a private altar, was a monument of the kind of martyrdom suffered by the Saint, according to her Acts. The existence of this sanctuary moreover supports the assertion contained in these Acts that St. Cecilia in dying bequeathed her house to Pope St. Urban, to be converted into a Basilica. There is no question here of one of those public baths, established near some of the churches in Rome and elsewhere, which were used by the faithful for certain mysterious ablutions. This was a *sudatorium,* used for vapor baths, totally different from those taken by the Christians of the first centuries in the sacred Thermae of the churches, Moreover, this oratory was constantly honored by the faithful. If we admit the veracity of the Acts, this veneration is easily understood, and becomes a fresh proof of the event which it commemorates. In the course of time, the primitive character of this oratory was totally destroyed by the numerous repairs made at different periods; so much so, that a few years before the discovery of Cecilia's tomb, a Christian archaeologist writing in Rome, expressed some doubts as to the truth of the tradition which specifies this sanctuary as the caldarium where the virgin had suffered martyrdom.

Sfondrato determined to restore this venerable place to its antique form, and ancient honors. Whilst superintending the repairing and embellishing of the Basilica, he ordered a search to be made under the floor of this chapel which was found to be built upon a vault. Shortly after, the hypocaust of a bath was discovered. The apertures which had been closed, were easily reopened, and a large boiler was found, with the remains of a leaden pipe, through which the vapor had formerly ascended to the caldarium. Sfondrato disposed the decorations of the chapel in such a manner that the destruction of a memorial so dear to his piety, should henceforth be an impossibility. He caused iron gratings to be placed over the openings, through which the pilgrims could look into the hypocaust and distinguish the boiler which had escaped the ravages of time. He cleared the terra cotta pipes through which the vapor had passed, as well as a leaden pipe, which, like the former, was carried above the floor of the room; both were protected by brass plates fastened to the wall. Nothing was neglected to restore this venerable monument to its original form — that of a *sudatorium,* the dimensions of which were much smaller than those of the ancient public hot baths, but in perfect accordance with the private dwelling to which it had belonged. [1]

We have before mentioned that Sfondrato preserved, until his death, the small splinter of bone which he had found adhering to the piece of linen with which Cecilia's wound had been staunched. He bequeathed it to his dear Basilica, and we have had the happiness of holding in our hands this precious pledge of the martyr's gratitude to her faithful servant. It is enclosed in a very elegant reliquary, bronze gilt, in the form of a tower. It stands upon a pedestal and is set with crystals.

In reviewing all these circumstances, brought to light, and certified so many centuries after the events to which they refer, is it not evident that they form a most imposing demonstration in favor of the Acts of St. Cecilia?

Would not such important archaeological discoveries be more than sufficient to banish all doubt respecting the truth of any recital handed down to us by antiquity? Would not all the academicians of Europe agree in acquitting its author of the charge of falsehood brought against him? Would they not be unanimous in condemning preceding generations for their injustice towards an author whose recital they had taken no pains to verify? Such has been the justification of the Acts of St. Cecilia. Their truth has been incontestably proved by the great discoveries of which we have spoken.

[1] Platner and Bunsen find no difficulty in recognizing in this chapel the Bath where Cecilia expired (Beschreibung der stadt Rom. Tome iii. 3re partie, pages 643 and 644.) The fact of their not seeing the boiler in the hypocaust, can be explained only by an error which they might have easily avoided. The room communicated with the furnace by two apertures; the boiler could only be seen through that on the right. These learned Germans may only have examined it through the aperture on the left, and seeing nothing, may have discontinued their search.

Chapter Thirty-Three - Sfondrato Discovers the Body of St. Agnes. His Piety towards the Mother of God and the Saints. His Will and Death. His Epitaph in the Basilica of St. Cecilia

The fervent piety of Sfondrato and his success in discovering Cecilia's tomb, inspired him, some years later, with the thought of trying to find the body of St. Agnes in her Basilica outside the walls, on the Nomentana road.

Martyred at the age of thirteen, under the Emperor Diocletian, about seventy years after the death of St. Cecilia, Agnes shares with her the homages of Home and of Catholicity. Sfondrato was destined to discover this new treasure, and to prepare a worthy triumph for this heroic child whose pure life and courageous death place her upon a level with the daughter of the Cecilii.

Clement VIII. had yielded his great soul to God. The pontificate of his successor, Leo XL, was very short, and in 1605, the Apostolic Senate confided the destinies of the Church to the powerful and faithful hands of Paul V. Scarcely was the Conclave over, when Sfondrato who had generously determined to restore at his own expense the Basilica of St. Agnes, commenced his work; he would not however permit the architects to begin, until he himself had directed a search for the relics of the holy martyr.

On Friday, the 7th of October, 1605, he repaired to the Church of St. Agnes, accompanied by the Chevalier Sasso-Ferrato, a gentleman of his household, and brother Nicostrato, an oblate of the monastery of St. Peter, *in Vincoli*. The presence of the latter was necessary, as the Nomentana Basilica was a dependency of the monastery of St. Peter. Sfondrato had considered it most probable that the main altar of the Basilica covered the bodies of Saints Agnes and Emerentiana, her foster-sister, and, like her, a virgin and martyr. He presumed that Honorius I. had deposited the sacred remains of both saints in this place.

The altar was lined with slabs of white marble, artistically inserted, one into the other, and the upper part was covered with a large plate of porphyry, which had not been removed since the seventh century. The face of the altar, on the side of the grand nave, was remarkable for the *fenestella* destined to receive the lamps which burned in honor of the Saints; the other side, facing the apsis, was covered with a solid slab of marble; and *this,* Sfondrato decided to remove.

After taking away the slab of porphyry which covered the altar, the workmen endeavored to remove the marble tablet which was laid vertically on the side of the hemicycle. It was only after repeated efforts that they succeeded in taking away enough cement to enable them to discern several white marble tablets arranged as if to protect some precious relic under the altar. Encouraged by the prospect of success, the workmen labored with increasing diligence, and before the end of the day, reached the tomb, which was built like a vault. But the marble slabs were joined with such strong cement, that it was almost impossible to break it. They were obliged to bore several places with instruments suited for the purpose. Through the apertures thus made, they were enabled, with the assistance of a light, to distinguish the bodies of the two virgins, lying side by side, under the little vault which was about five feet long. Night interrupted their labor. Sfondrato and his companions, after returning thanks to God for their success, retired, with the resolution of resuming their search the next morning.

The following day, Saturday, 8th of October, the Cardinal returned to the Basilica with the same persons. They were accompanied by Stephen Benassai, his auditor, Father Felix Veronico, Curate of the church of St. Lawrence *in Damaso,* and a gentleman from Modena, named Crigino. By some fortunate circumstance, Cardinal Aquaviva visited the Basilica towards evening, and thus another important witness was added to the number already present, as if to render the Invention of the sacred bodies still more solemn.

Intelligent and skilful workmen had been employed, but the cement was so solid that they were obliged to labor from two o'clock in the afternoon, until two o'clock at night, before they could open a sufficiently large space to enable them to reach the relics.

Finally, all obstacles being removed, Sfondrato was enabled to feast his eyes upon the eagerly longed-for treasure. The martyrs were each laid upon a tablet of white marble, supported at either end upon an iron bar. These tablets, which had been thus raised from the ground, to prevent the effects of humidity, had been also pierced with a number of holes, in order to give access to the air. Three other tablets, similar to the first, were elevated by iron bars above the holy bodies. The well-cemented marble vault had protected this glorious sepulchre for a thousand years.

The two virgins were lying on their backs, and turned towards the East, according to the Christian custom. The bones, which had rested directly upon the marble, had remained solid and joined; but the other bones had crumbled into dust. Near the figure on the right, they discovered a small quantity of some substance which they easily recognized as the coagulated remains of the blood collected by the faithful. This enabled them to distinguish Agnes from her companion. They also discovered near the two bodies, a little earth, which had doubtless been impregnated with their blood, and on this account, placed in their sepulchre. Some fragments of a light silken texture were found, which were evidently remnants of their veils.

Although the night was already far advanced, Sfondrato thought it would be very imprudent to leave these holy relics exposed to the indiscreet curiosity of those who would not fail to hasten to the Basilica the next morning, to see the result of the work which had been going on for two days. He had previously ordered a wooden box lined with purple silk embroidered with gold. With the assistance of his auditor and Father Felix Veronico, he deposited in this box the bones which had remained entire, carefully distinguishing the precious remains of the two martyrs. This operation required great precaution, for the bones would have crumbled into dust, if not very delicately handled. The box being closed and sealed, was carried to an inner chapel of the monastery adjoining the Basilica, and covered with drapery. The dust of the bones, the remains of coagulated blood, and the earth of which we have spoken, were carefully collected and placed in two beautiful antique vases which Sfondrato had brought for the purpose. One urn was consecrated to Agnes, the other to Emerentiana." [1]

Such were the circumstances attending the Invention of the body of St. Agnes. The reader will readily perceive that in many points it differs from the discovery of St. Cecilia's tomb. The precious remains of the Virgin Agnes had already partly suffered the common fate which condemns the body of man to return to the dust *of which it was originally formed;* the mortal remains of Cecilia were preserved intact in her sepulchre. The virgin who suffered martyrdom under Alexander Severus, could easily be recognized by the description given in her Acts; whereas the virgin, executed by command of Diocletian, could only be identified by means of antique documents which gave reason to suppose that Pope Honorius had buried her under the altar of the Nomentana Basilica.

We do not wish by this comparison to detract from the glory of the illustrious Agnes, whose memory is dear to us, and to whom we should be most happy to consecrate a biography worthy of her; but we cannot refrain from pointing out the preference shown by heaven for the daughter of the Cecilii.

172

Did she not herself reveal to Paschal that the Queen of Heaven watched over her forgotten tomb?

And if we would discover the motive of Mary's vigilance over Cecilia's remains, do we not find it in the ineffable resemblance between the Spouse of Valerian and the Spouse of Joseph, both having given the world the sublime example of virginity in the married state? The body of Mary, exempt from original sin, sanctified by the Divine Maternity, was assumed into heaven amidst choirs of angels; the body of Cecilia, participating in our fallen nature, but elevated by the immortal virtue of purity, remained thirteen centuries in the bowels of the earth without suffering dissolution. Let us return thanks to the heavenly Spouse who protected His beloved even in the tomb; and let us glorify the Queen of Virgins who honored in Cecilia one of her own most noble prerogatives.

Paul V. imitated the example of Clement VIII., and presented a silver casket to contain the relics of the glorious martyr whose Invention honored his Pontificate. *Emerentiana* was also placed in this splendid casket. The greater part of the glory of this new solemnity, which was far inferior to that offered Cecilia, was due to the exertions of the pious Cardinal, who seemed to have received the mission of presenting to the Holy City her most august and best beloved saints. Sfondrato was not satisfied with contributing to Cecilia's glory in the Basilica where she reposes; he desired to give the other sanctuaries dedicated to the illustrious Virgin, proofs of his pious solicitude. He commenced with the little Church of St. Cecilia *de domo* in the Campus Martius.

This sanctuary was once a dependency of the Basilica of St. Lawrence *in Damaso*; at a later period, it was attached to the Church of St. Lawrence *in Lucina*, on account of its neighborhood to the latter Basilica. But the divine service being carelessly performed, Sfondrato decided to place the church under the charge of two Dominican friars, for whose maintenance he would himself provide. After the Cardinal's death, Paul V. felt bound in honor to carry out his pious intention by Apostolic authority, and therefore issued a Brief, dated 23d of January, 1622, in which after commending Sfondrato's piety towards* the church, he first suppressed the title of Saint Blaise which had been attached to this sanctuary, and then taking it from the jurisdiction of the Church of St. Lawrence in Lucina, subjected it in perpetuity to the titulary Cardinal of Saint Cecilia. Finally, he assigned in favor of the two Dominican friars, a salary of three hundred and twenty-five Roman crowns, to be drawn from the revenues of the Abbot of "Our Lady of the Column," in the diocese of Piacenza. [2] We have spoken elsewhere of the Church of St. Cecilia a Monte-Giordano which also belonged to the Basilica of Saint Lawrence in Damaso. This Church was falling to ruins. Sfondrato had determined to rebuild it and had laid the first corner stone of the new edifice on the 21st of June, 1602. Later, in 1621, after Sfondrato's death, the Oratorian Fathers of Saint Philip de Neri, wishing to enlarge their house of Vellicella, earnestly begged Gregory XV. to permit them to demolish this church which interfered with their architect's plans. The Pontiff granted the request on condition that the principal altar of the celebrated chapel, called the *Oratory,* which was to be built on the site of the church, should be dedicated to St. Cecilia conjointly with St. Philip Neri; and that the altar piece should represent these two saints, the illustrious Virgin being on the right. [3] This condition was faithfully complied with. The picture was painted by Vanni. In the upper part, he has represented the Assumption of the Blessed Virgin. Every year on the 22d of November, the festival of St. Cecilia is celebrated as a patronal feast, and thus the beautiful thought of Sfondrato has been perpetuated to our day. The pious Cardinal who so zealously honored the memory of the Spouse of Christ, was no less devoted to the Queen of Heaven. We will illustrate this by a single incident.

Having been promoted by Paul V., to the Legation of Bologna, his first thought was to visit and venerate the house of Loretto. In the enthusiasm of his respectful love for the Virgin, he mounted to the ebony statue which represents the Queen of this Holy House, and taking from his finger a magnificent diamond ring, worth five hundred gold crowns, he placed it on the finger of the miraculous image. In returning to Rome, he passed by Loretto, and hung round the neck of the Madonna, a gold cross set with eight superb emeralds. He also desired to offer a worthy tribute to the divine Infant whom the Blessed Mother holds in her arms. Before starting for his legation, he presented the Son with a diamond ring far surpassing the one he had offered to the Mother. He himself placed it upon the finger of the Holy child, and until the spoliation of the sanctuary of Loretto in 1797, this diamond by its wonderful brilliancy attracted the admiration of all the pilgrims who visited the shrine. [4]

In 1607, Sfondrato was called to the Bishopric of Cremona, in the province of Milan, which had lately lost its great Archbishop St. Charles. The illustrious Cardinal Frederick Borromeo, nephew of the holy Archbishop, was faithfully imitating his uncle's virtues in the See of St. Ambrose. Sfondrato's arrival was a great consolation to Frederick, as they had both chosen for their model the celebrated Pontiff whose recent loss still deeply grieved the Church. Sfondrato, to whom the city of Rome owes the beautiful Church of St. Charles *al Corso,* obtained from Frederick for this sanctuary the heart of the invincible reformer of discipline and of Christian morals. In the year 1611, our pious Cardinal was recalled to Rome. Paul V elevated him to the Bishopric of Albano, and Sfondrato was obliged to leave his See of Cremona where his memory is still gratefully preserved. As he had been appointed Titulary of one of the Suburbicarian Sees, he could no longer, according to the ordinary rule, retain the simply Presbyterial Church of St. Cecilia; but Sfondrato could not think of confiding to another, the precious deposit which the Virgin herself had given *him.*

He therefore solicited and obtained from Paul V., as a reward for his generosity towards the trans-Tiberian Basilica, the favor of retaining it, *in commendam* together with the Bishopric which he had been forced to except.

His Administration of the Church of Albano was of 'short duration; but it was marked by his inexhaustible charity to the poor. Each year, he distributed among them the whole of his Episcopal revenue, without diminishing the alms he continued to bestow in Rome, whither the functions of his eminent dignity frequently called him. [5]

In 1614, the Roman Ritual, published by Paul V., completed the series of liturgical books, for the use of the Universal Church. The publication of this work had been left by the Council of Trent to the Sovereign Pontiff.

Catholicity owes it to Sfondrato's exertions. He induced Paul V., to undertake the compilation of this manual for the use of the priests in the administration of the Sacraments. He was one of the most assiduous members of the committee appointed by the Pope to prepare this important work; and he superintended its compilation with untiring solicitude.

Sfondrato [6] died at Tivoli, on the 14th of February, 1618, in the fifty seventh year of his age. The sad news reached the nuns of Santa Cecilia on the morning of the following day. Nothing can express their grief on hearing of this unexpected death; we find in the Chronicle of the Monastery: "That several of the Sisters fainted, and that the dinner of that day was untouched." [7]

Ever constant in his love for St. Cecilia, Sfondrato made his will in favor of her Basilica; he had for eighteen years renounced his own name, and assumed that of Cardinal of St. Cecilia. [8]

Some extracts from the will of this Cardinal, will probably, interest our readers, as his name will always be united with that of St. Cecilia in the annals of Christianity.

"In the first place," says Paul Emilius Sfondrato. "I recommend my soul with perfect submission to my gracious Redeemer, Jesus Christ; to his most Holy and ever Blessed Mother, the most pure Virgin Mary, the true advocate of sinners; to the glorious Apostles Peter and Paul; to my glorious and most faithful protectress, St. Cecilia; to St. Agnes, my special advocate; to St. Mary Magdalen, St. Thecla, St. Joseph, Sts. Lucius, Urban, Valerian, Tiburtius, and Maximus, and all the Saints towards whom I have any special devotion, or who have been my protectors; that I may be found worthy of the Divine Mercy, and may be admitted into their society forever. I wish my body to be buried in the Church of my beloved St. Cecilia, in the tomb I have caused to be made under the Confession before the altar of the Saint."

Then follow the Cardinal's directions relative to the religious services, and the alms to be distributed on the day of his funeral. After requesting the most simple obsequies, with merely twelve torches, he adds:

"I appoint as my sole legatee, the Church of St. Cecilia, in the Trastevere, where her holy body reposes." The legacy is to be employed in the following manner. First of all, ninety lamps are to be kept burning day and night, and fed with the purest oil. Four chaplains, one of whom is to have the title of guardian of St. Cecilia's body, are to officiate in the Basilica. They are to visit the chapel daily and are to be assisted by two clerks. Moreover, there is to be a layman charged with the care of the bronzes and marble of the Confession, as well as with the feeding and lighting of the lamps. The chaplains, clerks, and laymen, are forbidden to enter into the service of any other person, even though he be a Cardinal.

Sfondrato bequeathed to his Basilica all the relics he had collected in its treasury. The smallest portion of these can never be removed, and each Abbess, on entering upon her office, is obliged to take an oath faithfully to observe these directions. He also requested that there should be three keys to the treasury, one of which should be entrusted to the Abbess, the second to the Prioress, and the third to the Mistress of Novices.

The Cardinal also made other legacies to different persons or establishments. To the duke, his brother, his patrimonial estates; to his cathedral church of Albano, all his pontifical ornaments and all his silver church vessels; to the Madonna of Loretto, a gold heart worth one hundred crowns, and "I wish," he adds, "that it be suspended round her neck in memory of the love I have desired to feel for her." To this donation, the Cardinal adds the superb ring he was in the habit of wearing, and which was remarkable for a very valuable cameo.

The codicil contains the following legacies.

To his sister Angelica Agatha, a ring containing relics of St. Cecilia.

To the Duke Hercules, his brother, Vanni's picture of St. Cecilia expiring. This is a different one from that placed by the Cardinal in the Crypt of the Basilica, upon the altar of the holy martyr.

To his second brother, the marquis, a painting of St. Agnes.

To Cardinal Farnèse, his large painting of St. Peter weeping over his sin.

To Cardinal Giustiniani, the Ecce Homo of Sodomi.

To the Convent of The Minerva, a portrait of St. Thomas, life size. To the professed house of the Gesu, the painting in which the Cardinal is represented kneeling before St. Cecilia and the other saints to whom he had a special devotion.

To the barefoot Carmelites, an oval picture of the Madonna.

After this enumeration, Sfondrato adds, "I bequeath the remainder to the Saint." Then he concludes with the following directions: "For the honor and glory of my dear Saint Agnes and of her holy body, I leave two hundred and fifty measures (boccali) of oil annually, to feed ten lamps which arc to burn night and day, and I charge the Abbess of St. Cecilia with the execution of this bequest;'

This will, an everlasting memorial of the Cardinal's piety, bears the date of the 6th of August, 1615.

Sfondrato's body was carried from Tivoli to the. Church of St. Cecilia and placed near the Communion rail, so that the sisters might contemplate the mortal remains of him who had been their protector and their father. It was not deemed necessary to conform to the humble Cardinal's request respecting his obsequies. The Abbess and the religious of St. Cecilia desired that they should be celebrated with all possible pomp and solemnity.

So great a man could only be buried at the feet of the Virgin whom he had so tenderly loved. He had already caused his tomb to be prepared in the crypt where she reposes, and had had engraved upon a slab of porphyry the inscription he had composed as his last homage to the martyr. We have frequently, by the light of torches, read it in this gloomy vault, near Cecilia's body, and we have envied the happiness of him whose mortal remains it covers, and who sleeps, humbly buried under a pavement never trodden by the footsteps of the profane. It is thus conceived:

PALVS TITVLI S. CAECILLAE S. R. E. PRESB. CARD. SFONDRATVS MISERRI-
MVS PECCATOR ATQUE EIUSDEM VIRGINIS HVMUJS SERVVS HIC AD EIVS
PEDES HVMILITER REQVIESCIT. VIXIT ANNOS LVII. MENSES X. DIES XXV.
OBIIT ANNO MDCXVIII. MENSE FEBR. DIE XIV. ORATE DEVM PRO EO. [9]

This touching and simple epitaph, concealed from every eye in the depths of a crypt, was not sufficient to record the glory and merits of Sfondrato. The executors of his will erected a magnificent cenotaph to the Cardinal, under the right lateral nave, near the sacristy, at the spot where the Ponziani chapel formerly opened into the Basilica. On this monument is placed the bust of the Cardinal; the hands are joined, and the mozetta is of colored marble. On the right, is a statue of St. Cecilia, holding in her hand a miniature organ; on the left, one of St. Agnes with a lamb. A bass-relief on the upper part of the monument, represents Sfondrato presenting St. Cecilia's body to Clement VIII. These details are unfortunately very badly executed. The cenotaph is completed by an inscription recording the services rendered by Cardinal Paul Emilius Sfondrato to the Church and to St. Cecilia.

DEO. TRINO. VNI.
PAVLO. SFONDRATO. CARD. EPISC. ALBAN. GREG. XIV. FR. FIL. BONONIEN.
LEGATO. SIGNATVRAE. GRATLAE. PRAEFECTO. CREMONEN. PRAESVLI.
PIETATE. IN DEVM. DIVOSQVE. ANIMARVM. STVDIO. CHARITATE. IN. PAV-
PERES. PLANE. MEMORANDO. QVOD. SANCTAE. CECILLAE. CORPVS. INSIG-
NI. SEPVLCRO. LVMINIBUS. AD. CENTVM. PERPETVO. COLLVCENTIBVS.
TERRESTRI PROPE COELO. DECORAVIT. TEMPLVM EXORNATVM. SACER-
DOTIBVS. MINISTRIS. PRETIOSIS. VASIS. ET. RELIQVIIS AVCTVM.
HAEREDEM EX. ASSE. RELIQVIT. QVODQVE. OMNEM. EIVSMODI. RERVM.
MEMORIAM. VIVENS. REPVLIT. DEMORTVO. ANNO AETATIS. LVII. SAL.
MDCXVIII.
ORDOARDVS. CARD. FARNESIVS. ET. AVGVSTINVS. PACCINELLIVS. SENEN.
TESTAMENTARII. EXECVTORES. P. P. [10]

[1] An interesting account of this Invention may be found in Boldetti. Osserea-zioni. sopra. i., Cimiterj de Santi Martiri, pages 684-686.

[2] Biblioth. Vaticane. MSS. do Galetti. *Santa Cecilia.*

[3] Bref *Cum ad uberes*, du 7 des Kalondos do Novembre.

[4] Ciacconius *Vitae Romanorum Pontificum at S. R. E. Cardinalium.* Tome iv. p. 226.

[5] Ciacconius *Vitae Romanorum Pontificum et S. R. E. Cardinulium.* Tome iv. page 227.

[6] Ciacconius *Vitae Romanorum Pontificum et S. R. E. Cardinalium.* Tome iv. page 226. The Vatican Library is indebted to Sfondrato's generosity for the valuable Greek Menology, attributed to the Emperor Basil. It was published in 1727, with Byzantine illustrations, at the expense of Cardinal Annibal Albani. It is one of the most interesting monuments of the Melchite Liturgy.

[7] Chroniche del venerabile monasteri do Santa Cecilia.

[8] In the correspondence of Cardinal d'Ossat, we find two letters which Sfondra-to had addressed through this ambassador to Henry IV., and to Marie de Medicis, to obtain from France some relics for the Basilica. D'Ossat, in sending these let-ters, advised the king to address his reply to the Cardinal of St. Cecilia, because, he adds, he wishes to be called by this title and not by his surname! (Letters du Cardinal d'Ossat, 26 Aont 1602, tome iv. page 304). We find the same thing in a public document relating to the laying of the corner stone in the rebuilding of St. Cecilia's Church, a *Monto Giordano.* The following is an extract from the verbal process of this ceremony: Ob idqne Cardinalis Sanctae Caeciliae, relicta propria bus nobilissimae et antiquiasimae familiae denominatione, nuncupari et appel-lari voluit, amore atque devotionis zelo erga eamdem Beatam Caeciliam flagrans atque incensus. (MSS. du Vatican, Galletti.) Sfondrato in this respect followed the example of St. Charles Borromeo, who always signed himself Cardinal of St. Praxedes, and never Cardinal Borromeo.

[9] Paul Sfondrato, a Cardinal Priest of the Holy Roman Church, a Titulary of St. Cecilia, a poor sinner, and an humble servant of this holy Virgin, here lies humbly at her feet. He lived fifty-seven years, ten months, and twenty-five days, and died on the 14th of February, 1628. Pray to God for him.

[10] To the one God in three Divine Persons. To the memory of Paul Sfondrato, Cardinal Bishop of Albano, nephew of Gregory XIV., Legate of Bologna, Bishop of Cremona, Praefect of the Sign of Grace, worthy of all commendation for his piety towards God and the Saints, his zeal for the salvation of souls, and his charity towards the poor. Through his exertions the body of St. Cecilia was honored with a magnificent sepulture; one hundred lamps burn night and day before her tomb, presenting a faint image of the splendor which surrounds her in heaven. He named this temple, embellished through his largesses, heir of all his fortune, en-dowed its priests and ministers, and enriched it with valuable vases and holy relics. During his lifetime, he never permitted any one to speak in his presence, of the monuments of his piety. He died at the age of fifty-seven, in the year of salvation, 1618. Odoard, Cardinal Farnese, and Augustin Paccinelli, of Sienna, his executors, have erected this monument.

Chapter Thirty-Four - Facts Relating to St. Cecilia and Her Basilica throughout the Seventeenth Century. The Jansenistic School Attacks the Acts of the Holy Martyr

We are now near the close of our history. The Jansenists, ever eager to pluck from the brow of the Church, the ornaments with which it has pleased her divine Spouse to adorn her, seem to have taken pleasure in casting ridicule and contempt upon many of the touching traditions which have come down to us from the earliest ages. And, indeed, they have manifested as much earnestness in modifying history to suit their views as in reforming dogmas and Evangelical morals according to their own plans.

Their efforts have been fruitless. Jansenism has been supplanted by Voltarian philosophy, which, in its turn, is gradually falling into decay, and upon its ruin is rising a new and Catholic generation, clinging to the traditions of the early Church, sympathizing with it in faith and feeling, and trampling underfoot the prejudices which a succession of disastrous circumstances seemed to have rendered national. Truly, this generation exhibits a wonderful example of the unerring instinct of faith in matters regarding God and His Saints! Every thing is against us: Ecclesiastical History, the Lives of the Saints, the profound and systematic oblivion in which maliciously disposed persons have sought to bury a thousand traditions which nourished the faith of our fathers, and gave rise to the miracles of former ages.

It is alarming even to glance at the formidable task awaiting Catholic criticism; yet the church of France imperatively calls for the vindication of the authenticity of many grave and valuable documents, many historical details and Acts of the Saints, cruelly compromised in this conspiracy against truth. Such a task, considered in its full extent, is far beyond our power; we have merely touched upon a single point.

May the august Virgin Cecilia pardon us for having defended her so feebly; He, who has already indemnified her for the forgetfulness of mankind, will, in his own good time, raise up a powerful avenger of her cause.

The renown of the numerous miracles wrought in the trans-Tiberian Basilica^ during the latter part of the sixteenth century, was soon widely circulated, not only throughout France, but through the whole of Christendom, and resulted in the publication of several religious and literary works. We will cite among others a musical drama, entitled: *The Cecilian, or the Martyrdom of St. Cecilia,* published in Paris by Nicholas Soret, in 1606. The choruses were set to music by Abraham Blondet. In 1617, de Welles published at Arras, a French translation of a volume edited in Rome by Bosio, containing the Acts of St. Cecilia and an account of the two Inventions of the martyr's body. De Welles entitled his translation: *Chastity victorious in the admirable conversion of St. Valerian husband of St. Cecilia, Tiburtius, Maximus, and others.* [1] Later a member of the Oratory in France, Nicholas de Bralion, who resided at

Rome from 1625 to 1640, and who has left an interesting work upon the churches of this capital of the Christian world, [2] dedicated a volume to the glory of our holy Martyr in her tomb. He did not publish it until 1688, a short time before his death, under the title of: *The admirable Sepulture of St. Cecilia in her Church in Rome.* Even at this early period, hagiography was preparing the most magnificent tribute which the genius of Catholicity had ever dedicated to the honor of the Saints. The immense and erudite collection of the Acts of the Saints, commenced in 1643, at Anvers by Bollandus, successfully pursued its course; a new volume being annually published, worthy of those which had preceded it both in the importance of the matter and the erudition of the commentaries and notes. The work was arranged according to the plan of the "Ecclesiastical Cycle and the Martyrologies," but owing to many interruptions it is unfortunately still incomplete. It has been resumed in later years, much to the satifaction of all Catholic hearts; but the Acts of the 18th of October, upon this immense Calendar, will not be published for several years. It is more than probable that the present century will draw near to a close before the Acts of St. Cecilia will be given to the public.

In 1648, a new triumph was awarded to St. Cecilia, at the Capitol in Rome. The chapel of this magnificent palace was newly decorated, and the daughter of the Cecilii, as a Roman citizen and matron, was honored with a painting and accompanying inscription in this sanctuary. [3] This great Virgin is represented as the patroness of music: she is seated, playing a harpsicord. The painting is by Romanelli — the inscription as follows:

S. CAECILIAE VIRGINI ET MARTYRI
S. P. Q. R.
MDCXLVIII.

The idea of thus restoring the name and memory of Cecilia, in the very place where her ancestor Caia Cecili had for so many years been honored with a statue, is deeply touching and admirably blends Pagan and Christian Rome in the person of our heroine. A Christian Cecilia assuming in the Capitol the place of the Pagan Caia proves alike the triumph of Christianity and the eternity of Rome.

Before the close of the seventeenth century, the most eminent hagiographers had published their opinion respecting these Acts, against which so violent a tempest was about to break forth. Henschenius spoke in the highest terms of this venerable document, in commenting upon the 14th of April, dedicated to Sts. Tiburtius, Valerian and Maximus. [4]

The opinion of a man so well versed in the difficult art of comparing documents and deciding their respective merits, was certainly a powerful counterpoise to the arguments adduced by St. Cecilia's enemies; but the truth of her history was conclusively established in 1680, when Papebroke, who had shared the labors of Henschenius, announced to the public his decision in favor of her Acts. In the very beginning of the first volume of the Acts of the Saints for the month of May, this critic who certainly cannot be accused of credulity, declared the Acts of St. Cecilia most ancient and true. [5] Divine Providence doubtless permitted this fearless testimony as a counterpoise to the opinion of certain influential writers who would have consigned to oblivion one of the most precious recitals of the primitive Church.

The Acts of St. Cecilia, as the unprejudiced reader must have already perceived, are not wanting in intrinsic evidence of their own truth; still, Ave are no less happy to record in their favor the opinion of so competent a judge, a man who was censured throughout Europe for the severity of his criticism.

It is something to be able to prove that the very century which beheld the attack, saw also the most learned and reliable men coming forward to repress the audacity of a clique which felt itself called to exercise a lasting influence over the minds of men. The greater the number of Saints' lives which Papebroke has rejected, as doubtful or apocryphal, the stronger the weight of his authority in support of those which he has deemed it his duty to admit.

The impulse given to hagiography by the Bollandists, first called forth the *Acta Sanctorum Ordinis sancti Benedicti* published by Dom Mabillon, and then inspired Dom Ruinart with the idea of his *Acta primorum Martyrum sincera et selecta*. This precious collection, a treasure of erudition and criticism, appeared in 1689. The author's plan was to make a collection of what seemed to him the most authentic Acts of the Martyrs in order to set forth in its strongest light, the powerful argument which the Church derives from the courageous confession of those heroes of the Faith. The Acts of St. Cecilia are not in this collection, for as the school of Port Royal was then beginning to prepare its decrees of proscription against an innumerable number of Christian monuments, Dom Ruinart was unwilling to insert in his book any Acts that were not unhesitatingly admitted by men whose influence was already so strikingly felt. However, he thought himself bound to declare in the Preface that he was far from pretending that his collection contained all the genuine Acts of the Martyrs, or from branding as apocryphal those which he had not thought proper to insert; [6] and in the body of the work he qualifies as *excellent* (egregia) the Acts of St. Sebastian, which he had not dared to insert, on account of some trifling difficulties presented by them. This system offers serious inconveniences and if applied to historical records in general, would soon give birth to the most ridiculous and dangerous pyrrhonism. Among the best historians of ancient or even modern times, are there many whose narrations may not be contradicted in some particulars, and is it not the province of sound criticism to throw light upon doubtful statements, to explain inconsistencies, and in a word, to clear away the clouds which, through some fault, voluntary or involuntary, of the narrator, have veiled the truth? What would become of our knowledge of the past, if it were permitted to reject the testimony of an author whose honesty is undoubted, simply because his writings exhibit traces of haste and inaccuracy?

The favor with which Dom Ruinart's collection was received, and the esteem in which it is still held, enables us to draw from it rules of criticism which the severest critic *must* admit. The facts related in these Acts, which he declares to be absolutely unquestionable, are so many terms of comparison, whose value cannot be disputed, and we shall soon see that the Acts of St. Cecilia, when compared with those guaranteed as true by Dom Ruinart, come off triumphant from the trial.

We must also remember, that two thirds of the Acts published by Dom Ruinart were compiled after the age of Persecutions, from ancient memoirs long since lost. He even admits the Acts of St. Cyr and St. Julitte, although ho acknowledges that they were not compiled before the reign of Justinian. [7]

It is easy to perceive how strongly the example thus given by the severe Benedictine, tends to confirm the confidence of the Church in the Acts of St. Cecilia, although we no longer possess the primitive Acts compiled by the Notaries of Rome, nor other documents from which the compiler of the fifth century framed his narrative. But we will digress for a moment from the field of controversy, to congratulate the Roman Basilica of St. Cecilia upon an event which towards the end of the seventeenth century re-awakened its dearest and most brilliant reminiscences.

On the 12th of December, 1695, Innocent XII., elevated to the honors of the purple Celestin Sfondrato, Abbot of St. Gall. Celestin, who was born in 1644, was a nephew of Paul Emilius, and from his youth had aspired to the cloistered life. He pronounced his vows according to the Benedictine Rule, in this illustrious Abbey, where he consecrated his leisure hours to the study of sacred science, and' cultivated it with remarkable success. The heart of the young monk was inflamed with such ardent zeal for the liberty of the Church, that he was one of the most generous defenders of her independence against the encroachments of Louis XIV. And this, at a time when Catholic Europe was looking on these encroachments in silence.

Celestin had been sent to the Abbey of St. Peter, in Salzburg, to fill the chair of canonical law in the University of that city, when the assembly of the French Clergy, in 1682, published the famous Declaration respecting the rights of the Sovereign Pontiff in the constitution of the Church. A council of Bishops in Hungary, and several universities in Spain declaimed against the outrage thus offered in France to apostolic power. The University of Salzburg likewise published its disapproval of the four propositions of the Parisian Assembly. This courageous act was principally due to the influence of Sfondrato.

But he did not limit his zeal to the condemnation of novelties, of which he could easily foresee the disastrous influence upon religious and political society. He boldly entered the arena and whilst awaiting the "Defence of the Declaration," which Louis XIV., exacted from, the Bishop of Meaux, he avenged the liberty of the church in an excellent Treatise upon the *Regale,* against which this fatal storm had been directed; [8] in his *Sacerdoce Royal,* he elevated the apostolic monarchy, which had been degraded through the interested policy of several court prelates; [9] he proved the novelty of the principles of the French Clergy in a learned work against Mainbourg in which he brought forward the testimony and authority of ancient French authors; [10] and finally, when the scandalous conduct of the Marquis de Lavardin in regard to the privileges claimed by the French ambassador at the Court of Rome, bad manifested to the world the pride and obstinacy of Louis XIV., in his dealings with the Pope, Sfondrato transmitted to posterity a faithful account of these unworthy proceedings on the part of one, who called himself "the oldest son of the Church." [11]

This invincible zeal of Sfondrato excited the animosity of the heads of the French Clergy, who were accomplices in the work of 1652. But they failed in obtaining the condemnation of the book in which he treats all questions concerning grace, in a manner opposed to the theories of thomism. [12] Rome did not think that Sfondrato had advanced anything contrary to the decisions of the Church. At the same time the author could not be classed among those who were called in France the flatterers of the Roman Court; for although he energetically supported the sacred prerogatives of the supreme Pontiff, he was no less firm in censuring the abuses to which human frailty sometimes yielded in so elevated a position. There is a severe treatise against Nepotism which is a production of the courageous pen of Celestin Sfondrato. [13]

Such a man could not fail to interest the noble heart of Innocent XI., In 16SS, this Pontiff appointed Sfondrato, Bishop of Novare; this nomination was at first declined by the learned monk. He afterwards decided to accept it, but just as he was on the point of so doing, the Abbey of St. Gall became vacant, and the unanimous suffrage of the chapter elected Sfondrato to the dignity of Abbot, together with the honors of Prince of the Holy Empire. In this new dignity he was ever faithful to the Church, and to the Holy See, humble amidst the grandeur which surrounded him, zealous for the salvation of souls, assiduous in study, vigilant in the government of his principality, austere in his habits and remarkable, as his uncle Paul Emilius had been, for his inexhaustible charity towards the poor and suffering.

Such was Celestin Sfondrato, the most powerful Abbot of his time, as well as the most celebrated for his virtues and science, when he received the news of his elevation to the Cardinalate, Innocent XII. called him to Rome, and he was obliged to resign his Abbey. The Pope, in memory of his uncle, conferred upon him the Church of St. Cecilia. Celestin merited this glorious honor in reward for his attachment to the liberty of the Church; but he had scarcely arrived in Rome, when he was attacked by a serious illness, and scarcely had a year elapsed after his promotion, when he yielded his soul to God, on the 4th of September, JL 69 6, in the 52nd year of age. Like Paul Emilius, he desired to repose in the Basilica of the Holy Martyr, and gave orders that the humble epitaph composed by his uncle should be engraved upon his tomb. It is still to be seen and runs thus:

CAELESTINVS TITVLI S. CAECILLAE
S. R. E. PRESBYTER CARDIXALIS SFONDRATVS MISERRIMVS PECCATOR
ATQVE EIVSDEM VIRGINIS HVMILIS SERVVS AD CVIVS PEDES HIC HVMILI-
TER REQVIESCIT VIXIT ANNOS LII. OBIIT PRIDIE NONAS SEPTEMBRIS AN-
NO MDCXCVI. ORATE DEVM PRO EO.

This Prince of the Church, so lately a temporal Prince, did not have sufficient means to provide for his burial, and the Apostolic Chamber were
obliged to defray his funeral expenses. [14]

At the very moment when the Sovereign Pontiff invited Celestin Sfondrato
to take possession of the sanctuary, whence the heroic Cecilia has for centuries bestowed her blessings upon the defenders of the Church, the outrage
which had been long preparing in France against the memory of this incomparable Martyr, was consummated. In 1695, appeared the third volume of
the *Mèmoires pour servir a l'histoire Ecclèsiastique des six premiers siecles*, by
Le Nain de Tillemont, one of the most learned and dangerous adepts of Port
Royal. In this volume, as well as in those which precede and follow it, we find
a vein of profound and systematical contempt for the traditions most prized
by Catholics; the Acts of St. Cecilia are censured with a levity and partiality
which must call forth, sooner or later, the disapprobation of all impartial critics. Notwithstanding the popularity they had enjoyed for over a thousand
years, they are not deemed worthy a special chapter; in a simple note of the
two pages, Tillemont settles the question of their authenticity.

"These Acts," says he, "may be ancient, and are not badly written." [15]
Having admitted this, Tillemont goes on to assail these *grave* and *ancient* acts
with a multitude of objections, which we will refute in the ensuing chapter.
At present, we deem it a duty to lay before our readers the views entertained
concerning the Acts of St. Cecilia, by the majority of Christians during the
very century, which beheld them ridiculed and despised by bold and unscru-
pulous authors.

The Roman Church, the Ambrosian Church, the Gallican Church, the Gothic
Church of Spain, and the Greek Church had unanimously proclaimed these
Acts worthy the respect of all Christendom. From age to age, Pontiffs and
Doctors, who succeeded each other in their different Churches, venerated a
narration, many parts of which were then, and are still, used in different
parts of the Divine Service throughout the greater number of Christian countries. Can so many competent judges, so many nations, so many individuals,
be accused of having received, with undeviating respect, for thirteen centuries, a fabulous legend, which reason and criticism were always at liberty to
condemn, since it was not in any way connected with the Sacred Scriptures.

Shall we pass over, as a thing of no importance, the unanimous agreement
of hagiographers, for a period of a thousand years, beginning from the Venerable Bede and descending to Baronius and Papebroke? And shall we venture to assert, that the question, concerning the authenticity of St. Cecilia's

Acts, had never been discussed until the day when Port Royal was pleased to intimate to the Christian world its decisions against their truth?

If, after having cited the unanimous approbation of past ages, we now consider the Acts in themselves, will sound criticism, find any reason for discrediting the facts which they contain? Are not these facts in perfect accordance with the age in which they are said to have transpired? Do we find in them anything opposed to the customs of the early Christians of Rome? Is there anything either singular, or improbable, in the incidents related, or in the language of the speakers? Are we not, on the contrary, impressed with the similarity of these Acts to those given us by Dom Ruinart?

During the centuries that have elapsed since the publication of the Acts, St. Cecilia's tomb has been twice opened and her dwelling, now her Basilica, has been the constant object of pious and eager research. "What has been the result? The most evident proofs of the narrator's sincerity, the most striking confirmation of the facts he relates. Shall the satirical and gratuitous assertions of a writer who disdains to notice archaeological discoveries suffice to overthrow positive proofs, the least of which would be sufficient to reinstate in the minds of scientific men, a monument of profane antiquity no matter how decried; especially, proofs so strong as those furnished by the opening of Cecilia's tomb and the discovery of her *caldarium*?

If so, we must compliment the compiler of the Acts for all the beauties found in this astonishing work. That a man, who was ignorant even of the grammar of his native language and of all the rules of composition, could be the inventor of so sublime a drama, composed with such grace and energy, such delicacy and grandeur, never occurred to the Christian world, until it was informed of the fact by Tillemont; nor should we be surprised if the learned were still to reject it, in spite of the authority of Port Royal.

There are some men, who, slaves to pride, and to the spirit of system, have deadened that judgment which the Creator has given us to discern truth from falsehood; but it is strange that Tillemont, versed as he was in memorials of ecclesiastical antiquity, did not at once understand the difference between our Acts, which are so precise in their narration, so probable throughout, so easy in the developments of characters, and apocryphal recitals, the exaggerated style of which borders on the marvellous, and convinces the reader that the author has given full vent to his imagination, without troubling himself about circumstances, time, or place. Now there is as much difference between the two, as between a portrait taken from nature and a fancy sketch.

Even though we had been left without any documents concerning the first ages of Christianity, though the customs of the early Christians were perfectly unknown to us, what man, initiated in the religion of Christ, would not feel that the Martyrs led just such a life? And shall we, who, notwithstanding the ravages of time, can still represent to ourselves those heroic days, with the assistance of so many incontestable monuments, not recognize the Christians of the third century, the cotemporaries of Tertullian and Origen, in the noble yet simple characters of Cecilia, Tiburtius, and Valerian?

Insults and denials are not sufficient, proofs are requisite. The arguments so triumphantly adduced by Tillemont and his successors shall be discussed by us in that Catholic spirit which ought to have led them to treat with reverence, traditions admitted by learned and virtuous men, and proposed by the Church to the respectful admiration of her children. To root out a beautiful flower from the garden of the Church, to trample it under foot, to deprive Cecilia of all glory save her name and an uncertain martyrdom, must have required powerful reasons. Our Catholic readers may judge of their merits.

[1] One vol. in 12°.

[2] Curiositié de Tune et de l'autre Rome, 1655-1659. Three vols, in 8°.

[3] Three other personages, all Roman citizens, have been honored in this chapel of the Capitol. St. Eustace, St. Alexis, and Blessed Louise Albertoni.

[4] Haec pervetusta homm sanctorum solemnis veneratio, plurimum crevit ex certissima virtutum ac martyrii notitia, quam dabant antiqua S. Caeciliae Acta quae tunc temporis omnium manibus terebantur, et hactenus in praecipuis et perantiquis membranis conservantur. *Acta SS. Aprilis,* Tome ii. page 203.

[5] Antiquissima et sincerissima habentur hujus sanctae Virginia Acta, quorum notitia videtur admodum sero perlata ad Graecos, etc. *Ephemerides Graecorum et Moscorum,* page 51.

[6] Porro etsi nihil oniiserira, ut quantum in me fuit, haec Actorum collectio accurata atque numeris omnibus absoluta redderetur: non ita tamen rem me confecisse existimo, ut nulla penitus, praeter ea quae hic exhibemus sincera Martyrum Acta reperiri posse existimem. Nec etiam animus est, ea omnia inter spuria rejicere quae hic non habentur; quin et si aliquis nonnulla ex iis quae a me forte rejecta sunt sincera judicaverit, non refragabor, modo id argumentis certis probare queat: alias unusquisque in suo sensu abundet. *Acta sincera Martyrum:* Praefatio. page 12.

[7] Acta Martyrum sincera et selecta, page 526.

[8] Tractatus Regaliae contra Rlerum Gallicanum, 1682 in 4°.

[9] Regale Sacerdotium Comano Pontifici assertum, et quatuor propositionibus explicatum, *sous le pseudonyme* d'Eugenius Lombardus, 1684, in-1.

[10] Gallia vindicata. 1688, in-4.

[11] Legatio Marchionis Lavardini Romam, ejusque cum Innocentio XI dissidium. 1688. in-12.

[12] Nodus praedestinationis dissolutus, 1697. in-4.

[13] Nepotismus theologiae expensus. 1692 in-12.

[14] Guarnacci. *Vitae et res gestae Pontificum Romanorum. et S. R. E, Cardinalium,* tome 1, page 443-446.

[15] Tillemont. Memoires pour servin a l'Hist Ecclesiastique, tome iii. p. 259. It is perhaps well to observe that the expression *badly written* which Tillemont uses, should not be understood in its present signification. In the seventeenth century, it signified a compilation faulty in matter, not in style.

Chapter Thirty-Five - Examination and Reputation of the Arguments of the Jansenists against the Acts of St. Cecilia

Tillemont begins by attacking the Acts of St. Cecilia, as well as those of Sts. Callistus and Urban, because they imply a persecution against the Christians, during the reign of Alexander Severus, who is well known to have been favorably disposed to Christianity. [1] This objection might have some weight, if the author of the Acts had alleged any edicts or hostile disposition of the Emperor towards the Christians; but Alexander is not once mentioned in the Acts; the violent persecutions against the Christians are attributed solely to the personal hatred of his prefect, Turchius Almachius. The Acts of Saints Callistus and Martina are more open to criticism on this point, because Alexander Severus is personally spoken of in connection with the persecutions.

Now it is certain that, during the reign of this weak-minded prince, the Christians Buffered local persecutions from the magistrates, who were hostile to the Church, and who took advantage of the laws which the son of Julia Mammaea had not the courage to revoke. We can prove this assertion not only by the opinion of Baronius, [2] but also by the express admission of Petau, [3] Dom Buinart, [4] Fleury, [5] Baillet, [6] and, strange to say, Tillemont himself, who, finding it impossible to deny the martyrdom of Pope Callistus, which assuredly took place daring the reign of Alexander Severus, agrees that several Christians may have received the crown of martyrdom at this period. He even goes so far as to explain how such persecutions took place, and in doing so, makes use of the very arguments which we presented to the reader in the commencement of this history. [7]

The opinion of so many learned men as to the kind of persecution the Christians of Rome suffered under Alexander, is confirmed by the Acts of St. Cecilia, with a precision, the force of which Tillemont does not seem to have even perceived. It is evident from every circumstance mentioned in these Acts, that the Prefect Almachius, in his process against the brothers, is very reluctant to bring forward the charge of their being Christians; that his hesitation in condemning them to death is very marked; and that he dares not sentence Cecilia to a public execution. Let these Acts be compared with those of other martyrs who suffered in consequence of edicts of persecution, and see if in the latter case the magistrates acted with so much indecision. Add to this the emperor's absence in the year 230, which was the last of Urban's pontificate, and the temporary persecution of the Roman magistrate will be easily understood. His violence was at first directed only against the plebeians; but a patrician family becoming accidentally implicated, the magistrate feared to commit himself. We have admitted that five thousand persons fell victims in this persecution, and if the number be exaggerated, our readers must remember that we do not quote it from the Acts of St. Cecilia, but from those of Urban, which, although doubtless reliable, have not the authority of the Acts of the Roman Virgin. The fact that the latter were compiled during the peace of the Church, is a sufficient proof of the purity of the sources whence the writer drew his story. Entirely ignorant of chronology, he does not seem to know the name of the emperor under whom the events which he relates took place; and, nevertheless, his narrative perfectly accords with the reign of a weak-minded prince, who, although favorable to Christianity, still permitted his magistrates to enforce laws which had been suspended, but not abolished. If our writer had not had tradition to guide him, he would, like the authors of apocryphal acts, have cited in his history edicts and emperors; he would have imitated the Acts of other martyrs, instead of showing that originality, which is in perfect keeping with the condition of the Church of Rome under Alexander Severus. Tillemont probably felt this, for he seeks to throw discredit upon the Acts by pointing out circumstances contained in them, which appear to him difficult to reconcile with what we know of the period.

"We find," he says, "in the Acts of St. Cecilia, that the emperors had commanded that all who would not renounce Christianity should be punished; consequently there must have been a declared persecution. The mention made in many places of several emperors is out of place at a period when but one prince was reigning." It is easy to explain this latter difficulty, if it can be called one.

Almachius became so involved in judiciary acts of violence against the Church, that he was forced to refer to some law, in order to authorize his prosecutions. The laws which had been promulgated against the Christians, by the predecessors of Alexander, were his only refuge. It was very natural that the Prefect should express himself in the plural when alleging the edicts of former emperors; had he presumed to use Alexander's name, the latter might have brought him to account for abusing his name and authority in support of actions which were totally foreign to his own line of conduct. If, therefore, Almachius mentioned several emperors, he did not necessarily imply that the empire was at this time governed by several heads. This form of judiciary style is constantly found in the acts of legal tribunals, both of ancient and modern times. Tillemont was perfectly aware of this. He lived during the reign of Louis XIV., a prince who assuredly reigned alone; did he then think that France had suddenly fallen into the hands of several monarchs, when lie met with some decree of Parliament, appealing to the edicts and ordinances of our lungs? Tillemont is not satisfied with declaring our acts a romance, solely because they seem to him incompatible with the reign of Alexander Severus; he, moreover, considers the very name of Almachius, which he says is not Roman, [8] sufficient to invalidate the whole narration. He even adds that such is the opinion of Fathers Gamier and Sirmond, deeming that in *such* a cause even *Jesuits* may be considered reliable authority. The reply to this pretended difficulty is very easy. Without dwelling upon the possibility of some alteration having been made in Almachius' name during the two centuries which elapsed between the martyrdom of St. Cecilia and the compilation of her Acts, we will simply say that the prefect who condemned our martyrs was named *Turcius* Almachius, and not merely *Almachius.* Can Tillemont deny that *Turcius* is a Roman name? The Roman inscription given by Gruter, would be sufficient to convict him of falsehood.

Moreover, Tillemont himself, in his study of the Martyrs of Italy, met with the name of Turcius and quietly registered it. He relates that in 274, the Emperor Aurelian sent a magistrate, named Turcius, to Sutri in Tuscany, [9] with orders to persecute the Christians; and he even positively asserts that the name of Turcius was quite common in ancient times, several persons, named Turcius Asterius, having been elevated to the first offices of the Empire. [10] Moreover, he mentions that in 303, during the persecution of Diocletian, a Proconsul Turcius prosecuted the Christians in Perugia. [11] It matters little, however, whether the name of Almachius was the exact surname of the prefect, or whether it is a corruption of the true surname, we have used it simply because it is more popular. Tillemont, after attempting to prove that Cecilia did not live during the reign of Alexander, and after trying to obliterate even the name of the judge to whom she owed her crown of martyrdom, takes the trouble to find her a place in the chronology of the saints. Now, as he refused to accept the epoch determined by the Acts, he found it necessary to choose between two dates. In order to avoid embarrassment he adopted both, neither being the one received by the Church. The following are his proofs: "Usuard and several others, for instance Ado, place St. Cecilia under the Emperors Marcus Aurelius and Commodus who reigned conjointly, from 176 to 180. The Greeks place her under Diocletian." [11]

The reader may now choose between these two equally reliable dates. It is indeed true that Usuard and St. Ado place St. Cecilia under Marcus Aurelius and Commodus; but the historian of Port Royal does not add that they also mention her during Urban's pontificate, that in their martyrology of the 14th of April, they note the martyrdom of St. Tiburtius, Maximus, and Cecilia, under the same Pontiff, from whose hands they affirm the two former received Baptism, and that on the 25th of May, in the notice on St. Urban, they relate the interviews between this Pope and Cecilia. Usuard and Ado have therefore erred in placing Cecilia under Marcus Aurelius and Commodus; this mistake may perhaps be accounted for by the name of Alexander Severus, which was in full, Marcus Aurelius Severus Alexander. The liturgists of the ninth century had not the facility we have of knowing the different imperial names, which are now found upon bronzes and medals. Moreover, on any other occasion, Tillemont would not have considered their opinion of any value; he only quotes it here because it helps to prove his assertions. As to the Greeks, who did not know the Acts of St. Cecilia before the ninth century, and who refer her martyrdom to the persecution of Diocletian, this is the only occasion upon which Tillemont quotes their books which are proverbial for their extreme imperfection and open in many points to criticism. In this case, they

189

are evidently wrong, since they relate the interviews between Cecilia and Pope Urban who governed the Church fifty years before Diocletian.

We frequently find this arbitrary use of the rules of criticism in Tillemont's work. The reader has already seen the Hymn we copied from the Gothic Breviary; it is a perfect abridgment of our Acts, and by its antiquity, of sufficient importance to confirm them Tillemont does not deign to notice it, whereas he mentions in the following terms a Hymn of the same liturgy, which embodies the Acts of St. Marciana. "We have a hymn to St. Marciana, taken from the Gothic or Mozarabic Breviary of Toledo, and from the Acts given by Bollandus. We cannot assert that these Acts are original, since they seem to have been written several years after the death of the Saint, and contain some particulars which give us reason to doubt their truth. However, the Hymn found in the Breviary of Toledo, is sufficiently ancient and beautiful to authorize us in receiving the Acts." [12] The Acts of St. Marciana are not certainly wanting in authority; nevertheless they are far from having been so universally received as those of St. Cecilia; the details in them were never so publicly known; nor are they confirmed by such striking monuments; and still Tillemont is very liberal to them, and disdainfully rejects the others.

This author, not satisfied with trying to invalidate the chronology of our Acts, also attacks them in their topographical bearing. We will cite the words of this celebrated critic. "It is very singular," he says, "that both the Greeks and Latins mention St. Cecilia as being a Roman, even the Martyrologies attributed to St. Jerome; whereas Fortunatus, who is probably our most ancient author upon these subjects, places her in Sicily:

CAECILIAM SICULA PROFERT, SELEUCIA TECLAM.

"Neither he, nor any one else, says that she was a native of Sicily, for we see, from St. Thecla and others, that Fortunatus only mentions that island as the place of her death. It is probable, therefore, that she was martyred there, and that her body having been carried to Rome in the early ages, some have called her a Roman, from this circumstance, as in the case of St. Sabina, who died at Umbria; others believed that she lived and died in Rome, and consequently composed her Acts upon this supposition, probably transforming a Governor and a Bishop of Sicily into a Prefect of Rome and a Pope. It is certain that this would be easy for those who have not received the love of truth. [13]

Conformably to the doctrines of Port Royal, which the author exposes with so much naiveté, a writer is truthful or deceitful in his narrations, not according to his own free will, but according to whether he has or has not received *the love of truth*. Such doctrines should render those who believe in them, indulgent to false writers, and historical imposters; they should not reject them with too much disdain; but should wait patiently for the love of truth to descend into them, and render them sincere and faithful, without their own

190

co-operation. We who are Catholics and believe man to be endowed with personal responsibility, find it difficult to recognize in Tillemont that *love of truth* which he refuses to the compiler of St. Cecilia's Acts, and we do not hesitate to call him to an account for it. He agrees that all *the authors who mention St. Cecilia call her a Roman,* and yet all these venerable names are effaced by that of a single individual, Fortunatus, Bishop of Poictiers. And what do we find in his writings, so conclusive as to overthrow the testimony of ages? One single line of poetry! And that line, defective in quantity, which naturally leads us to suppose the copyist in fault, at least in some degree. On the authority of this one line, Tillemont would have us believe that St. Cecilia died in Sicily, because, forsooth, "Fortunatus is *probably* the most ancient author who speaks of the holy martyr!" This *probably* is, to Tillemont's mind, sufficiently weighty to counterbalance the Martyrology attributed to St. Jerome; the Leonian, Gelasian, Ambrosian and Galilean Sacramentaries; the Papal Chronicle of Felix IV., and all the historical monuments of St. Cecilia, founded upon the Acts, and prior to Fortunatus.

But even supposing the famous line to be original, does Tillemont know of *what* Cecilia, Fortunatus speaks? It is very certain that the Bishop does not say. Many learned Sicilians, among others Octavio Gaetano, who have written the lives of the Saints of Sicily, have frankly acknowledged that they could not find the slightest vestige of a St. Cecilia, born or martyred on that island; or even of one whose relics had been brought there. It is therefore natural to think that, if Fortunatus composed this line, he erred; or perhaps he confounded one island of the Mediterranean with another. There was a St. Cecilia martyred at Cagliari in Sardinia; [14] the similarity of name may have led to this mistake. However this may be, the spirit of system alone, could transform into an oracle these unexplained words of an author who wrote at a distance from the theatre of events, and whose words had passed unnoticed for more than a thousand years.

But Tillemont not only prefers this solitary line of poetry, to the unanimous testimony of Roman authors, both anterior and posterior to Fortunatus; but, with it for his guide, he proceeds to relate Cecilia's history. He cannot deny that hei body is at Rome; but he explains this circumstance by an imaginary translation of her relics, which was never heard of before. That the Saint suffered in Sicily, he deems incontestably proved by Fortunatus' words. It is equally certain that her body is now in Rome. Therefore it must have been carried thither. This is Tillemont's proposition. Now for his proof. St. Sabina, who suffered martyrdom in Umbria, was transported to the capital of the Christian world. [15] Wherefore, Cecilia's body may also have been translated thither. Such is the logic of this relentless critic of Cecilia's Acts.

The above reasoning, however, is opposed by a grave difficulty, which Port Royal did not perceive in the exultation of its triumph. The body of St. Sabina was indeed brought to Rome; but it was for the purpose of being honorably placed in a church built under the invocation of the saint, upon Mount Aventine. St. John Chrysostom was also transferred from Constantinople, to St. Peter's in Rome; St. Jerome from Bethlehem to St. Mary Major; and many other foreign saints to the different churches of the same city; but besides the fact of history having preserved the memory of all these translations, altars and Basilicas awaited these sacred remains. St. Cecilia, on the contrary, arrives, and no one is aware of her coming; this great martyr, to whom Sicily with regret confesses itself a stranger, comes nevertheless, from that island, and the Roman Church which coveted her relics, thinks them of so little importance, that she buries them in the depths of a crypt on the Appian Way. She inscribes Cecilia's name in the Canon of her Mass, and yet clandestinely conceals her sacred body, brought from such a distance, in a vault, where Tillemont is forced to acknowledge, Paschal found it in the beginning of the ninth century, together with Sts. Tiburtius, Valerian, and Maximus, who were, it is to be presumed, brought from Sicily with the holy virgin.

Is not this nonsensical? Is it not humiliating to see Catholics carried away by such reasoning, in spite of the most convincing proofs of its falsehood?

But Tillemont does not stop here. Since he has received the *love of truth* more than any one who lived during the twelve centuries when Cecilia was supposed to be a Roman virgin, we naturally expect him to explain to us how it was that Urban was transformed from a Sicilian bishop into a Pope, and Turcius Almachius, from a governor of Sicily, into a Roman prefect. But Tillemont contents himself with asserting this transformation; he does not condescend to prove it. We must then conclude that the compiler of the Acts is an impostor, and that Port Royal is an infallible judge of places and persons no matter how ancient. Nothing remains now but to assign the date of this famous translation upon which the system depends. It must have taken place before the end of the fifth century, since Tillemont says that, during the, Pontificate of Pope Symmachus, there was a church of St. Cecilia in Rome. [16] Otherwise it would be Impossible to explain why the saint "had not been placed in her church. There was however, remarks Tillemont, time enough to bring her relics to Rome, between the cessation of the persecutions and the pontificate of Symmachus, and the fact of no one having heard of this Translation, does not prevent its having taken place. It is astounding to find so intelligent and learned a man as Tillemont ignorant of the fact that the very existence of a Church of St. Cecilia in Rome, is a sufficient proof that she lived in that city; yet Tillemont must have known that at the period of which he was writing, the canonical rules forbade the erecting of churches in honor of saints, except in those places where their relics reposed, or which had been sanctified by their lives and sufferings. Now, in the time of Pope Symmachus, the virgin's body was reposing in the Catacombs; the trans-Tiberian Basilica was, therefore a monument which commemorated her residence in Rome, and also, as we learn from her Acts, and from tradition, marked the place of her martyrdom. It was, therefore, useless to imagine the translation of Cecilia's body, together with those of her companions, from the isle of Sicily to the

Catacombs of Rome, unless the origin of this church was first accounted for. We are perfectly willing to agree that the bodies of foreign martyrs were brought to Rome after the persecution, and deposited in the Catacombs, provided it be proved that previous to this time, no church in Rome had been dedicated to them. But we have lost sufficient time over these Jansenistic fancies. Their boldness and cunning will not surprise those who are acquainted with the subterfuges of this wily sect; but the above remarks may prevent others less informed, from being deceived by the plausible statements of the Jansenist authors, who for more than a century, have monopolized, in France, the compilation of works upon the history of Christianity.

[1] See Tillemont's "Memoires pour serrir a l'Histoire Ecclèsiastique dea six premiers siccles.' Tome iii. p, 679.

[2] See his notes upon the Roman Martyrology of the 1st of January.

[3] Alexandro Imperatore pacem habuit Ecclesia. Nam et Christianis ille favisse dicitur. Verum cum eos in consilium adhiberet qui, ut juris peritissimi, ita christianis iniquissimi erant, nonnullae Martyrum caedes extiterunt, quos inter Caecilia claruit cum Tiburtio et Valeriano. *Rationarium temporum,* part, i., lib. v., cap. xi.

[4] Alexandrum Heliogabali successorum Christianis favisse nemo potest inficiari, nisi omnes antiquos scriptores rejicere velit. Unde mirum est, tot Martyres sub ejus imperio passos a nonnullis recenseri. An id ad Praefectos, quos sub ejus imperio saevissimos fuisse aiunt referendum est? An forte dicendum, aliquot Martyres, qui sub Severi persecutione passi sunt, ad Alexandri tempora incaute transferri, quod et ipse Severus fuerit appellatus? At Callixtus Papa, qui eo imperante vivere desiit, inter Martyres in Kalendario Bucheriano recensetur. *Praefatio in Acta Martyrum,* §iii., page 38.

[5] Although Alexander was favorable to the Christians, we can count several martyrs during his time, among others, Pope Callistus, who died the first year of his reign, A.D. 122., and his successor, St. Urban. But we may believe that the persecutions took place without the knowledge of the Emperor, by the sole authority of the magistrates, who were bitter enemies to the Christian name. *Hist. Ecclesiastique.* lib. v. n° xlix.

[6] However great was the peace of the Church under so good an Emperor as Alexander Severus, who permitted himself to be governed by his mother, Julia Mammaea, supposed to be a Christian, and who esteemed our Redeemer so much as to propose ranking Him among the gods and erecting a temple in His honor; still many martyrs suffered during his reign, either in popular tumults excited by the Pagans, or through the malignity of the heathen priests and magistrates. We can assert with sufficient authority, that Callistus was of this number. Vies des Saints, tome vii. in-4° 14 *Octobre.*

[7] But this peace did not prevent that either in consequence of some sedition among the people, or from other causes, there may have been some cases of martyrdom during the reign of Alexander Severus, as there had been during that of Philip, who passed for a Christian, and of other emperors who openly protected the Church. We have even many proofs that St. Callistus suffered martyrdom un-

der Alexander Severus. *Memoires pour servir a l'Histoire, Ecclesiastique,* tome iii. p. 231. See also *Ibid* in the notes, p. 681.

[8] Memoires, tome iii., page 690.

[9] Memoires tome iv. p. 352.

[10] Memoires dans les notes p. 682.

[11] Memoires, Tome v. p, 119.

[12] Memoires, tome v. page 263.

[13] Memoirs, tome iii. page 690.

[14] Macedo. *De Divis tutelaribus orbit christiani,* page 215.

[15] Memoires, tome iii. page 690.

[16] Memoirs, tome iii. page 690.

Chapter Thirty-Six - Continuation of the Same Subject

We must now consider the objections to the Acts of St. Cecilia, which Tillemont pretends to find in these Acts, considered in themselves. This discussion will not be less instructive than the preceding.

We will begin with the critic's own words: "These Acts are composed of extraordinary miracles, and other matters which have little appearance of truth. The discourses are long. There are, indeed, some beautiful passages, evidently taken from Tertullian; but he who wrote them should have learned from the same author to treat princes with more respect." [1]

Hence, sound criticism must reject the Acts of St. Cecilia on account of the extraordinary miracles recorded therein! Had Tillemont plainly said that the conversion of the Pagan world to Christianity, was effected without miracles, Ave could refer him to the' illustrious Doctor St. Augustin, who would teach him that in that case, so incomprehensible a transformation would be the greatest of miracles. But Tillemont does not deny miracles in general; he merely distinguishes between those which he calls *extraordinary,* and those which he deems *ordinary.* Unfortunately, he *has left us no theoretical rules* whereby we may discern one from the other. We have no resource left but to study his manner of appreciating supernatural facts.

Let us first remark that this critic admits all the miracles contained in the *genuine* Acts of Dom Ruinart. He cannot, however, deny that this authentic collection contains many miracles more *extraordinary,* to use his own expression, than those related in the Acts of St. Cecilia. The latter are among the most simple recorded in the annals of primitive Christianity. Nothing more than the apparition of St. Paul and several visions of Angels. We learn from Origen, who wrote at that time, and who was certainly not a weak minded man, that such apparitions were very frequent. Tertullian, a contemporary of Origen, attests that the greater part of those who embraced Christianity were converted by visions. [2]

Tillemont relates and admits all the facts of this nature mentioned in the Acts of Sts. Vincent, Agnes, Theodotus of Ancyra, etc. Most of these apparitions are much more marvellous than those recorded in the Acts of St. Cecilia. Is it reasonable then to contest the latter? Beside the apparitions there is no mention in the Acts of any miracle except the prolongation of Cecilia's life after the severe wounds inflicted by the lictor's sword. Were these wounds sufficiently serious to produce death in a short time? We think so. But, however this may be, it should not surprise Tillemont who must remember that the Acts of Dom Ruinart, all of which he admits, frequently speak of Martyrs, whose bodies, rendered invulnerable by divine power, resisted all torments; whose dislocated limbs and gaping wounds were often suddenly and miraculously healed, filling the Pagans with rage and confusion.

The principles of the Port Royal School paved the way for those of anti-Christian rationalism. To refuse to believe in miracles because they are *extraordinary*, is senseless logic, since a miracle is only a miracle from the fact of being *extraordinary*. For this reason, supernatural facts are not proved by internal evidence, but by human testimony. Can we measure the limits of God's Omnipotence? What answer will Tillemont make to those whose rejection of the Bible, is grounded on the very argument which he addresses against the truth of Cecilia's Acts, viz.: that the miracles mentioned therein, are too *extraordinary* to be believed?

Our critic brings forward the lengthy discourses in the Acts of St. Cecilia, as another argument against them. He probably desires to infer that such lengthy discourses could not have been preserved; but this reasoning might carry him too far. To be consistent, he must begin by rejecting the *genuine* Acts of Saints Pionius, Victor of Marseilles, Philip of Heraclius, Patrick, etc., all of which he admits, and which, nevertheless, contain longer discourses than those of St. Cecilia's Acts.

Even though it be granted for a moment that these discourses have no historical value, would this concession invalidate the Acts themselves? This would be treating the Acts of the Martyrs with more severity than has ever been shown to any of the historians of antiquity. The latter have embellished their writings with harangues of their own composition; no one ever questioned their veracity on this account. Is historical pyrrhonism to be our rule, *only* when examining the history of Christianity?

The sole discourse of considerable length in the Acts, is the harangue to Tiburtius, when Cecilia explains to him the Christian faith. Tiburtius may have committed this discourse to writing. It would not be the first time that a man has thus preserved words which have deeply impressed his mind and heart. In such occasions, which are not so rare as Tillemont imagines, the memory may sometimes be at fault; but the writer who has thus noted down his remembrances, knows that his account is a faithful one, because it gives the sense of the discourse and the thoughts which have most forcibly struck him. Besides, this speech had an historical bearing; the conversion of Tiburtius, which was due to Cecilia, was an event in the history of the Roman

Church, and well merited a page in the annals of Christian Borne. Would it not be more surprising if it had *not* been handed down to posterity?

The rest of the Acts contain rather dialogues than discourses. The questions and replies in the interrogatory do not exceed the length of those found in the Acts published by Dom Ruinart. Valerian's parable is long; but improvisations of equal length are frequently found in the most authentic interrogatories. The Registrars noted down all that the martyrs said; whilst the notaries of the Church compiled their Acts upon notes made by faithful persons, accustomed to the charge; in many cases, the official interrogatories were purchased with money. The Christians valued every word uttered by the martyrs before the judges, considering them as inspired by the Holy Ghost, according to the promise of our Saviour in the Gospel: "And you shall be brought before governors, and before kings, for my sake. But when they shall deliver you up, be not thoughtful how or what to speak; for it shall be given you in that hour what to speak. For it is not you that speak, but the spirit of your Father that speaketh in you." [3]

Tillemont could not avoid seeing the beauty of our Acts, and the acknowledgement of it involuntarily escaped his pen; but he found an ingenious means of turning this remark against the probity of the historian: "There are some beautiful passages," he says, "but evidently taken from Tertullian," implying that the narrator made use of Tertullian in composing the speeches of his heroes. It is very true that some points of resemblance may be found between the Apology of the eloquent African and the dialogues and responses of the interrogatories; but what inference can be drawn from this except an additional confirmation of the truth of the Acts?

At this time, all Rome was speaking of that magnificent Defence of Christianity, which, combining all the arguments of preceding Apologies, had elevated the Christian cause to the highest degree of moral grandeur. It was only natural, therefore, that the Christians, in their replies to the magistrates of the Empire, should repeat the energetic sentences which had so lately thrilled the Senate. Our heroes were contemporaries of Tertullian, and, consequently, might have spoken like him; but we find it difficult to believe that the compiler of the Acts, whose careless and unadorned style bears no resemblance to the powerful diction of the Apology, could even have conceived the idea of borrowing from such a masterpiece.

Tillemont considers Cecilia's manner of addressing the prefect, and her invectives against the princes, another improbable circumstance. Her freedom of language scandalized him, and we can readily understand that more than one Catholic in the reign of Louis XIV., thought it a sufficient argument for rejecting Acts in which Christian liberty is so fearlessly proclaimed. This may be accounted for by a confusion of ideas which had become prevalent, respecting the spirit and manners of the early Christians, a confusion which still exists in many minds. A more liberal appreciation of the actions and words of the saints, would have enabled the world to understand, that if it be glorious to suffer death with the meekness of a lamb, led to the slaughter, [4] it is no less glorious to protest against iniquity, and to denounce to earthly rulers, the nullity of their rights, and the injustice of their actions, when they use against God and His Church, that power which they could not have received unless it had been given them from above.

Moreover, Cecilia did not in her energetic replies, spit in the face of her judge, as Eulalia did; [5] nor did she, like St Andronicus, answer the prefect who reproached him with insulting the Emperors: "Yes, I have cursed and will curse these Emperors who overturn the world in their thirst for blood. May God overthrow them with His mighty arm; may He crush and annihilate them; may He visit them with His anger, that they may know of what crimes they are guilty in persecuting the Christians." [6]

Is it necessary to give other examples? Julian, uncle of the Apostate, and created by him governor of the province of the East, when cruelly tormenting St. Theodoret, a priest of the Church of Antioch, dared to demand his obedience to the Emperor's edict, by quoting the following text of Scripture: "The hearts of kings are in the hand of God." The martyr replied: "These words are written of a king who knows and serves God, but not of a tyrant who adores and serves idols." "Fool!" exclaimed the governor, "do you dare to call the emperor a tyrant?" [7] "If he gives such orders as you say, and if he be the man you represent him," answered Theodoret, "he is not only a tyrant, but the most wretched of men."

Christian liberty was no less fearlessly asserted in the peaceful days that succeeded the age of Persecutions. Saint Hilary of Poitiers, in his sublime invective against Constantius, branded this prince with the name of tyrant, and did not fear to add: "What I say to thee, Constantius, I would have said to Nero. Decius and Maximian [8] should have heard it from my lips." We find in every century, similar traits of courage. The recital of them would startle the universal effeminacy of the present generation. We need to study diligently, the manners of our ancestors in the faith, who so generously defended that precious deposit, which we find it so difficult to preserve. These public protestations of Christian liberty, far exceed Cecilia's courageous replies to Almachius, which Tillemont considers a proof of the falsity of her Acts. He nevertheless, defends the holy audacity of St. Andronicus, and is only scandalized when he encounters that same audacity in a much milder form in the Acts of St. Cecilia. We will cite his own words: "We find in nearly all the authentic histories of the martyrs, now extant, that they were very respectful to the sovereign powers, and practiced that meekness so frequently recommended by St. Paul. But St. Paul himself fearlessly called his judge a *whited wall*, and threatened him with the anger of God. St. Stephen, and even our Saviour, speak to the Jews with seeming harshness. The frightful cruelties practised against the Christians were sufficient to excite the just indignation of the martyrs. These Saints hated what God hates, without losing their repose and tranquillity of soul, and they are not to be blamed for expressing their condemnation of what they felt to be wrong. We speak of the fire, as well as of the oil, of charity; and the more justice is loved, the greater zeal and horror is felt for injustice. It is certain that God acted and suffered too visibly in His saints, to permit us to doubt for a moment that His spirit was with them, according to His promise. Therefore we cannot but respect the apparent harshness of their words, although this harshness should not be unadvisedly imitated, lest impatience, bitterness, or hatred, rather than zeal for God and for justice, should actuate us in following this example of the Saints." [9]

In thus exposing the entire system of Tillemont in its bearing upon the Acts of St. Cecilia, we think we have enabled the reader to estimate the value of the criticism and the intention of the critic. We are writing in a country where many honest men persist in considering Jansenism as only a system of exaggerated morality. This is not the place to explain to such men to what an extent the dogmas of this sect, condemned by the Church, are opposed to Catholicity. Let them study the history of Catholic truth and the perils to which it has been exposed from a heresy which so artfully insinuates the most odious theories of Calvin. In a question of mere criticism, our duty is simply to remove all doubts concerning the truth of an historical narrative, dear to the Church and to the faithful at all times, for the sanctification of Christian souls. It does not enter into our plan to expose the reasons which have induced the Jansenists to suppress all the precious, charming, and soul-inspiring traditions offered by the Catholic Church to her children; we prefer concluding this chapter with the beautiful words of St. Paul to the Philippians: "Finally, brethren, whatsoever things are true, whatsoever things are honest, whatsoever things are just, whatsoever things are pure, whatsoever things are lovely, whatsoever things are of good report; if there be any virtue, and if there be any praise, think on these things." Phil, iv., 8.

[1] Memoirs, tome iii. page 689.
[2] Major pene vis hominum visionibus Deum discunt *De anima,* cap xlvii.
[3] Matt, x. 18-20.
[4] Isaiah, liii. 7.
[5]   Martyr ad ista nihil: sed enim
      Infremit, inque tyranni oculos
      Sputa jacit.
   Ruinart. *Acta sincera. Martyrium S. Eulaliae Virginis,* p. 499.
[6] Ego maledixi et maledico potestates, et sanguibibulos qui saeculum evert-erunt, quos Deus brachio suo alto evertat, et conterat, et perdat, et det super eos iram; ut seiant quid agant in servos Dei. Ruinart. *Acta SS. Tarachi, Prohi et Andro-nici, page* 487.
[7] Julianus dixit: Vol nunc time deos, et fac quae ab Imperatore sunt jussa, quia soriptum est tibi: *Cor regis in manu Dei.* Theodoritus respondit: Cos Regis cogno-scentis Deum scriptum est esse in manu Dei, non cor tyranni adorantis idola.

Julianus dixit: Stulte, tyrannum vocas Imperatorem. Theodoritus respondit: Si talia jubet, et talis est ut dicis: non solum tyrannus ditendus est, sed miserrimus omnium hominum. *Passio sancti Theodoriti*, page 659.

[8] Proclamo tibi, Constanti, quod Neroni locuturus fuissem, quod ex me Decius et Maximianus audirent. *Adversus Constantium*, lib. i. page 113.

[9] Memoires pour servir a l'Histoire Ecclesiastique, tome v., page 286.

Chapter Thirty-Seven - Events Relating to Cecilia and Her Basilica throughout the Eighteenth Century

It is refreshing to return from the field of controversy and rest for a moment under the shadow of our dear Basilica, so justly proud of its noble treasure. In the first half of the eighteenth century, it was entrusted to two titulary Cardinals, who gloried in imitating the munificence of Paul Emilius Sfondrato. The first was Francis Aquaviva, born of an illustrious Neapolitan family. Before receiving the purple, he had occupied with distinction several important offices of the Roman Court. He was sent as Nuncio to Spain, where he faithfully fulfilled the duties of his elevated and important mission. He was residing in that country when the war of the Succession broke out. Aquaviva embraced the cause of Philip V., who reposed such confidence in his devotedness and firmness, that at one time, when he was trembling for his crown, he entrusted to the Nuncio's care the Queen Maria Louisa of Savoy. Aquaviva, with an escort of five hundred cavaliers, traversed the hostile territory, and never left the queen until he had placed her in safety from the scene of war. [1]

Created Cardinal by Clement on the 17th of May 1706, he was at first appointed Titulary of St. Bartholomew's Church *on the island;* but three years after he changed this church for that of St. Cecilia, on account of his great devotion to this holy Martyr. The Basilica at this period needed a restoration which Aquaviva executed according to the prevailing taste. Sfondrato had at one time conceived the idea of concealing the wood work of the nave by a rich *soffit,* ornamented with gilded panels and paintings; but he was deterred by the fear that the columns were not sufficiently strong to support this additional weight. Aquaviva made the experiment and succeeded perfectly. The *soffit,* which still exists, was painted and decorated by Sebastian Conca. [2] Unfortunately it was impossible to execute the plan without nearly destroying the antique and venerable aspect of the Basilica. The columns were totally concealed by heavy masonry, and the nave was transformed into a series of arches. The triumphal arch was sacrificed together with its mosaics; and the paintings representing the succession of the Popes, and scenes from the Old and New Testament, painted by order of Paschal and restored by Sfondrato, were irretrievably annihilated "to the deep regret of the amateurs of venerable antiquity," says Marangoni, who witnessed this deplorable ruin. This same author likewise tells us that the antique inscriptions forming the pavement, many of which were Christian, were pitilessly destroyed. [3] This restoration, which might have been more wisely planned, was nevertheless a testimony of the Cardinal's devotion to Saint Cecilia. He faithfully prayed at the martyr's tomb, and had the consolation of seeing his own mother and his niece join the community of religious who took charge of this sanctuary. He was so renowned for his piety towards the illustrious virgin, that the Queen of Spain desiring to offer him a present as a proof of her esteem and gratitude, sent him a picture of St. Cecilia which she had painted herself. [4]

The great works undertaken in the Basilica by Paul Emilius Sfondrato, had inspired Bosio with the idea of editing his Acts of St. Cecilia; the labors of Francis Aquaviva suggested to James Laderchi of the Roman Oratory, the thought of offering the Cardinal a more complete life of the holy Martyr. His intention was to insert, century by century, all that had been written concerning St. Cecilia, the whole to be comprised in three quarto volumes; only the first two appeared. They are entitled: S. Caeciliae Virginiset Martyris Acta et trans-Tiberina Basilica, sseculorum singulorum monumentis asserta et illustrata, 1723. The author reproduces Bosio's work, literally introducing, in chronological order, all the documents and quotations which refer to his subject. This work, which has become very rare even in Italy, is remarkable for its typographical beauty; it is much to be regretted that the two volumes given to the public, do not bring us down to the Invention of Cecilia's body in 1599. The notes added by the compiler, are unfortunately few in number. The third volume was intended to embrace many details, the loss of which we must deeply regret. Notwithstanding this, Laderchi merits, by this important compilation, a distinguished place among the authors who have dedicated their efforts to the glory of Saint Cecilia. Two years had scarcely elapsed after the publication of the first volume of this work, when Francis Aquaviva died, on the eighth of January, 1725. He had been elevated to the Suburbioary Bishopric of Sabina; but Benedict XIII. had permitted him to retain *in commendam,* as Paul Kmilius Sfondrato had done, the Presbyterial Title of St Cecilia. Aquaviva was interred in this Church near his uncle, Cardinal Octavio who had been Titulary of the Basilica in the preceding century. The following epitaph was placed over his tomb:

FRANCISVS S. R. E. CARDINALIS DE ACQVAVIVA ET ARAGONIA EPISCOPVS SABINENSIS HVIVS ECCLESIAE COMMENDATARIVS SACRIQVE CAENOBII AC OMNIVM HISPANIAE REGNORVM APVD SANCTAM SEDEM PROTECTOR. IN TEMPLO DECOREM DILEXIT ET AVXIT. PROPE CARDINALIS OCTAVII PATRVI SVI CINERES HIC MONVMENTVM SIBI VIVENS POSVIT ANNO IVBILAEI MDCCXXV. OBIIT DIE VIII. MENSIS JANVARII MDCCXXV. AETATIS SVAE AN. LIX. MENS. XI. DIE. XXV.

Trojano Aqua viva, a nephew of Francis, was promoted to the Cardinalate by Clement XII., on the 1st October, 1732. The same Pope appointed him Titulary of St. Cecilia. [5] He appears to have continued the works commenced by his uncle in the Basilica; it is certain that the exterior porch, which was constructed upon the plan of Ferdinand Fuga, is due to his munificence. [6] The porch is quite modern, but not wanting in grandeur. We should at least give credit to the different restorers of the Basilica, for having respected the old brick cupola which towers above all their modern constructions, as a memorial of the devotion of the middle age towards Cecilia. They have also faithfully preserved the interior arrangement of the edifice, which even since the taking away of the ambons and the substituting of arcades for columns, bears a strong resemblance to the Christian Churches of the primitive ages.

In the year, 1729, the sanctuary of St. Cecilia, on the Campus Martius, attracted the attention of the Roman Pontiff. The little Church was falling into ruins; it needed rebuilding. Benedict XIII., who proved his devotion to the Saints by many monuments still existing in Rome, was unwilling to yield to another the honor of laying the corner stone of the new edifice. In thus venerating the dwelling where Cecilia had passed her youth, he thought it his duty to favor the devotion testified by a confraternity in honor of St. Blaise, to one of the altars of this Church. The Pontiff ordered that the new temple should be placed under the joint invocation of St. Cecilia and St. Blaise; and as if to prove, that in admitting another Saint to share the honor of the great Martyr, he intended no disparagement to the latter, he decided that the Church should bear the name of the Queen of Virgins. From that time, it was called: *Santa Maria del divino amore:* An inscription placed in the nave of this Church, records the Pontiff's intention. It is as follows:

BENEDICTO XIII. PONT. OPT. MAX.
QVOD PATERNAM DOMVM CAECILIAE DOMVM IN EIVSDEM VIRGINIS ET
MARTYRIS HONOREM ET DIVI BLASSII DICTAM INIVRIA TEMPORVM PENE
COLLAPSAM IACTO SOLEMNITER PRIMO LAPIDE
DIE XXV. IVLII. ANNO MDCCXXIX. A FVNDAMENTIS RESTITVERIT ET DEIP-
ARAE MARIAE SACRAM QVOQVE IN POSTERVM ESSE IVSSERIT. [7]

The Pontiff removed to the sacristy, the charming fresco of the fifteenth century, which we have already mentioned; as well as a marble tablet discovered in 1504, in rebuilding the principal altar of this sanctuary. This tablet bore an inscription, attesting a consecration of the Church of St. Cecilia *de domo,* on the Campus Martius, in the year 1131, probably the period at which it was rebuilt. The zeal of the pious confraternity, which assembled in this church, led it to perpetuate the memory of these facts:

VETVSTISSIMAM IMAGINEM
AC LAPIDEM HVNC CONSECRATIONIS
ANTIQVAE HVIVS ECCLESIAE

S. CAECILIAE VIRG. ET M.
ANNO MCXXXI PERACTAE TESTEM
SVB EIVSDEM ARA MAXIMA ANNO MDIV REPERTVM
BENEDICTVS XIII P. M. ORD. PRAEDICAT.
ANNO MDCCXXIX HVG TRANSFERRI MANDAVIT [8]

Another glorious fact relating to St. Cecilia and proving at the same time the homage rendered by France to the great martyr, may be referred to the year 1741. Our readers have not forgotten the mysterious tomb of the Callistus Cemetery, where Cecilia reposed for six centuries, until Paschal transferred her remains to the trans-Tiberian Basilica. This humble cell, excavated horizontally in the tufo, was lined with four slabs of white marble. In 1741, the upper one, which had been solidly fastened to the stone with a thick coating of lime, was the only one left.

Paul Hippolytede Bovilliers, Duke of St. Aignan, Ambassador from the King of France to the Holy See, in his ardent devotion to St. Cecilia, solicited and obtained from Benedict XIV., the favor of removing to his private chapel in France, this piece of marble, which had been sanctified by the presence of the virgin's body. The marble was respectfully detached in presence of two learned Roman archaeologists, Boldetti and Marangoni, and presented to the Duke of St. Aignan. Guadagni, the Cardinal Vicar, affixed his seal to it; [9] and the precious monument was carried to France, and deposited in the chapel of a castle, belonging to the family of Bovilliers, where it is still preserved. We find the preceding facts in a document of great interest under the name of Cardinal Guadagni [10] We are most happy to mention these testimonies of the piety of France towards St. Cecilia, at a period when Jansenism was endeavoring to blot out her very memory from among us.

Tillemont's principles were carried to scandalous lengths by Adrian Baillet, in his "Lives of the Saints," published in 1701. A prudent and learned writer recently said, in regard to certain insinuations by which Baillet seemed desirous of sapping the truth of evangelical facts: "These assertions would be sufficient to create serious doubts respecting the orthodoxy of the writer, if it were not notorious that he has frequently sacrificed historical truth to the interest of the sect whose principles he advocates; and were it not also well known that by his bold freedom of thought and expression, he prepares the minds of his partisans for open infidelity." [11]

This is not the place to examine the character of Baillet's genius, such as we find it in his biographies of Descartes, [12] Eicher, [13] and in his account of the difficulties between Boniface VIII. and Philip the Fair; [14] nor to speak of his work upon "Devotion to the Blessed Virgin, and the veneration which should be paid her;" [15] but we must acknowledge that his "Lives of the Saints," replete with erudition and with errors, influenced the public much more than the Memoirs of Tillemont. Although all the works of Baillet are on the Roman *Index*, this author still ranks in France as the highest authority in all matters pertaining to hagiography. Happily, his influence has been some-what lessened in our days by the translation of Alban Butler's "Lives of the Saints."

Baillet's article upon St. Cecilia, is nothing more than a violent tirade, in which he reproduces with his accustomed acrimony, the objections of Til-lemont. We would fear to soil our pages by quoting his contemptuous and disdainful expressions in speaking of a Spouse and Martyr of Christ, whose name is daily pronounced in the Holy Sacrifice. Baillet mentions, however, Sfondrato's discovery of Cecilia's body, and declares that the account of this discovery, is the most ancient record we have of her. But he relates the cir-cumstances of this event in a very abridged manner; frequently deviating from the truth, as if he feared to meet with some confirmation of the Acts whose authority he wished to destroy. [16]

But the influence of Tillemont and Bailiet produced one fatal result which they had not probably anticipated. Not only, thanks to their efforts, did the name of St. Cecilia lose in France the aureole of glory which had hitherto sur-rounded it, but the moment had arrived when even the Liturgy took part in this singular conspiracy against the holy martyr.

Until then, the Roman tradition of the Divine Office had held full sway in France, and, consequently, the glory of Cecilia shone with undiminished lus-tre within the precincts of the Church. But in the eighteenth century, the French Liturgy was revised, and all those saints excluded who were not hon-orably mentioned by Tillemont and Bailiet.

In 1680, the Archbishop of Paris, Francois de Harley, had appointed a committee to correct the Breviary of his church. The Abbe Chastelain, who was the soul of this committee, insisted upon retaining the record of St. Cecil-ia's life, with the Anthems and Responses taken from her Acts. This will not appear strange, if we remember the intimacy existing between Chastelain and Father Papebrook, both bold critics, but far removed from the scandal-ous audacity of the Jansenistic school. The Jesuits of Anvers, as we before stated, had pronounced in favor of our Acts, that they were both *ancient* and *genuine.* Owing to the influence of these two learned and strong-minded men, the record of St. Cecilia's life was retained in the Parisian Liturgy. [17]

But when this generation of learned men had descended into the tomb, and when the Church of Paris had called upon sectaries to revise her Breviary, all the Catholic traditions relating to St. Cecilia were sacrificed. The instincts of the sect and the oracles of Port Royal, required it. The Parisian Breviary of 1736, contained a record of St. Cecilia's life, which was successively intro-duced into the greater number of the Dioceses of France. In it, the actions of St. Cecilia are passed over in silence. There is some mention in the latter part, of the Invention of Cecilia's body by Sfondrato, but it is given according to the inaccurate relation of Baillet.

From that time, these heroic scenes, blotted out from the Breviary of the priests, were never recalled to the memory of the faithful. The *abridged Lives of the Saints* were thenceforth compiled according to the same plan, and we are fully aware that our attempt to avenge an insult offered as much to history as to the Roman Church, will awaken much surprise in the breasts of our readers. Such is the legitimate fruit of that artful silence which the Jansenists so often employed, and with so much success.

The ill-will of modern liturgists was not satisfied with effacing the account of Cecilia's virtues and actions from the French Breviary, it also strove to despoil the modest virgin of the beautiful title of Queen of Harmony, with which for nearly three centuries, Catholic piety had loved to salute her. The Abbe Lebeuf, composer of the new French Liturgical music, was the first to dispute Cecilia's title to the crown of harmony. In a memoir, under the form of an anonymous letter inserted in the *Mercure de France,* [18] this academician, who is celebrated for his erudition, assumed the very easy task of demonstrating that in the Acts of St. Cecilia, there is nothing to prove that she ever performed upon any musical instrument; but this was not the question, and we are surprised that an antiquarian, like Lebeuf, should have found it necessary to waste so much time in proving to us that the symbolical attributes assigned to the saints, by Christian artists, have not always their origin in history. Determined to seek material reasons for a fact which springs only from sentiment, the Abbé Lebeuf, after criticising the Acts of St. Cecilia, in Tillemont's spirit, and often in Tillemont's own words, comes to the conclusion that the idea of styling St. Cecilia patroness of music, arises from the fact that one of the Anthems in her Office commences with these words: *Cantantibus organis.* He then seeks the origin of this Anthem in that passage of the Acts which speaks of the musical concert at the wedding feast of Valerian and Cecilia. He did not comprehend the meaning of these touching words: "During the concert, *Cecilia sang also in her heart* to the Lord." He understood nothing of that melody of the soul which ascends to the Divine fountain of all harmony, and sings to its Creator, even amidst the profane concerts of earth. He translates the sentence in the following manner: "Cecilia paid no attention to the music, but was interiorly absorbed in God;" and he even pities those who blend the idea of harmony with Cecilia's name. In his zeal for reformation, he offers musicians their choice among the following patrons: St. Arnold of Juliers, Sts. Dunstan, Ado, Nizier, Gall and Prix of Clermont, Germain of Paris, and Aldric of Mans. The Abbé forgets none but St. Gregory the Great; however this omission can scarcely surprise us in the avowed enemy of the Gregorian chant.

We do not dwell upon the tone of superiority with which the Abbé Lebeuf criticises and censures all that was composed before his time; happily, Christian instinct has preserved what the Abbé would have gladly annihilated, and notwithstanding his efforts to bury St. Cecilia in the seclusion of convents, with the Agneses, the Lucys, and the Agathas [19] of antiquity, the Roman virgin still retains one of her most touching prerogatives. The Abbé did not succeed better in pointing out the period when she was first honored as patroness of music; according to him it was about the beginning of the seventeenth century. [20] On being reminded that Raphael's St. Cecilia, painted in 1513, represents her seated, with a musical instrument resting upon her knees, while her soul is absorbed in listening to the concert of angels, he was somewhat embarrassed; but he defended himself in a second letter [21] by saying that he knew the picture perfectly well, and that he had had reference to it, when he asserted that St. Cecilia was first proclaimed patroness of music in Italy. This reply did not, however, vindicate the learned academician from the charge of anachronism.

Besides, Raphael was not the only artist of the sixteenth century who represented St. Cecilia with the attributes of music. At the same period, the German artist, Laike of Leyden, painted her, accompanied by an angel holding a little organ upon which she plays. The picture is in the royal gallery at Munich. About the middle of the same century, Garofolo painted a magnificent picture in which he represents St. Cecilia playing the organ in presence of the Blessed Virgin and St. Anthony of Padua. [22]

We have yet to show the facts which characterize the progress of hagiographical writings throughout the eighteenth century, relative to the Acts of St. Cecilia. We shall begin with the Bollandists. Papebrok was no more, but his successors continued with zeal and erudition the great work to which he has so gloriously attached his name. It was not, however, until the nineteenth century, that they were ready to enter into the lists with Tillemont and Baillet on the controverted question of St. Cecilia's Acts, which the authority of the two learned Jansenists seemed to have settled forever in Catholic France. We see the sad influence of these hagiographers in the following fact. When Father du Sollier published his edition of Usuard's Martyrology, he spoke of the Acts of St. Cecilia with moderation, indeed, since he could not forget the respect which he owed to his predecessors, Henschenius and Papebrok, but at the same time, with a reserve which proved the influence exercised by the boldness of French criticism over the best disposed minds. When speaking of the martyrdom of Sts. Tiburtius and Valerian, the learned Jesuit contents himself with remarking that this is not the place to enter into a discussion which properly belongs to the Acts of St. Cecilia. [23] He repeats the same assertion when relating the martyrdom of St. Urban. [24] But when he comes at length to St. Cecilia, he merely lays before its the controversy concerning her Acts, without entering into a discussion of its merits. Tillemont's objection as to the improbability of a persecution against the Christians under Alexander Severus, seems to make some impression on his mind: [25] "however," he frankly adds, "the opinion of Baronius, of Florentini, of the others whom I have cited, and of the whole Catholic world, are all in favor of the Acts of St. Cecilia. [26] With respect to Tillemont's idea of calling our Saint a Sicilian virgin, on the authority of Fortunatus, Du Sollier considers the proposition perfectly paradoxical, [27] but, again deserting the arena, he refers the decision of this controversy to himself or his successors at a later period.

Laderchi, more courageous and probably more frank than du Sollier, energetically undertook the defence of the Acts of Saint Cecilia, and devoted an
essay in the work we have mentioned to this object; but Tillemont and Baillet
were so highly respected even in Italy, that he did not venture to give their
names, although he translated their objections word for word. At the same
time, he did not hesitate to attribute to the influence of Jansenism, the incredulity of certain men with regard to these venerable Acts, and asked "if the
Church and historical science had definitively passed under the dominion of
the new sect?" Francis Bianchini, in his commentary upon Anastasius, was
equally sincere and firm, and brought to the support of the ancient cause, the
weight of his authority and profound erudition. *He* also thought that the
opinions of Baronius, Bosio, and Papebrok, might be accepted without disgrace. In 1752, appeared a new champion of St. Cecilia. The learned Canon
Moretti undertook to write the history of St. Callistus and of the Basilica of St.
Mary beyond the Tiber. The plan of this work compelled him to examine the
great controversy concerning the Martyrs under Alexander Severus. In so
doing, this learned and talented man rendered an invaluable service to the
Acts of St. Cecilia, although the question concerning them entered but indirectly into his thesis.

The martyrdom of St. Callistus was incontestable, as well as the fact that he
suffered under Alexander Severus; therefore, there were Martyrs in Rome
even under this prince, otherwise so favorable to Christianity. The demonstration of this particular fact, led to that of the general thesis. Moretti takes
up that thesis, and with resistless erudition, demonstrates it step by step,
until he triumphantly settles the controversy in a manner conformable to the
opinion of Baronius. Although Moretti had not investigated the Acts of St.
Cecilia individually, yet his triumphant solution of the great question with
which they are so intimately connected, tended much to prove their authenticity.

At Naples, several years previously, in 1744, the Acts of St. Cecilia had been
directly subjected to the critical and literary examination of Alexia Mazochi, a
most skilful hagiographer. His conclusions were far from according with
those of Tillemont and Baillet. In his valuable commentary upon the celebrated Neapolitan Calendar of the eighth century, Masochi makes particular
mention of certain latinisms in the Acts of St. Cecilia, which prove that these
Acts date back to the fourth century. The compiler of the fifth, whose style is
very careless, must then have made use of manuscripts previously written,
and must have transcribed whole passages from them. Hence the Acts are
not entirely his own composition.

Mazochi then points out several incidents and allusions which characterize
the account, and shows how perfectly they accord with the manners and language of antiquity. He accounts in several w; for the name of Almachius, and
is far from considering this name as an invalidation of the Acts. He next energetically attacks the system by which Tillemont endeavors, from a single

hemistich in the works of Fortunatus, to prove Cecilia a Sicilian. He plainly shows that the most conclusive evidence designates Rome as the theatre of the illustrious Virgin's martyrdom: "To deny a fact so well attested." he remarks, "is contrary to common sense, to say nothing more. And yet, Baillet and other Frenchmen still cling to Tillemont's opinion." [28]

Such is Mazochi's appreciation of the Acts. The learned and courageous critic makes, it is true, some concessions to his adversaries with regard to the dialogues and discourses which he thinks may have been interpolated; but he forgets that the very part of the Acts, from which he quotes expressions to prove their antiquity, is precisely that of the discourses and dialogues. Notwithstanding these restrictions, the favorable judgment of Mazochi is remarkable at a time when the French prejudice against hagiographical monuments was so prevalent in Europe.

The Neapolitan author finds it difficult, however, to reconcile a persecution against the Christians with the character of Alexander Severus; yet he is unwilling to invalidate St. Cecilia's Acts, and therefore adopts the opinion of Usuard and St. Ado who refer her martyrdom to the reign of Marcus Aurelius. This involves him in some difficulty with regard to her interviews with Pope Urban; but Mazochi thinks he can solve the problem by supposing that St. Urban was but a simple priest at the time of Cecilia's martyrdom; and that having been appointed Pope about fifty years later, the actions of Urban as priest, were attributed to Urban as Pope. [29]

This solution, although more ingenious than satisfactory, is at least a proof of the seriousness with which Mazochi studied Cecilia's Acts. Nor is it more fanciful than that which was proposed later by the learned Jesuit, Lesley, in his commentary upon the Mozarabic Missal, published in 1755. This critic, also desirous to place St. Cecilia's martyrdom under Marcus Aurelius, after relating Mazochi's theory, proposes his own. It consists in admitting that Bishops were established in the *Pagi* around Rome, and that St. Urban was probably Bishop of a Pagus on the Appian Way, during the reign of Marcus Aurelius [30] Unfortunately, no one has ever heard of Bishops being established in the *Pagi* of the environs of Rome, and an explanation based upon so gratuitous a conjecture, cannot have much weight. [31] Had the Acts ot St. Cecilia been more thoroughly studied, learned men would have perceived that the persecution mentioned in them, was precisely such as might have been expected in the reign of such a prince as Alexander Severus. The unity, the probability, and the natural succession of the various incidents, all perfectly in accordance with what we should expect in the reign of a prince, who, though tolerant to the Christians, was weak, and served by magistrates who despised them; were above the comprehension of an author so simple hearted as the compiler of the Acts in the fifth century. His narration proves, therefore, the existence of previous memoirs from which he gives his details. If our Martyrs had suffered during the persecution of Marcus Aurelius and Commodus, in consequence of an edict issued by these Emperors, the conduct of the Roman Prefect, his trial of the culprits, and Cecilia's death, would have presented a totally different character. But if it be granted, on the contrary, that this great drama took place during the reign of Alexander Severus, then, all that would appear extraordinary under a persecuting Emperor, becomes perfectly natural; we feel that the events *could* not have been different.

But this method of appreciating an historical document, was not familiar to the hagiographers of the period; and we are therefore deeply indebted to Mazochi and Lesley for having seriously defended the Acts of St. Cecilia at a time when it required no little courage to contest even the most trifling of Tillemont's decisions in regard to monuments which had once been universally respected. The gravity of the narrative, the universal assent of all nations, the palpable facts stated in the account of the two Inventions, everything, even to the philological study of the Acts, had induced these learned men to accept a document which seemed to them so worthy of respect; their only study was to fix the date of the events mentioned in it; we have just explained why they were deceived as to the period of Cecilia's martyrdom.

The close of the eighteenth century, beheld the persecuted successors of Bollandus, wandering through the world, without a resting place. These noble exiles took refuge for some time in the abbey of Tougerloo. Whilst there, they published in 1794, the sixth volume of the Acts of the Saints, for October. It contained the Acts of St. Callistus, whose festival falls on the 14th of October. This article was compiled by James de Buc, one of the Bollandists. He openly adopted Moretti's conclusions, and the famous question which had puzzled du Sollier, was finally decided according to Baronius and our Acts. In 1845, the Bollandists resumed their work amidst the applause of Europe. After fifty years of suspension, the seventh and eighth volumes appeared. May heaven grant that the present editors may bring the immortal work to a glorious conclusion, and avenge the Arts of St. Cecilia in a manner worthy of the erudition and piety of the illustrious Society of Jesus!

We have still to speak of a celebrated English hagiographer, Alban Butler, whose work is known in France under the name of Godescard, Canon of Saint Honore, who translated and completed it. This book neither merits the great reputation which it has obtained, nor the contempt with which it is now frequently treated. We shall only dwell upon the carelessness with which the question concerning St. Cecilia, is examined. Butler and Godescard, generally so eager to seek and cite every work, treating of the Saints, consulted neither Bosio nor Laderchi. In 1763, they seemed to consider the question as finally settled. Had not the French Liturgists decided it? They therefore merely state that the Acts of St. Cecilia are of little authority, an observation which they attempt to justify by a short exposition of Tillemont's assertions; they agree, however, that there may have been Martyrs under Alexander Severus.

The inconceivable carelessness with which this notice was compiled, is clearly proved by the following phrase: "We learn from the Acts of St. Cecilia, that in chanting the praises of God, she frequently added instrumental to vocal music." [32] Hence, it is clear that Butler and Godescard, before compiling St. Cecilia's life, had not even taken the trouble to read her Acts, since these do not contain a single expression which could lead to such a conclusion. The only authority which these learned men could allege, in favor of the fact they thus advance, is the legitimate license with which artists have represented St. Cecilia playing upon musical instruments, to indicate that she is patroness of Music. They might have shown at least some deference for Acts which were written nearly a thousand years before the paintings in question were executed. [33]

In concluding this chapter upon the events relating to the Holy Martyr throughout the eighteenth century, we again gladly take refuge in our dear Basilica, the history of which is so intimately united with that of St. Cecilia.

Whilst the erudites were agitating the learned questions we have mentioned, multiplied homages of piety were offered the illustrious Virgin. The trans-Tiberian Basilica was devoutly visited by pilgrims; and the devotion of the Romans to this august sanctuary and the valuable treasures it contained, had not grown cold. Among all Cecilia's clients, towards the end of the eighteenth century, the pious Joseph Mazzolari held the first place. He was a member of the Society of Jesus, before its suppression. He was a distinguished scholar and full of zeal for the glory of the Blessed Virgin and the Saints. This zeal led him to write under the assumed name of *Mariano Partenio*. Among the Ciceronian harangues found in his literary works, there is one, styled *pro domo Lauretana,* [34] which he caused to be engraved upon a plate of silver as an offering to the sanctuary of our Lady of Loretto. He particularly venerated the Martyrs of Rome, and it was principally on account of this devotion, that he published a little work entitled *Diario sagro;* [35] but Cecilia was Mazzolari's special favorite. Through his exertions, an Italian translation of her Acts was published in Rome, [36] in 1775, preceded by a preface proving their authenticity.

In the year 1785, Mazzolari, at his own expense, caused the fresco, representing upon one of its compartments Cecilia's interment, and upon the other her apparition to Paschal, to be detached from the exterior portico of the Basilica. He removed this valuable painting to the interior of the Church, placed it in front of the large altar, and added to it the following inscription:

MONVMENTVM VETVSTISSIMVM INVENTIONIS ET DEPOSITIONIS SACRAE
CHRISTI SPONSAE ET INCLYTAE MARTYRIS CAECILIAE NE AERIS INIVRIA
PRORSVS INTERIRET HVC E PORTICV IOSEPHVS MARIANVS PARTHENIVS
PRO SVO ERGA S. VIRGINEM ET MARTYREM STVDIO TRANSFERENDVM
CVRAVIT A. D. M. DCC. LXXXV. [37]

This was not the only proof of Mazzolari's devotion to St. Cecilia. He thought that Paschal's document, in which the holy Pope describes the apparition of the illustrious virgin, should be publicly exposed in the Basilica. He had it engraved, therefore, upon a large white marble tablet, and placed it opposite the antique fresco of which we have just spoken. It bears the following inscription:

HAS LITTERAS E COD. VATIC. DESCRIPTAS JOSEPHVS MARIANVS PARTHE-
NIUS INCIDENDAS CVRAVIT A. D. M. DCC. LXXXVI. [38]

A third memorial of Mazzolari's devotion to St. Cecilia, was a large silver gilt heart, which was placed near the Confession. The following words are engraved upon it:

JOSEPHVS MARIANVS PARTHENIVS CAECILIAE VIRGINI SANCTAE MARTYRI
INVICTAE D. D. PATRONAE COELESTI ANNO MDCCLXXV. ORAT OBSECRAT
SUPPLICAT VT HABERE MEREATUR PARTEM CVM EA. [39]

While these pious offerings were being placed upon Cecilia's tomb, disastrous days wore looming over the holy city, and the treasures of her Basilicas were soon to fall into the hands of wicked men. The pontificate of Pius VI. was almost at an end, when the Directory of the French Republic, having conceived the odious project of deposing the Lord's anointed, announced to the Pontiff that Christian Home was condemned to destruction, and that nothing could avert its ruin but the greatest sacrifices. Pius VI., by the armistice of Milan, and soon after, by the treaty of Tolentino, was forced to cede a portion of his territory, to deliver up his most beautiful pictures and finest statuary, and to pay thirty-one million francs.

To satisfy this enormous demand, the Pontiff sent the treasures of gold and silver that still remained in the Castle of St. Angelo, and, moreover, added to them all the gold and silver ornaments belonging to the churches of Home.

We have read with much emotion in the archives of the Basilica of St. Cecilia, an order issued by the Cardinal Vicar, in the name of his Holiness, dated July 6th, 1796, to all the superiors of the churches in Rome, commanding, under the severest penalties, an inventory to be made of all the gold and silver plate entrusted to their keeping. [40] A document of later date, mentioned that on the seventeenth of that same month, the Abbess delivered up three hundred and ninety-five pounds of silver to the pontifical commissary Livaldini; on the 29th of August, sixty-nine pounds; and on the 9th of the following March, one hundred and sixty-nine. [41]

This cruel spoliation, to which the Pontiff wag forced by extreme necessity, deprived the Basilica of its three precious caskets, in which Sfondrato had enclosed the heads of Valerian, Tiburtius, and Maximus. These holy relics were then placed in the copper cylinders in which they have since remained. Besides the three caskets sent by the Abbess, there were silver chalices, candelabra, and other altar furniture; the greater number of the reliquaries, presented by Sfondrato, were merely bronze-gilt.

Notwithstanding this enormous sacrifice, the liberty of the Pope was not long respected. In less than two years, the holy old man was dragged into exile. Then followed new spoliations of the churches of Rome, under the immediate supervision of the French authorities. We find in the Archives of St. Cecilia's Basilica, a French document, headed with the words *Liberty, Equality*, and dated 16 *Ventose of the sixth year of the Republic*. This document attested that the citizen Valette, charged by the financial administration of Italy, to *receive* the gold and silver taken from churches, required the *citizen* Sebastian Bartoletti, a Roman priest, to enumerate, *upon oath*, all the silver articles which remained in the Church and monastery of St. Cecilia, of which he was chaplain.

"We may form an idea of the state of destitution to which the sanctuary of St. Cecilia was thus reduced, and at the same time picture to ourselves the rapacity of the spoliators of Rome, by reading in this document the list of precious articles which were reluctantly left in the Basilica. They consisted of an altar cloth embroidered with gold, an ostensorium, four reliquaries, two chalices, and a censor.

Whilst the trans-Tiberian Basilica was being thus despoiled of even its most trifling ornaments, the illustrious Cardinal, Hyacinth Sigismond Gerdil, to whose care the Pope had entrusted it, was, like the other members of the Sacred College, forced to leave Rome. This austere religious and eminent theologian, a worthy successor of so many great cardinals, was renowned for his learning and virtue. He had successfully combated all the errors of his time, and had compiled the immortal Constitution *Auctorem fidei* which annihilated Jansenism.

Gerdil was eighty years of age when thus forced to leave Rome and the pious sanctuary which had been committed to his care. We have read with deep emotion the autograph letter which he addressed, previous to his departure, to his dear daughters, the Abbess and Religious of St. Cecilia, whom he left exposed to every danger. This letter breathes throughout the most heroic resignation and paternal charity. After the miraculous election of Pius VII., at Venice, Gerdil returned to Rome and once more had the consolation of praying at Cecilia's tomb. But he was soon called to receive the recompense he had merited by his noble and holy life. He died on the 12th of August, 1802.

Our Basilica, towards the end of the eighteenth century, shared in the general tribulations of the Church. We will close this chapter with a single incident characteristic of this epoch, no less fruitful in virtues than in crimes. We are confident that our readers honor the angelic memory of the amiable and pious Madame Elizabeth, sister of Louis XVI. This princess, whose murder was one of the greatest crimes of the French Revolution, venerated St. Cecilia with special devotion. Perhaps she felt a secret presentiment that she too would one day add the rose of martyrdom to the lily of virginity. When her brother, the Count of Provence, before leaving France, bade adieu to his dearly loved sister, Elizabeth presented him with a picture of St. Cecilia, entreating him never to part with it. "I am aware," said she, "that your mind and heart have been misled by a false and dangerous philosophy. I trust that this holy martyr will obtain your conversion. [42] Elizabeth did not seek to escape from a country where a cruel fate awaited her. Her devoted attachment to the royal family did not suffer her to abandon them. She consoled the last moments of the Queen; and when her own turn arrived, she calmly ascended the scaffold, after encouraging with angelic words the numerous victims, who, one by one, preceded her to death on that mournful day.

[1] Guarnacci, tome ii., p. 73.

[2] Platner and Bunsen err in attributing the destruction of the portico paintings, and the taking away of the ambons, to the two Cardinals Aquaviva.

[3] Non senza dolore degliamanti della venerabile antichita. Marangoni Cose gentilesche ad uso delle chiese, p. 311.

[4] For this fact see Laderchi in his dedicatory epistle of the Acts of St. Cecilia to the same Cardinal.

[5] He died on the 21st of March. 1747, and was buried in the Church of St. Cecilia.

[6] Platner and Bunsen, tome iii. p. 639.

[7] To Benedict XIII. a great and good Pontiff, for having rebuilt the paternal dwelling of S. Cecilia, consecrated in honor of this Virgin and of St. Blaise; for having on the 25th of July, 1729, solemnly laid the first stone, the ancient edifice having been almost entirely destroyed by the ravages of time; and for having decreed that the Church should, henceforth be dedicated to Mary, the Mother of God.

[8] Benedict XIII., the Sovereign Pontiff, transferred this painting to this place, as well as the stone attesting the consecration of this antique church of St. Cecilia, Virgin and Martyr, in the year 1131; the stone was discovered in 1504, under the main altar.

[9] The marble was in two pieces, having probably been fractured in detaching it from the wall. It was a Little over live feet long, and somewhat more than two feel broad.

[10] See the certificate in Marangoni, Cose gentilesche ad uso delle Chiese, page 426-429.

[11] Unpublished Memoirs upon the Apostolate of St. Mary Magdalen, vol. ii. p. 154.

[12] 1691. Two volumes in 4°

[13] 1714. Two volumes in 12°

[14] 1717. Two volumes in 12°

[15] 1694. Two volumes in 12°

[16] The only argument produced by him against the Acts, and neglected by Tillemont, consists in saying: "That the Roman Calendar arranged under Pope Liberius, about the middle of the fourth century, makes no mention of Cecilia; which show," he adds, "that she did not suffer martyrdom in Rome." It is easy to prove that this objection has no weight. This Calendar, although very valuable, does not

represent the complete Martyrology of the Roman Church in the fourth century. It is true that Cecilia is not mentioned; but neither are the holy Topes Linus, Cletus, Evaristus, Alexander, Telesphorus, Hyginus, Anicetus, Soter, Eleutherius, etc., nor the holy martyrs Processus and Martinian, Nereus and Achilleus, Primus and Felicianus, Marcellinus and Peter, Boniface, Chrysogonus, etc., nor the holy virgins, Flavia, Domitilla, Petronilla, Prisca, Praxedes, Pudentiana, etc., nor the holy women Symphorosa, Felicitas, etc. Baillet agrees, nevertheless, that all these saints belonged to the Church of Rome.

[17] About the time of the publication of Harlay's Breviary, Santeuil published several hymns for the Office of St. Cecilia, They are not among his best compositions, but they at least celebrate the virtues and actions of the holy martyr according to the facts recorded in her Acts.

[18] Jan. 1732, pages 21-46.

[19] Page 43.

[20] Page 24.

[21] Mercure de France, June, 1732, pages 1081-1088.

[22] St. Cecilia was acknowledged patroness of music long before the foundation of the Academies of Music which were placed under her protection. Nevertheless, we see in the year 1601, a celebrated musical confraternity at Rouen bearing the title of St. Cecilia, upon a deed by which they renew their previous statutes. (Ouin Lacroix. *Histoire des corporations et des confreries de Rouen,* page 453.) At the same period, the musicians of Rouen established their Academy of St. Cecilia. (Alfieri, N*otizie storiche sulla Congregazione et Academia di Santa Cecilia,* and an excellent article of M. Morelot, in the *Revue de Musique religieuse* de M. Danjou, November, 1845.

[23] Nec locus hic, necotium est controversiam illam expendere, de qua in Actis nostris disputari poterit xxii. Novembris. *Sollerius. Martyrologium Usuardi illustratum,* tome i., page 210.

[24] Ne quid hic temore definiamus, aut extra propositum eyagemur, omnia tutius ad xxii. Novembris, de integro examinanda explicandaque remittimus. *Ibid.* page 294.

[25] Praecipua quae a recentioribus objicitur eaque capitalis difficultas, in eo consistit potissimum quod ut alibi etiam insinuavi, Alexandrit emporibus, tam acerba immanisque persecutio, qualis in istis Actis describitur, tam atrocia passim tormenta Christianis illata, quadrare prorsus non videantur. *Martyrologium Usuardi illustratum,* tome ii., page 692.

[26] Pro his (Actis) cum Baronio, Florentinio, aliisque certant laudati scriptores, certat totius orbis catholici pervulgata opinio. *Ibid.*

[27] Paradoxa multis aeque ac mihi videtur hujusmodi sententia. *Ibid.*

[28] Rem vero ita testatam negare, id, ne quid gravius dicam, *communi sensu plane caret.* Et tamen Tillemontii sententiam Bailletus, aliique passim Gallorum, adhuc admirantur. *Mazochi. In vetus marmoreum S. Neapolitanae Ecclcsiae Kalendarium commentarius.* Tome i, page 211.

[29] Mazochi. Pages 211, 212.

[30] Missale mixtum, dictum Mozarabes, praefatione, notis et appendice ornatum, page 608.

[31] Sue Riccy. Pago Lemonio, page 104.

[32] Vies des Peres et des Martyrs, tome xi. an 22 Novembre.

[33] Tabaraud, the author of the article upon St. Cecilia, in *la Biographic universelle*, has merely abridged the notice of Butler and Godescard; but he faithfully quotes the sentence in which these two authors assert that Cecilia's proficiency in music, is formally expressed in her Acts.

[34] Mazzolari opera, tome i.

[35] An interesting edition of this work appeared at Rome, in 1805, with excellent notes by Adami.

[36] In 8°, chez Solomoni.

[37] That this very ancient monument of the Invention and Deposition of the holy Spouse of Christ, the illustrious Martyr, St. Cecilia, might not be totally destroyed by the inclemency of the weather, Joseph Mariano Partenio, through devotion to the holy virgin and martyr, removed it from the portico to this place, A.D., 1785.

[38] This letter was copied from a manuscript of the Vatican, Joseph Mariano Partenio caused it to be engraved A.D. 1786.

[39] Joseph Mariano Partenio dedicated this heart to the holy Virgin and invincible martyr St. Caeciliae his heavenly patroness, A. D. 1775. He prays, he beseeches, he implores, that he may merit a share in her happiness.

[40] Archives of St. Cecilia. Lossier 94, No. 30.

[41] *Ibid.*, No. 31.

[42] Relation of a voyage to Brussels and Coblentz In 1791. Paris 1823. This pamphlet was written by the Count of Provence, afterwards Louis XVIII.

Chapter Thirty-Eight - Events Relating to St. Cecilia and Her Basilica throughout the Nineteenth Century

The nineteenth century opened with the elevation of Pius VII. During his pontificate, the churches resumed something of their ancient splendor, through the generosity and pious zeal of the faithful; but long years must pass away, ere the Basilica of Saint Cecilia, despoiled of nearly all its riches, and impoverished in its revenues, will again surround the tomb of the saint with the magnificence it displayed in Sfondrato's time. Instead of a hundred lamps burning day and night, there are now only fifty, and these are extinguished at sunset. The edifice itself was beginning to decay, and there was every reason to fear that the holy dwelling of Cecilia, which had been so frequently restored and embellished, would fall to ruins before the close of the century. Joseph Doria, who had been Secretary of State during the troubled pontificate of Pius VI., was now titulary of St. Cecilia. But the short time which elapsed between his nomination and the fresh troubles which fell upon the Church, was not sufficiently long to permit him to undertake, much less to execute, any repairs in the Basilica. He had been named Secretary of State to Pius VII.; but he did not remain long in this dangerous office. He was soon exiled to Genoa, in consequence of his fidelity to the sovereign Pontiff*. He died on the 10th of February, shortly after the return of Pius VII. to Rome. His nephew, Cardinal George Doria, succeeded him as Titulary of St. Cecilia, and profiting by the happy revolution which had restored to Rome her Pontiff* and Master, he determined to devote his first care to the Basilica, which sadly needed restoring. He strengthened the arcades of the ground nave, consolidated the falling arch, and renewed the painting and gilding. The Abbess and religious of St. Cecilia, wishing to hand down to posterity, a remembrance of the pious munificence of George Doria, caused the following inscription to be engraved upon a marble tablet:

GEOKGIVS AB AVRIA PAMPHILIVS
PRESBYTER CARDINALIS HVIVS TITVLI PERINSIGNE DIVAE CAECILLE E
DOMO TEMPLVM IN QVO ETIAM PIISSIMORVM CARDINALIVM GEORGII
PATRVI MAGNI ET IOSEPHI PATRVI SVI CINERES QVIESCVNT QVVM
TEMPORIS INIVRIA FATISCERET PERISTYLIO LATERICIIS MOLIBUS
SVBFVLTO SVPERIORI CONCAMERATIONE SOLIDATA OMNIBUS DENIQVE
AD ELEGANTEM FORMAM PERFECTIS VRGINVM SACRARVM RELIGIOSO
CVLTVI RESTITVENDVM SVA IMPENSA CVRAVIT ABBATISSA ET MONIALES
EMINENTISSIMI VIRI MUNIFICENTIAM GRATO ANIMO PROSEQVVTAE
REI MEMORIAM LAPIDE SIGNATAM VOLVERVNT ANNO M. DCCC XXIII. [1]

The Basilica thus restored, resumed its superiority over all the other churches of the city; and although still preserving traces of the cruel spoliation it had suffered, cheered by its splendor and elegance, the hearts of the pilgrims who visited the virgin's tomb. There were no events of any importance in the annals of St. Cecilia, until the disastrous days when Rome was profaned by sacrilege and revolt. No change was made in the trans-Tiberian Basilica during the pontificates of Leo XII., Pius VIII., and Gregory XVI.; under this last Pope, the church was entrusted to the pious Cardinal James Louis Brignole, a Genoese, who, upon his elevation to the Suburbicary Church of Sabine, obtained permission to retain this Basilica *in commendam*, as Sfondrato and Aquaviva had done. It was therefore under his administration, that the events we are about to relate, took place. We shall have occasion to admire the wonderful manner in which the holy martyr protected the house consecrated by her blood, and by the actual presence of her body. When, in November, 1848, the angelic Pius IX. had been forced to seek safety in flight, the fury of his enemies vented itself upon churches and monasteries. The venerable sanctuary of St. Cecilia was not spared; but nowhere throughout the holy city, was the protection of heaven more clearly or more constantly manifested. Before the arrival of the French army, the faction who governed the city, conceived the idea of taking away from the churches, some paintings which needed restoration, under the pretext of giving occupation to the artists. A party came to the Church of St. Cecilia, and took possession of the altar piece in the Chapel of the Bath. They were carrying it away in triumph, when an energetic band of Trasteverini, thinking they were despoiling the Basilica, suddenly rushed upon them, and by menaces which they would have carried into effect, forced them to return the picture they had so imprudently detached from the wall. In revenge, the minister of fine arts established his artists in this very chapel, with orders to restore the frescos of Paul Brill, which were in reality much defaced; but which are now completely destroyed, thanks to the pencils of these wretched artists. The tyrants of Rome had ordered that a number of the church bells should be taken down and cast into cannon for their service. The Basilica of St. Cecilia was one of the churches mentioned, but it was protected in a most unlooked-for manner. The President of the trans-Tiberian region, Vincent Cortesi, obtained from the triumvirate that the bells should not be disturbed. His influence likewise obtained for the Monastery and the Basilica an exemption from the decree, ordaining an inventory of all church furniture and monastic property.

The news that the French army was approaching, redoubled the rage of the factious party, while it increased the terror of peaceable citizens, who dreaded the horrors of a siege. On the 28th of April, 1849, the Benedictines of Campus Martius, begged admittance to the monastery of St. Cecilia, their convent having been seized by the republican administration and converted into barracks.

The daughters of St. Cecilia received their sisters with the most heartfelt kindness, their mutual afffection being increased by the common peril to which they were exposed; and the two communities, henceforth united in one, endeavored to assist each other in preparing for the trials in store for them.

Three days had scarcely elapsed, when a troop of armed men broke into the convent, at midnight, under pretext of seeking for a concealed priest. These ruffians searched every part of the house, but not finding the priest, they departed, threatening the religious with every kind of cruelty, assuring them that these threats would soon be put into execution. A few days later, the republican commissary of the Trastevere Region, accompanied by two of his satellites and a mason, forced his way into the convent and demanded the treasures which he declared the Titulary Cardinal had entrusted to the religious. He, and his companions, pierced the walls, broke open the doors, and examined all the furniture; but found no treasure. Such unheard of outrages committed in a house of unprotected women, were but preludes to greater insults. On the 14th of May, two commissaries of the government, presented themselves to the Abbess, Giuseppa Beneggi, after having broken open the doors of the monastery. They compelled her to assemble all her religions in the parlor, and then, in the presence of these holy virgins, they read a decree of the triumvirate, annulling the vows of all religious, and declaring them free to return to the world. The daughters of St. Cecilia listened to this insolent and sacrilegious decree, with silent indignation, and the commissaries retired.

The next evening, at ten o'clock, the commissary of the Trastevere Region, escorted by ten men, again entered the convent, and imperiously demanded the treasures of the Titulary Cardinal. After a fruit, less search, this man, furious at his non-success, summoned the Abbess before him, and told her that he considered her responsible for the missing treasures. He finally threatened to carry off the Abbess as a hostage, a menace which he would have executed, had not Providence interposed.

The month of June having arrived, the French resolved to press the siege. The fury of the assault, as well as of the defence, was confined principally to the Trastevere Region.

There was a constant cross fire from the Aventine Hill and the summit of Mount Janiculum, above the Basilica and Monastery of St. Cecilia. The balls struck against the august temple of the Roman Virgin in every direction, and the religious, who had been successively driven from one room of the monastery to another, finally took refuge in that part of the building erected on the Piazza de Santa Cecila. We have seen, in the monastery, a heap of balls which were picked up in the garden, by the religious, after the siege.

The intervention of heaven was marvellously shown by the miraculous preservation, not only of the religious, but also of the Basilica. Not one of the sisters was injured, although the balls frequently pierced the walls of the rooms where they were assembled; whilst the Basilica, though exposed on all sides to bomb shells and balls was not damaged in the slightest degree.

Christ visibly protected this sacred house, and the virgins who dwelt under its roof, because the tomb of Cecilia His spouse, is ever dear to His heart. This was proved by the following incident.

On the 10th of June, after one of the most fearful days of the siege, four religious had remained after matins in the tribune of the choir, directly in front of the main altar and of the Confession of St. Cecilia. They were the RR. MM. Donna Flavia Celeste Cecconi, Donna Electa Benedetti, Donna Gertrude Benedetti, and Donna Scholastica Rosa; the first three were exiles from St. Mary of the Campus Martins; the last belonged to the monastery of St. Cecilia. After the severe trials of the day, they remained to pray and to implore Almighty God to put an end to the disastrous events which were devastating the holy city. The Basilica was plunged in almost total darkness, the only light being that of four small tapers placed upon the upper balustrade, near the altar, on the Epistle side.

The four sisters were praying devoutly, when their attention was attracted to the sanctuary, suddenly illuminated by a brilliant light, issuing from the crypt under the altar where Cecilia's body reposed. This light ascended slowly to the foot of the statue, crossed the altar on the Gospel side, and after reaching the tabernacle, again descended, and vanished. The marvellous apparition was repeated twice. The four sisters were so impressed at such an unexpected sight, that at first they did not venture to communicate their feelings to one another. The Sisters of St. Mary were the first to speak; turning towards Donna Scholastica Rosa, they said: "Do you see that light? — "I do see it," replied the religions of St. Cecilia. "But what can it mean?" asked the other sisters." "I know not," answered Donna Scholastica, "let us see if it will reappear." A few moments after, the same brilliant light returned, and again ascending to the tabernacle, slowly descended, and disappeared as before. The Sisters remained a long time, respectfully waiting for another apparition; but the mysterious light appeared no more. This extraordinary fact, which we have heard from the lips of the above named religious, was certainly most significant.

Who does not see in it a touching indication of Cecilia's prayers, ascending to her divine Spouse, interceding for the cessation of the scourge and for the salvation of Rome and her Pontiff? The light emanated from the virgin's tomb like a fervent aspiration; it ascended towards Him who alone can give peace, and returned to the tomb, after having obtained the favor it implored. What greater proof could there be of the intercession of the Saints in our favor; and does it not likewise show that this intercession is more readily granted when prayed for in the places where their bodies repose?

Cecilia was truly watching over the salvation and deliverance of her children in the trans-Tiberian regions; for the wonderful preservation of the Basilica and monastery could only be attributed to her powerful intercession. Their trials, however, were not yet at an end; Cecilia's vigilance was still required over her august temple and her devoted children.

On the 15th of June, the Abbess received an imperious order to leave the house within three hours, and to send some of her daughters to the monastery of St. Bernardin, the rest to that of St. Susanna. The military engineers had selected the Church and monastery of St. Cecilia as a point of defence from which they could return the enemy's fire. We may easily conceive the desolation into which the religious were plunged by this unexpected expulsion from the sanctuary, rendered doubly dear by the terrors, the heartbreakings, and the dangers of the preceding months. Their souls were oppressed with the sad prospect of the sacred temple exposed to frightful profanations, the body of Cecilia, their faithful patroness, abandoned to these sacrilegious men,, the asylum of consecrated virgins converted into a barrack; the convent, within which they had practised the humble virtues of the cloister, and which they considered their home, desolated, perhaps destroyed, by the cannon of the besiegers, whilst they were wandering through the streets of the city.

Tears and supplications would have been lost upon the agents of the triumvirate; but Cecilia's protection was again sensibly felt. A private gentleman, Joseph Costa, who lived near the convent, and whose three daughters had been educated by the religious, interceded in their favor. He obtained permission for the Sisters to remain in their house, only giving up the part of the building which faced the Janiculum.

The religious immediately walled up the communicating doors between the part of the building which they were forced to relinquish, and that which they were permitted to retain, and continued to trust in the power of their heavenly protectress. The project of converting the Basilica and monastery into a place of defence, was never carried into execution; a sufficient proof that cupidity was the principal cause of this new vexation. In fact, two days later, some commissaries having thoroughly explored that part of the monastery given up to them, entered the Basilica about seven o'clock in the morning, with the intention of searching everywhere for the hidden treasures, of the Titulary Cardinal. As there was no one to oppose them, everything was to be feared from their audacity and avidity. The commissaries were accompanied by workmen, and they immediately commenced their search. Thinking that the treasures might be buried in the vault where the religious were interred, they hesitated not to violate this sacred place, and to disturb the ashes of the consecrated dead. Finding nothing in the first vault, they directed their steps to another, situated in the chapel of the Crucifix, and long used as a burial place for seculars. This search proved as unsuccessful as the former, and finally, after twelve hours of fruitless labor, the commissaries retired, uttering a thousand imprecations against the religious, and threatening in their fury, to force the cloister of the monastery. Joseph Costa again interceded in behalf of the Sisters, and obtained a detachment of the civic guard for their protection. This guard continued in service until the taking of Rome, and were disbanded by General Oudinot on the very day of his triumphal entrance into the city. We will now close these annals of the Roman virgin, hoping that by the mercy of Christ, they will be enriched throughout the course of time, for the consolation of Christianity and the honor of our invincible heroine. The Romans, especially those dwelling in the trans-Tiberian regions, pay her the most devoted homage, and she reigns over all Christendom as Queen of Harmony.

It is true, that for more than a century, neither poet nor artist has laid at her feet a tribute worthy of her acceptance; but this must be attributed to that general decline of true Catholic inspiration in the fine arts which commenced at a much earlier period. In France, another cause may be assigned, viz., the conspiracy of our hagiographers against the honor of the Saint.

Better days are in store, when devotion to the Saints will become more lively and practical. All must acknowledge that little was thought of St. Elizabeth of Hungary, until the pen of Montalembert had so vividly painted her beautiful virtues. Cecilia lived at a much earlier period, but her name has always been popular and her feast annually celebrated. Christ will deign to glorify His Spouse still more. He will infuse new life into the homages paid her, and will incite the faithful to imitate her glorious example.

What thanks do we not owe thee, Cecilia! for having permitted us to trace thy hallowed memory throughout sixteen ages; for having assisted us in our narration, and above all, for the favor thrice repeated of prostrating ourselves before thy august tomb, and celebrating the Sacrifice of the Lamb, thy Spouse, upon the altar which covers and protects thy remains!

In the first of these pilgrimages, we conceived the idea of rendering thee this public homage of our tender veneration; of consecrating to thy glory this humble work as a memorial of the holy joy we have experienced when kneeling at thy feet. Deign, O Virgin, Apostle, Martyr, amidst the many gifts offered at thy Confession by purer hands than ours, to accept this feeble tribute of our love!

Angels alone can worthily celebrate thy praise, O Spouse of Christ! We can but address thee in the trembling accents of fallen and sinful humanity.

Deign to look favorably upon us, O glorious queen! from the throne of glory whereon thou sittest, clothed with the dazzling robe of which the Psalmist speaks. Vouchsafe to accept our humble offering. [2]

Deign also to hear our prayer for that holy Church, whose glory and support thou art.

In the profound night of the present century, the Spouse delays His coming. Amidst the solemn silence, He permits the virgin to slumber until the day of His advent. [3] We honor thy repose upon thy mysterious couch, rendered glorious by thy victories, O Cecilia! but we know that thou dost not forget us; for thus speaks the Spouse in the sacred Canticle: "I sleep, but my heart watches!" [4]

The hour approaches when the Spouse will appear, and rally his followers around the standard of the Cross. Soon the cry will be heard: "Behold the bridegroom cometh; go ye forth to meet him." [5] O Cecilia! then wilt thou exclaim to the Christians of our generation, as thou formerly didst to the faithful band, who surrounded thee in the hour of combat: "Soldiers of Christ, cast off the works of darkness and clothe yourselves with the armor of light!" [6]

The Church daily pronounces thy name with love and confidence in the most sacred part of her Mysteries, firmly confiding in thy assistance, O, Cecilia! which she knows will never fail her. Raise up Christian hearts to the contemplation of those eternal truths which they too often forget in their vain pursuit of those earthly vanities, which held captive the heart of Tiburtius, until thy sublime eloquence had undeceived his noble soul. Thus wilt thou prepare the triumph of the Church; for when thoughts of eternity shall predominate in the heart of man, then will the salvation and the peace of nations be secured.

Our task is accomplished: we must now resume less pleasing labors. Mayest thou. Cecilia! ever be the delight of the Heavenly Spouse. Mayest thou ever breathe the divine perfume of his roses and lilies, and be charmed with the ineffable harmony of His Sacred Heart. From thy throne of glory, watch over us during life; aid us at the hour of death, and bear our souls to their immortal home. There shall we behold thee, crowned with glory, and radiant with ineffable happiness; and in the light of that refulgent vision, we shall comprehend the exalted excellence of Virginity, Apostolic zeal, and Martyrdom.

[1] George Doria Pampliili, Cardinal Priest and Titulary of this church, caused to be restored at his own expense, for the divine office chanted here by sacred virgins, this august temple, dedicated to St. Cecilia, and formerly the house in which she lived. The remains of George, the great uncle, and of Joseph, the undo of the present Titulary, repose hero. Seeing that this sanctuary was falling to ruins, Cardinal Doria supported the arcades with brickwork, consolidated the arch, and restored to the church its primitive beauty. As a token of gratitude for the munificence of this eminent Cardinal, the Abbess and religious have caused this inscription to be engraved.

[2] Psalms xliv. 2.

[3] Moram autem faciente sponso, dormitavorunt omnes (virgines) et dormierunt. *Matth.* xxv. 5.

[4] Cant., v. 2.

[5] Matt. xxv. 6.

[6] Eia milites Christi, abjicite opera tenebrarum et induamini arma lucis. *Acta S. Caeciliae.*

Appendix

The following are the two Hymns in honor of St. Cecilia which His Holiness has approved for Liturgical use.

DIE XXII NOVEMBRIS.
IN FESTO

S. CAECILIAE VIRGINIS ET MARTYRIS.

———

AD MATUTINUM,
tiam ad Vesperas, quoties festum transferatur.

HYMNUS.

Terrena cessent organa,
Cor aestuans Caeciliae
Caeleste fundit canticum,
Deoque totum jubilat

Dum nuptiali nobilis
Domus resultat gaudio;
Haec sola tristis candido
Gemit columba pectore.

O Christe mi dulcissime,
Cui me sacravit charitas,
Serva pudoris integram,
Averte labem corpore.

Ovis leonem sedula
Agnum facit mitissimum;
Hic fonte lotus mystico
Coelo repente militat.

Solvit Tiburtium soror
Erroris e caligine,
Factoque fratris asseclae
Ad astra pandit semitam.

Seges per illam plurima
Superna replet horrea:
Verbo potens, fit particeps
Apostolorum gloriae.

Delapsus arce siderum
Illam tuetur Angelus,
Rosaeque mixtae liliis
Ambire crines gestiunt.

Sertum rubens et candidum
Affertur una conjugi,
Quem castitatis aemulum
Coelestis ardor efficit.

Te sponse Jesu, virginum
Beata laudent agmina
Patrique cum Paraclito
Par sit per aevum gloria
Amen:

———

AD LAUDES.

HYMNUS.

Nunc ad coronas pergite,
Clamat suis Caecilia;
Mox ipsa Virgo sistitur
Ad judicis praetorium.

Minantis iram despicit,
Et falsa ridet numina;
Jam morte digna ducitur
Puella culpae nescia.

Inclusa perstat balneo,
Ardent calore fornices;
Ast urit intus Virginem
Divinus ignis fortior.

Intaminatam barbarus
Ter ense lictor percutit;
Scelus tamen non perficit,
Christus moras dat Martyri.

Horae supremae proxima,
Deo sacrandas devovet
Aedes avitas, libera,
Volatque ad Agni nuptias.

Salveto, corpus Martyris
Diu sub antris abditum!
Nova refulgens gloria

Romae parenti redderis.

Ne fios tenebris areat,
Te Virgo servat virginum;
Rubens cruoris purpura,
Stola micante cingeris.

Dormi silenti marmore,
Dum sede laetus caelica
Indulget hymnis spiritus,
Votisque dexter annuit.

Te sponse Jesu, virginum
Beata laudant agmina;
Patrique cum Paraclito
Par sit per oevum gloria.

Amen.

Decretum

Ordinis Sancti Benedicti in Galliis.

Certamen apprime forte disposuit Deus in Urbe inclytae Virgini et Martyri sanctae Caeciliae, quae dum in Christianae religionis proposito Deo devotam virginitatem saam singulari Angeli praesidio incontaminatam servare promeruit, illud insimul obtinuit, ut verae fidei lumine collustrati Valerianus sponsus sibi datus, ejusque frater Tiburtius, in libera religionis ipsius confessione ad mortem usque immobiles perseverarent, et gloriae corona redimiti coelitum felicitate potirentur, donec et ipsa Dominum Regem Salvatorem collaudare non desinens, innumeris superatis tormentis, iisdem sociaretur in perpetuas aeternitates triumphatura. Sanctae Caeciliae cultus longe lateque diffusus, quum in dies magis in Gallia inclareat, praesertim penes alumnos Ordinis Sancti Benedicti ibi degentes, Reverendissimus Pater Domnus Prosper Guèranger, Abbas Solesmensis, constituit in divina Psalmodia ejusdem Sanctae laudes ampliori solemnitate commemorari; ac proinde Sanctissimo Domino Nostro Pio IX. Pontifici Maximo supplicavit enixe, ut pro alumnis sui Ordinis in Gallia adprobare dignaretur Hymnos proprios in honorem sanctae Caeciliae Officio ipsius addendos. Sanctitas Sua hujusmodi preces peramanter excipiens, referente me subscripto Sacrorum Rituum Congregationis Pro-Secretario, de speciali gratia benigne annuit juxta preces, propositosque Hymnos proprios Officio sanctae Caeciliae Virginia Martyris a Benedictinis in Gallia addendos, uti superiore in exemplari adnotantur adprobavit, die duodecima Februarii M DCCC LII

A. card. LAMBRUSCHINI,
S, R. C. Praefectus.

Locus Sigilli

Dom. Grigli. S. R. C. Pro-Seer

Printed in the USA
CPSIA information can be obtained
at www.ICGtesting.com
LVHW051959270124
769807LV00002B/262